IN THE
HORNETS'
NEST

IN THE
HORNETS'
NEST

Charlotte and
Its First Year
in the NBA

JOE DRAPE

St. Martin's Press
New York

IN THE HORNETS' NEST: CHARLOTTE AND ITS FIRST YEAR IN THE NBA. Copyright © 1989 by Joe Drape. All rights reserved. Printed in the United States of America. No part of this book may be used or reproduced in any manner whatsoever without written permission except in the case of brief quotations embodied in critical articles or reviews. For information, address St. Martin's Press, 175 Fifth Avenue, New York, N.Y. 10010.

Library of Congress Cataloging-in-Publication Data

Drape, Joe.
    In the Hornets' nest : Charlotte's first year in the N.B.A. / Joe Drape.
        p.   cm.
    ISBN 0-312-03366-4
    1. Charlotte Hornets (Basketball team)   2. Charlotte (N.C.)—History.   I. Title.
GV885.52.C4D73   1989
796.323'64'0975676—dc20   89-32897
                                                                  CIP

First Edition

10 9 8 7 6 5 4 3 2 1

For My Mother and Father
—this isn't enough.

CONTENTS

CONTENTS

ACKNOWLEDGMENTS

S O many people gave me their time, support, and direction in researching and writing this book that many thanks are due. There were dozens of stops in NBA ports and at each, people who allowed me into their world.

I'd like to thank the entire Charlotte Hornets' organization for the unlimited access they allowed me—especially team owners George Shinn, Cy Bahakel, Felix Sabates, and Rick Hendrick, and vice-president and general manager Carl Scheer. Their publicity department, in particular Harold Kaufman, proved to be an invaluable guide.

The Hornets coaching staff and players were especially willing to share countless hours and many insights on their profession, their league, and their love of the game. They are truly professionals and great bunch of guys who made a long, grueling season more pleasurable than I deserve. They all deserve thanks: Muggsy Bogues, Rex Chapman, Dave Hoppen, Tim Kempton, Sidney Lowe, Greg Kite, Dell Curry, Brian

Rowsom, Kelly Tripucka, Ralph Lewis, Rickey Green, Michael Holton, Earl Cureton, Gene Littles, Ed Badger, Tom Jorgensen, and Terry Kofler. My sincerest thanks to coach Dick Harter, Robert Reid, and Kurt Rambis, all of whom's love for the game was apparent in their passion when speaking of basketball. I thank them for sharing their stories.

Many players, league officials, and people connected with the game contributed their time and thoughts to this project, but several need to be singled out for answering that perpetual last question: NBA commissioner David Stern, Denver's Doug Moe, Houston owner Charlie Thomas, Andrew Brandt, and David Falk. I greatly appreciate the Dallas Mavericks' Norm Sonju for the candor and enthusiasm that he maintained for long hours as he spoke of the birth of an NBA franchise.

So many people in Charlotte took the time to help put this story in the context of their city that a list would be futile. I am indebted, however, to Lloyd Scher, Harvey Gantt, and Max Muhleman for imparting their sense of Charlotte. In addition, colleagues such as Tucker Mitchell, Leonard Laye, Bruce Martin, Tom Sorensen, Rick Bonnell, Steve Martin, and Gil McGregor were more helpful than they were required to be.

Special thanks are in order for my newspaper, *The Atlanta Constitution,* especially managing editor Glenn McCutchen, photographer Jim Gund, and national editors Plott Brice and Pat Yack for granting the time needed to follow this story. I am forever grateful for their understanding. My agent, David Black, got this thing rolling and was a friend throughout. My editor, Jim Fitzgerald, picked up the dice and remained ever patient. Many thanks to them both.

I'd be remiss if I failed to extend my warmest thanks to my family and friends who prevented me from caving in to the travel and anxiety. John, Tim, Tom, and Mary Ann Drape came through, as I knew they would, with sizable and critical contributions. All of us know I couldn't have done it without them, and I'm glad I'll never have to. Eileen, Marian, and Andrew (more Drapes) were at once careful readers, tolerant spouses, and pillars of stability. Mom, Dad et al., can't be thanked enough.

Judy Williamson hung tough through the endless frantic days and with unerring kindness and support made me see the end was at sight. I'm forever grateful. Steve Blow, Mark Edgar, and Dave Tarrant were needed friends and mentors. Peter Meyer helped me expect the unexpected. In addition, there were many who provided jolts of kindness and much needed levity. These are the people who kept me smiling on the road: David Boul, John and Marianne Trabold, Grant Pace, David Gentsch, Denny and Kelly Trabold, Bill Adams, Jorge Canseco, Winston Talbert, Mike and Lori Higgins, Barb Jaccodine, Chuck and Alta Asmar. And at home: Sean Lanham, Wendell Helms, Stu Owens, and Bo McDonald. Shelley Pendleton worked overtime on the copying machine and at tapes. J. P. Olsen kept things running smooth for me at St. Martin's. Many thanks to them all.

IN THE
HORNETS'
NEST

1

OPENING

NIGHT

THIS was the city's grandest moment, according to the front-page headline in the morning newspaper. As dusk muted the glimmer of downtown skyscrapers, a pilgrimage of sorts was beginning. There were traffic snarls and impatient motorists, of course, but there were mostly joyous Carolinians. For the most part, they were Charlotteans making the six-mile trek south on Billy Graham Parkway to the city's new $52-million state-of-the-art Coliseum. Many were fleeing the office towers of Uptown Charlotte—the city center, which until the 1970s was called plain old downtown. But there were also cars filled with folks from the nearby communities in South Carolina, and a few came from as far away as Tobacco Road some 100 miles up I-85. All were converging on this immaculate new structure for a single event. A grand event.

Fireworks sprayed the skies outside the gleaming new Charlotte Coliseum, shaped befittingly like a crown made of red brick, with columns and a sparkling glass facade. The upbeat rhythm of a jazz band wafted majestically along its veranda and welcomed those who emerged from the acres of dark, asphalt parking lots. Many wore tuxedos and evening gowns, others simply opted for jeans and T-shirts, but virtually all had donned some hint of the color teal. This shade of green was a show of solidarity for their new basketball team whose official colors—teal purple and Carolina blue—had already become a symbol in itself.

The way those 20,000-plus Carolinians edged their way toward the arena gates this special night was eerie. It was as if some extraterrestrial force had summoned them there for a mysterious close encounter. Chatter bubbled along with their soaring spirits as they neared the entrance.

For on this crisp autumn night, twelve professional athletes were going to put this Southeastern city on the map or at least indelibly print it in the nation's box scores. In less than an hour, the newly formed Charlotte Hornets would tip off their first regular-season game in the National Basketball Association. The NBA. The major leagues. The basketball players who pulled on Charlotte jerseys for the season opener were still relatively new in town—virtual strangers—but they would be loved no matter what they did on the basketball floor after that first glorious jump ball flew into the air. This was Charlotte's team playing North Carolina's most beloved game. The morning newspapers tomorrow from New York to Los Angeles, and especially those of much-envied Atlanta, would give some account, however brief, of how this Bible-Belt expansion team fared against tonight's opponent, the Cleveland Cavaliers, on November 4, 1988. They would continue to do so for eighty-one mornings hence in this inaugural season. The Charlotte Hornets would be right there beside Chicago, Detroit, Boston, and Philadelphia in the standings. Granted they'd be at, or near, the bottom for at least the next several years, but the point was, they'd be there.

But this evening wasn't only about basketball even though Carolinians worshiped the sport fiercely. God entrusted *the game* to the University of North Carolina's Dean Smith, they'd tell you. Before that Everett Case was its keeper, as was Bones McKinney, Frank McGuire, Vic Bubas, and Lefty

Driesell—all Carolina college coaching giants in the revered Atlantic Coast Conference.

This basketball game was a celebration of what people in a proud city could accomplish when issued a challenge. The NBA had issued that challenge three years ago by asking them to prove that they were major league. What the league probably didn't realize at the time was that these were the sort of people who'd change their downtown's name to Uptown just because the mayor asked them to. Most of the denizens had agreed that it was more cosmopolitan sounding and indicative of the towering office buildings, upscale retail stores, and nifty walkways being built in its center. Besides, that's what old-timers had once called the town's most elevated natural point—which Uptown still was.

As the noisy and ebullient crowd poured into the arena, scuffing their feet along the freshly polished terazzo floors of the city's new shrine, they admired the carved-out concession stands with bright Formica countertops and applauded the images on the closed-circuit television monitors. The $47-million bond issue these people had voted for back in 1985—before anyone had ever dreamed of an NBA franchise playing here—was now being touched, walked across, sat in. Charlotte was really turning out tonight to cheer for itself. That it was basketball they were here for just made it that much sweeter.

The shots weren't falling yet, but Robert Reid kept working at it anyway.

He had started about four feet away from the basket, flipping the ball off the glass backboard, and had moved in a tight arc from right to left. It was almost 6:45 P.M. and Reid was already dressed for the game, underneath his teal warm-up pants and gray sweatshirt. The Charlotte Symphony Orchestra was already settled in at one end of the court, striking notes on their violins and blowing their horns, preparing to welcome the Hornets with a musical flourish. Workmen on video and news crews were dragging hundreds of yards of cable along the periphery of the court while technicians hurriedly prepared an indoor fireworks display. Nothing distracted Reid, though. He moved a couple steps back after completing each rotation, gradually picking up his jog as he went to retrieve each shot whether it swished or clanged to the sidelines. His shots were barely jumpers at first, but by the time Reid passed the foul line during his ritual shoot-around he was easily lifting off the floor. His legs were getting warm and his body was beginning to glisten. Reid was old by NBA standards and conscious that his thirty-three-year-old body needed extra attention.

Reid had played 762 NBA regular-season and 72 post-season games going into tonight's contest against the Cavaliers. Twice, he had played in the Championship Series—and played well. Reid had averaged a solid 11.2 points a game over his ten-year career. He had done all of this with the Houston Rockets in his more or less native state of Texas, where he continued to live with his wife and two children. He was a military brat who had lived in Georgia and Hawaii but clung to his Texas roots. This was his eleventh opening night and he needed just 1,177 points over the next 82 games to reach the 10,000 career-point mark. It was a modest NBA milestone, but one that signified that a player's years in the league, if not spectacular, had been well spent. His new teammate, Kelly Tripucka, would probably reach that mark several games before Reid this year, which was only Tripucka's eighth NBA season. But Tripucka was a bona-fide scorer who earlier in his career had averaged 26 points and earned two trips to the NBA All-Star Game for the offensive talent he had displayed with the Detroit Pistons.

Tripucka was expected to do the same now for the Hornets, while Reid, it was hoped, would play some defense, dig out rebounds, dish the ball off to his teammates, as well as score from the perimeter—all things that Reid was pretty good at. It wasn't that Tripucka wouldn't also do the rest, but he was paid mainly to score and that took up a lot of energy. Even if over the next three years, Tripucka was able to match his own career-high numbers in the rebound, assist, and steal categories—which was doubtful since he'd achieved those as a twenty-two-year-old rookie—he would not be able to match the 3,706 rebounds, 2,253 assists, and 881 steals that Reid had posted in his ten NBA seasons. They were different players with different talents and were paid accordingly. Where Tripucka was paid almost $1 million per season to score, the 6'8" Reid was paid $450,000 a year to do a little bit of everything.

The salary difference didn't bother Reid as much as the fact that he'd only recently moved out of the nearby Registry Hotel. Since his salary wasn't guaranteed, and there were no assurances on how long he'd be a Charlotte Hornet, the team had waited until the last moment to move him into an apartment. He was still bitter about the way the Rockets had dumped him over the summer. They had traded him and a second-round draft choice in 1990 for a journeyman forward named Bernard Thompson. It was bad enough to be peddled to an expansion team, he thought, but what really ticked him off was that he believed Rockets general manager Ray Patterson had reneged on a handshake deal that would have guaranteed the final two years of his contract.

Hornets general manager Carl Scheer had compounded the insult by touting the deal in the newspapers as a way to pick up future draft choices. Scheer had insinuated in the newspaper that Reid was just an old body who'd been brought in cheaply as an afterthought to the team's preseason training camp. They'd only pay him as long as they kept him around. It was hoped that the veteran's savvy might provide some order to what promised to be an unruly camp filled with rookies, last-shot free agents, Continental Basketball Association fugitives, and assorted veterans the Hornets had managed to pluck off the end of other NBA benches. The thinking was that Reid would most likely be gone before the season's start and that the twelve other players with guaranteed salaries would be the charter Hornets.

But here Reid was, starting the season in a new town with a ragtag bunch of kids. There were big guys named Tim Kempton and Dave Hoppen, who between them had barely registered in the box scores during two NBA seasons. Baby-faced kids like Tyrone "Muggsy" Bogues who, at 5'3", was getting a second season in the league to prove that he was more than a physical oddity and gate attraction. And the rookie Rex Chapman who had been a ten-year-old boy hoisting a basketball at the hoop on the playgrounds of his native Owensboro, Kentucky, when Reid first stepped on an NBA court eleven years ago alongside the likes of Moses Malone, Rudy Tomjanovich, and Calvin Murphy.

There were other veterans here besides Reid and Tripucka, though. There was Earl Cureton, who owned an NBA championship ring and had signed on over the summer. Kurt Rambis had four rings from the champion Los Angeles Lakers and had been voted a cocaptain by his new teammates. The season that was about to begin in less than an hour was approaching and Reid was going to be a starter and the other captain of the brand-new Charlotte Hornets.

Reid was well aware of the irony of the situation but did not give it much thought as he approached the three-point line. He was looking forward to another professional basketball season and the opportunity to reach an important milestone in the world's greatest roundball league. Reid mused that they'd probably stop the game and present him with the basketball that ripped through for his 10,000th point. He'd keep it as he did all his mementos of the game in a chest tucked away in the basement of his Houston home. The team pictures, the clippings, and the odd souvenirs that were signposts of a pretty considerable basketball career would soon be all that was left of his career. The reason he kept it all was simple. According to Reid: "This is the best part of my life and I want to remember every part of it. In the NBA, when you're finished they don't let you hang around the office."

He finished his shoot-around by swishing two more jumpers from beyond the three-point line, just as another veteran was beginning his. Rickey Green had also been in the league for ten years and still was arguably the fastest man in the NBA. Now he was showing why, as he launched jump shots erratically from all over the court, catching up with the ball on a dead run, then dribbling it frantically to another spot before uncoiling those springy legs for another jumper.

Green interrupted his drill to stop Reid for a moment near the mid-court line. He nodded to the arena chairs that were beginning to fill up with fans. They stood next to each other for several moments without speaking and watched as fans streamed through the portals and made their way down the drab concrete steps to their appointed seats. For the first time since stepping on the court, Reid flashed the easy smile that was already beginning to make him a local celebrity. "This is going to be some kind of season, Rickey," he said. But it was too late; Green had already bounded off to the bucket to continue his haphazard warm-up.

George Shinn was perhaps the proudest man in the Coliseum this opening night. But true to his single-minded nature, he was busily darting about the arena attending to the many details that accompany the start-up of a multimillion dollar sports franchise. Shinn was a detail guy driven by a result-oriented ego. He had already studied a game log that precisely laid out the evening's program—down to the sixty seconds former Blood, Sweat & Tears singer David Clayton Thomas would be allowed for his rendition of "The Star Spangled Banner." This was Shinn's operation and it was going to be run tightly. That's why he had settled a dispute at the Coliseum with a season ticket holder by asking his general manager, Carl Scheer, to give the tickets earmarked for Scheer's wife to him. The gentleman claimed he had not yet received his tickets and Shinn believed him. The Hornets' new owner had even been at courtside earlier in the day when two Coliseum workers flipped through an NBA rule book and decided that the 3-point line that they had taped on the court was much shorter than it should be. Their basketball experience was at the college level, thus the line had been taped almost 4-feet shorter than NBA requirement. Big-league shooters launched three-pointers from twenty-three feet nine inches. A few Cleveland players had noticed the discrepancy during their morning shoot-around and had mercifully pointed it out to building officials.

Shinn was born in Kannapolis, North Carolina—a gritty textile town twenty-five miles up I-85 entirely dominated by the Cannon Mills company. His father, George Sr., had died owing $20,000 for an unfinished subdivision when Shinn was eight years old, forcing him and his mother, Irene, to auction off a gas station, six acres, a house, and a duplex. Only the family home had been saved, and that was after a friend of the family volunteered to buy the house and let Irene Shinn pay him off. Shinn had been something of a ne'er-do-well at A. L. Brown High School, more interested in fast cars and pretty girls than his school work. He had made the football team, but because he was small—only 5'6"—he didn't play much and eventually quit. He received most of his schoolboy notoriety for his wit and pranks. He graduated last in his high school class and went on to work at Cannon Mills, content to settle for an unremarkable life. Shinn might have remained a mill hand tearing up his hometown on the weekends if back problems hadn't started plaguing him after two-and-a-half years of lugging bolts of fabric. He thought of landing a job in the insurance field but was turned down. With his limited options he entered the two-year Evans Business College in nearby Concord, North Carolina. But he soon ran out of money and was forced to work as school janitor so he could finish his courses. He graduated from the college with the basic skills of an office manager. But Shinn had always been personable, and the tenacity with which he set about a task prompted the school's owner to hire him first as a recruiter, and then finally as manager. By 1968, Shinn was co-owner of the Evans Business School.

Shinn's obsession with every aspect of a project was sometimes maddening to those who worked with him to bring the NBA to Charlotte. Harvey Gantt, who as former mayor of Charlotte was called on several times to smooth troubled public waters in the NBA quest, can remember numerous dawn or midnight calls from the would-be owner, who simply wanted to discuss another aspect of the project. Early on

Shinn railed about why the Coliseum Authority, not he, should have control of the ushers at the new facility, or debated what would be the best way to present the city to visiting NBA dignitaries. Gantt thought that at times Shinn showed little regard for the process of decision-making public officials had to follow—especially when it didn't suit his entrepreneurial purposes.

George Shinn first came to the attention of the city of Charlotte after making a ripple about going to Los Angeles to discuss buying the United States Football League's Los Angeles Express franchise. Shinn had amassed a fortune with his vocational business and trade schools and other investments and was just getting serious about becoming a sports mogul. First, he had wanted a baseball team, but it was apparent that any major league expansion was many years down the road. Football was his second choice, but he soon discovered that the National Football League wasn't talking expansion yet either. The fledgling United States Football League (USFL), however, needed help.

After Shinn expressed interest in the short-lived league, he was courted by Eddie Einhorn of the Chicago Stings. Sports impressario John Bassett soon took him under his wing as well and he still likes to speak about how he was dazzled by "power lunching" in a boardroom with the irascible Donald Trump. The late Bassett was the owner of the Tampa Bay Bandits, and Trump, who owned the New Jersey Generals, were ready to welcome the aspiring franchise owner into their fledgling fraternity, but Shinn had simply been testing the waters. What he wanted to see was how interested the city of Charlotte might be in becoming a major-league sports franchise. Shinn was admittedly naive when he took a financial team with him to investigate the Express's operation. But, as he has since pointed out, not that naive.

In the course of his USFL networking, Shinn and the various owners agreed that Charlotte would be allowed to host two exhibition games in February 1985.

Lloyd Scher was just a guy running a small business when

he first met the man who was trying to launch the USFL in Charlotte. Scher's tiny Video Taping Services was starting to succeed when an acquaintance—Max Muhleman, a local sports consultant who'd handled much of the NASCAR promotion—recommended Scher and his services to Shinn. The two were trying to make arrangements for the football exhibitions. Muhleman would later become Shinn's right-hand man in landing the NBA franchise, before being dumped by Shinn as the result of a business disagreement.

Scher was a sports fan and in fact believed that he owed the success of his modest business to basketball. As an undergraduate manager for the University of North Carolina's Tarheels in 1973, he'd spent much of his time filming and videotaping games for Dean Smith. During that time he got interested in how the state's most glorified coach used videotapes in coaching. He became a lot better acquainted with the just-budding videotape industry. He also gained a greater understanding of the game and a familiarity with video hardware, all under Smith's tutelage. The wristwatch bearing the inscription, "New York's National Invitational Tournament (NIT)," that he still wears during the roundball season is a bonus he earned for these efforts.

After college Scher bounced around before returning to the basketball and video world. He completed a stint in the military, then worked for the Mecklenburg County Utility Service, as well as coaching and counseling at Charlotte junior high schools. He even headed North—he was born in New York before moving to Charlotte at age eleven—to sell tickets at the Capitol Centre in Washington, D.C. But he was back in Charlotte by 1978, watching his city take shape.

Scher was a doer, though, and when something caught his fancy, his burly frame, curly hair, and conivival personality usually followed. He dove into projects—at his synagogue or in the sports world. It was during one of these forays that he'd first met George Shinn. Tonight he privately shared some of the credit for laying the foundation for the Charlotte Hornets. There wouldn't have been an NBA basketball game tonight if Scher and others hadn't pushed for the new Coliseum.

For Lloyd Scher, Shinn's need for control exemplified the creed by which the Charlotte Hornets would operate. The NBA was a highly profitable entertainment and Shinn insisted that all aspects of his operation be handled professionally and with class. The bottom line was simple: for the city and the Hornets, professional basketball was a business.

Along with Gantt, Scher liked and admired Shinn. Both men were at the Coliseum this opening night. Gantt had returned from Clemson, South Carolina, where, as a member of Clemson University's board of directors, he'd been attending a special meeting. No longer the mayor of Charlotte he had allowed himself the luxury of wearing a blue suit instead of black tie to sit at midcourt, where he had purchased season tickets. Scher's rented tuxedo was already a little dirty by 7 P.M. His size-50 jacket was dusty from scurrying about in the bowels of the Coliseum hooking up—sometimes having to hot-wire—the video equipment he had hocked his convertible for in order to start up his business. The Hornets had contracted him to handle most of the video link-ups and to do whatever recording was necessary in this first season.

Scher's crusade to bring a major-league facility had come a long way since 1979, when Max Muhleman had staged the McDonald's All-Star game in April at the old Charlotte Coliseum. He had been a volunteer then, readying the old building for basketball's high school showcase. Isiah Thomas, Ralph Sampson, and Steve Stipanovich were just fuzzy-cheeked youngsters then, but they were among the best high school ballplayers of that year and they were coming to Charlotte, where more than 10,000 people would pay to see them play. The game was to be televised by ESPN and an already image-conscious town wanted things to go off without a hitch. But one notorious Carolinian downpour dampened the festivities. The old 11,000-seat Coliseum that had opened in 1955 was at the time thought to be quite a design marvel. It was a minidome that would later serve as a scaled-down model for Houston's Astrodome. But on this day in April 1979, the Coliseum was just an outdated, leaky old auditorium. Rain seeped through the roof and onto the court, causing a delay in the nationally aired telecast.

This mishap alerted at least a few people to the fact that something new had to be built if Charlotte was to realize its major-league aspirations. One of those people was Lloyd Scher.

His video shop was starting to get more business from basketball programs. Nearby Davidson University was a good customer and when NCAA regional tournament games came to Charlotte in 1980, Scher got yet another boost. He was starting to make his four-person payroll with greater ease, thus giving him more time to get involved in the city's future. In 1983, there was a movement to investigate the plausibility of building a new multipurpose arena. A private developer had come forward with an improbable proposal to fashion a 60,000-seat Carodome out of Memorial Stadium, an old football and soccer stadium on the edge of Uptown. It was outlandish, but it simply whetted the appetite of city planners. Mayor Eddie Knox decided in January of 1983 to appoint a Committee of 100 to come up with a viable way of building a new facility. Scher wangled his way onto the committee alongside the city's prominent corporate executives, lawyers, and architects. He had sensed that there was a new attitude in Charlotte and the town was ready to do something first rate— Scher wanted to be part of it all.

Basketball had already been a century-old institution in the state. But that was college basketball. There was absolutely no idea of an NBA team coming to North Carolina, much less to Charlotte. Instead, all sights were set on capturing the Atlantic Coast Conference Tournament. The ACC. God's conference. The Duke Blue Devils. The Wolfpack from North Carolina State. The Maryland Terrapins. The Demon Deacons of Wake Forest. The Clemson Tigers. The Rambling Wreck of Georgia Tech. The Virginia Cavaliers. And of course, the Tarheels.

The ACC's postseason tournament was basketball country's crown jewel. For three days, school allegiances and a pure love for the game converged at the tournament site where fans would line up, paying up to $250 for the opportunity to see their own Larry Miller, Tree Rollins, David Thompson, Phil Ford, Ralph Sampson, James Worthy, or Michael Jordan take on others of similar talent and prestige in arguably the nation's most competitive tournament. The ACC has always been a coach's conference and its present rulers, Jim Valvano of North Carolina State, Mike Krzyzewski of Duke, and Dean Smith, always make sure their teams were ready to snatch undisputed bragging rights. Charlotte had hosted the tournament for only three brief years—1968, 1969, and 1970—in the ACC's thirty-six-year history. The first twelve tournaments, dating back to 1954, were played at North Carolina State's Reynolds Coliseum. Greensboro had hosted it thirteen times, and by the late 1970s, Landover, Maryland, and Atlanta each got a shot to host a handful of tournaments.

ACC fans from all eight schools can usually agree on only two things: that the greatest basketball game ever was between North Carolina and Maryland in the 1974 championship; and that Dean Smith earned deification that same season by bringing the Tarheels back eight points in seventeen seconds against Duke with a series of brilliant coaching maneuvers and pushing the Tarheels to a triple overtime win. The former feat pitted the high-flying David Thompson and his circus side-kicks, 7'4" Tommy Burleson and 5'4" Monte Towe, against Maryland's Tom McMillen, John Lucas, and Len Elmore in a thrilling 103–100 overtime victory. The Wolfpack went on to claim the NCAA title, while the Terrapins voted to turn down an invitation to the NIT lest they sully a glorious season.

When Charlotte was bypassed for the ACC's postseason festivities, most Charlotteans were shut out from being a part of basketball lore. In addition, Greensboro looked as if it was thumbing its nose at the "Queen City." Even worse, when the ACC started moving the tournament around, it chose Atlanta and Landover—relatively neutral sites that seemingly had little roots in and respect for God's conference. Georgia Tech didn't join the ACC until 1982, and Landover was just a suburb of Washington, D.C.

In typical fashion, Scher threw himself into the project and took over the tedious conceptual work of cost analysis and plausible construction designs for the city's committee. His work was tireless and soon he was elevated from mere committee member to a valued voice on the executive committee. He even paid his own way to Indianapolis to assess the advantages of the Hoosier Dome. Early on in the planning, he and several other members were vocal about overruling the hired consultant who recommended that an 18,000-seat facility be erected. That seating capacity was the result of crunching current population and building statistics. Scher recognized that Charlotte was changing. The influx of well-heeled corporations was bringing more cosmopolitan people into the area. Northeasterners and Midwesterners were used to traveling to a facility to see a major sporting event or concert. These were people who appreciated first-rate entertainment. These newcomers would dictate the rhythms of Charlotte's future as much as the natives and older transplants, like Scher. The consultant was overruled and a 25,000-seat facility was planned. It was to be the centerpiece of a new, booming city.

There were two great entrances on opening night.

The first came at about 7:10 P.M. when the tiny one, Muggsy Bogues, led the Hornets onto the court for pregame warm-ups. The Coliseum erupted as these twelve professional basketball players entered what would become their home office for the first of many long work days. They were an unlikely collection of heroes, most either too old, too young, or too much trouble for established NBA teams. But there they were, shooting lay-ups while Michael Jackson's "Thriller" pumped over the loud speaker and 23,000-plus fans roared at their every movement. A few moments later their coaches, Dick Harter, Ed Badger, and Gene Littles walked out of the tunnel. Harter was starting his first season as an NBA head coach. He was grateful to be directing his own team, but he knew that this was an unseasoned bunch and that in the grueling 82-game schedule ahead there wouldn't be many opportunities to match the high of opening night, especially with these brand-new, adoring fans. He was smiling ever so slightly.

Less than thirty minutes later, George Shinn stepped to center court. The place thundered, drowning out the final strains of the theme from *Rocky*. Shinn's eyes misted as Governors Jim Martin and Carroll Campbell of North and South Carolina declared it *his* day. He finally was at the end of his rainbow and could barely hold back his tears.

In front of the 23,000 fans he said, "Thank you for supporting the Hornets." As the spotlight bore down on him he whispered, "I love you all very much."

2

THE HUSTLE

L IKE many business deals, the negotiations for the Hornets' franchise started in a roundabout way. A friend of a friend calls someone else who in turn calls someone he knows to arrange a meeting with the friend now twice removed. In the Hornets' case, Maxwell L. Muhleman, a Charlotte marketing consultant, called a California lawyer to ask him if he knew anyone in the office of the National Basketball Association who could arrange a meeting for George Shinn. Muhleman knew the lawyer from his days doing public relations and marketing work on the auto-racing circuit out West. He came back to Charlotte in 1977, where he had started as a sportswriter in 1955. Muhleman had left newspapers for public relations and advertising, but he'd kept the journalist's habit of cultivating sources. It had served him well in the marketing business, and he had a reputation for knowing somebody somewhere who might help or who might know somebody who could help.

Muhleman made the call after having produced the two

USFL exhibition games the previous February for Shinn. The enthusiasm the games had created, and the talk that a successful crowd showing might lead to a USFL team in Charlotte, had convinced Muhleman that the city was ready for major-league sports. It was a surprise to him because when he returned to Charlotte in 1977 he'd joined an advertising firm. "When I left Charlotte, you couldn't run a sports marketing business very easily from here," he recalled. "When I came back the reputation of the South had changed quite a bit."

Muhleman had started his sports marketing business in 1972 in Southern California, after working with Carroll Shelby, who was building the Cobra sports car for Ford. He then joined Shelby and Dan Gurney when they went back into racing. Once on his own, Muhleman added marketing work for the World Hockey Association, the World Football League, and found national sponsors for motor sports teams and other sporting events. When he began, sports marketing was still a fledgling industry. He kept his interest in his California operation because he expected to return to sports marketing someday.

Muhleman met George Shinn through Rick Hendrick, a Charlotte-based auto dealer who hired him to help him start a NASCAR racing team. Hendrick was Muhleman's first significant client when he decided to bring Muhleman Marketing to Charlotte. First, Shinn wanted to use Muhleman's acquaintance with baseball commissioner Peter Ueberroth, whom he had met when Ueberroth was in the travel agency business, to find out about major league baseball's expansion plans. Baseball was Shinn's first ambition. Besides the NFL's not having immediate expansion plans, football was just too expensive for Shinn. But by coincidence, the city of Charlotte was going ahead with its plans to build a new arena and the NBA was talking expansion. Shinn asked Muhleman to arrange a meeting with NBA officials.

That call resulted in a May 8, 1985 meeting with David Stern. The NBA commissioner was added to an already-full schedule of appointments for the would-be sports mogul. Shinn and Muhleman were in New York to talk to Ueberroth,

American League president Bobby Brown, and Bowie Kuhn, the former baseball commissioner. They also were going to discuss pro football with USFL commissioner Harry Usher. These meetings were to take all afternoon. Stern agreed to see them at 10:00 A.M. What was to be a brief introductory meeting turned into a two-hour discussion of why Shinn wanted to be a major-league sports owner.

At that time, David Stern did not have a timetable for expansion. Like major-league baseball and the NFL, the NBA approached growth gingerly. The game was on the upswing in popularity and business was good. The twenty-three owners Stern represented weren't wild about adding new members, but the commissioner thought the league was ready for growth. He was accepting visitors. In other words, Stern was pumped up by the idea of taking his league a step further, choosing the arenas, the market, and the owners.

"One of the most wondrous things about expansion for commissioners," Stern said later, "is that you're able to start at the very beginning for everything. We didn't need to expand or have to expand, but we had the wonderful luxury of expanding under exactly the right conditions."

Both Shinn and Stern walked away from the wide-ranging meeting with strong impressions of each other. Their differences were immediate as they faced off on separate sofas in the commissioner's fifteenth-floor corner office that overlooked Fifth Avenue. Stern, a native of Manhattan, had his coat off, tie loosened, and he was smoking a cigar. Seated at one side was Gary Bettman, the league's vice-president and general counsel. He was framed on the other by a Kermit the Frog telephone resting on a table. Stern's colleagues in the office believed he resembled the Muppett character when he was wheeling and dealing on the phone. Shinn sat on the edge of the sofa next to Muhleman. When Stern asked him to tell him about himself, Shinn wound up to deliver the George Shinn story, knowing full well that he had already mailed biographical information to the league. The Shinn story worked. It was an often told spiel, a combination of rags-to-riches and Christian commitment, that Shinn had polished over the years. Shinn believed in the hardsell and this was his way of personalizing his sales pitches.

Stern waved him off politely. There was no need to go back that far. He just wanted the pertinent information about the town and why Shinn wanted to be an NBA franchise owner—the bottom line. Shinn settled back, regrouped, and launched into what would prove to be the NBA hook: the demographics. One million people lived within thirty minutes of a $52-million, 23,000-seat coliseum under construction; another 800,000 were within fifty miles; all told a potential customer base of 5.5 million, some in medium-size cities such as Greensboro, North Carolina, and Columbia, South Carolina, lived within a one hundred-mile radius. The Southern guy sitting across from him, whom he had never met before, had done his homework. At first glance, he fit the owner's profile Stern was trying to develop. Stern was interested, but noncommittal. The NBA hadn't decided yet when or if they would expand. He made it clear that a significant portion of the owners were against it, and if they agreed, joining would be a pricey proposition—costing at least $20 million. In the meantime, he recommended that Shinn visit some of the league's other franchises.

Shinn walked out onto Fifth Avenue satisfied. This was the beginning of a long sports day with baseball and football discussions still to come. He wanted a sports franchise—any franchise. He was encouraged by the NBA commissioner's attentiveness. Baseball was his first love, football was more prestigious, but he sensed the real opportunity was in basketball. The sports moguling had gone well. Only one thing was amiss. "If it had been in my office," he recalled, "I would have reached over and put out that cigar."

Commissioner Stern steered Shinn and all other franchise seekers toward the teams in Portland, Salt Lake City, and Dallas as case studies in Basketball Operations 101. The NBA owners had at last added an expansion team in 1980 when they voted Dallas into the league. At the time, the NBA was in the doldrums—attendance was down and so were the television ratings. But the Mavericks had become a model franchise. Norm Sonju, the chief operating officer and general manager, had come to Dallas from Buffalo and had operated as a one-man band, generating interest and investors. He had talked to 146 Texas businessmen before finding someone to put up the money—at a time when interest rates were on the way up and the Texas oil boom was on the way down. He had also faced down the nay-sayers who contended that a basketball team couldn't dent the hold the Dallas Cowboys had on the city's sports dollars.

Sonju was skeptical when Stern called and asked him to speak to a representative from Charlotte. Sonju had already spent considerable time several months before with two Miami businessmen only to see the dream of a South Florida franchise fade when the two had a falling out. "I asked Stern if this guy was a viable candidate," Sonju said. Sonju was getting used to being the resident expert on NBA expansion, but he was also trying to run the Mavericks. Assured that Shinn was the real thing, Sonju had another thought. "I have been around the league a lot of years," Sonju recalled, "and I have to tell you that I've never heard anyone say, 'What this league needs is a team in Charlotte.' "

Shinn traveled alone when he visited Dallas in October 1985 for an introductory meeting. The tenor of previous meetings Sonju had had with prospective owners from Minneapolis, Orlando, and Miami was business-driven and impersonal. Most of the groups were hard-charging businessmen who had narrowed their sights only on landing a franchise. But Shinn and Sonju talked little business over a leisurely Mexican dinner. They had exchanged letters before the meeting and each were aware of their shared religious values. Sonju had made much of his Christian commitment in the start-up and operation of the Mavericks. The soft-spoken, courtly Southerner had done the same with his business schools and intended to run his sports franchise the exact following manner. The two hit it off instantly.

"I liked him in a minute. He's not the 'type A' kind of

guy, but quiet, a little laid-back but strong-willed," Sonju said later.

They talked about their wives and children, about how they both grew up poor and their sports business ambitions. As it turned out, Sonju found that Shinn had never been to an NBA game. Sonju was hooked, though. The next day he called the commissioner's office enthusiastically. "I told them 'Wow, do I like this guy,'" Sonju recalled. "This guy belongs in our league."

Sonju had not yet seen Charlotte, and remained skeptical about its major-league status. Recalling the odds he had overcome in Dallas, Sonju told Shinn that "Charlotte had to be the 'Spud Webb' of cities if they were going to get a franchise. If you're five-six in a league that averages six-seven, you have to run a little faster, jump a little higher, and work a little harder."

Charlotte had grown hard and fast since the 1970s, propelled by the town's leading industry: banking. NCNB Corporation and First Union Corporation, headquartered in Charlotte, are the two largest bank-holding companies between Los Angeles and the Northeast. As interstate banking laws in the Southeast began loosening up, they began aggressively acquiring businesses and banks in South Carolina, Florida, and most recently Texas. Since the 1950s, the two had been responsible for shaping the skyline and geography of the city. The two banks, in a spirited, intramural competition, had rebuilt Charlotte's center city. When First Union built a thirty-two-story tower in Uptown in 1970, NCNB countered four years later with the forty-story NCNB Plaza two blocks away. Then in 1988, First Union moved into its new forty-two-story headquarters, prompting NCNB to announce plans for a new sixty-story NCNB Corporate Center to be completed in 1992. This was great for Tryon Street, Uptown's main thoroughfare and stomping ground for the button-down bankers who tumbled out of its formidable towers at lunchtime.

This one-upmanship, however, was only a sidelight to the philanthropic and civic contributions of Charlotte's banking executives, and the bucks the financial institutes were pouring into their community. NCNB had made low-interest loans available to early pioneers of Uptown's seedy fringes so that they could build upscale condominiums and Victorian-style homes. First Union was in the process of sinking $10 million into an Uptown park. At the same time, the town's financial giants were amassing more than $56.5 billion in assets and becoming the nation's seventh-largest banking center, shoving Dallas aside in the process.

The changes Charlotte was going through were consistent with its history since it was founded in the early 1760s and took the name of King George III's wife. The city had always tied its fortune to the business interests of the region. Over the years, it had been the capital of cotton, tobacco, and textiles. Since becoming the state's most populous city at the turn of the century, it had maintained its size by serving as the hub for North and South Carolina, whose border was only a few miles away. But the changes created by the banking industry had given Charlotte an urban profile. While shopping centers were anchoring the growing suburbs, downtown, now called Uptown, was coming back and it had a big-city feel—a mix of business, shopping, and street life. Attractive homes were being built within walking distance of the center of city. And it was also developing big-city problems—traffic congestion and expensive parking.

Charlotte had its critics. Some thought its push to become a New South City sacrificed the courtly, hospitable Southern ways of doing business. In the skyscraper building boom, Charlotte's historic architecture came down leaving it with few identifiable landmarks. It was becoming less courtly, less languid, and, consequently, less Southern. Bankers had introduced the three-piece suit as the business uniform. Charlotte was no longer a "sport coat" kind of town.

Mayor Upchurch of Raleigh, North Carolina's capital city, claimed that Charlotte was getting too big for North Carolina. Charlotte took such criticism lightly. It wasn't interested in intrastate competition. It had its sights set on becoming a bigger capital. When the city's boosters took out their demographic maps and counted all the residents within one hundred miles of the city, the number they came up with 5.6 million, slightly more than Atlanta.

George Shinn was far removed from the Fortune 500 and banking set in Charlotte. He ran a successful string of vocational schools, the Rutledge Educational System, and had made a fortune in an essential, but unglamorous, business. He was a friendly and accessible man, with perfectly coiffed preacher's hair and an easy manner. Shinn was a salesman who sold himself, fashioning a rags-to-riches tale that he told in two books, *The American Dream Still Works,* published in 1977, and *The Miracle of Motivation,* which appeared in 1981.

Shinn's books can be found in the inspirational section of bookstores. They contain a mix of autobiography, positive-thinking dictums, salesmanship tips, and "Praise The Lord-isms." Shinn fashioned himself as the regional spokesperson who utilized the Norman Vincent Peale/W. Clement Stone brand of business pep talks that he believed were validated by his own experience.

At thirty-one, on the brink of bankruptcy and failure, Shinn says that he had a religious experience. Facing a dozen or so lawsuits and a $67,000 tax bill on his business schools in Concord, Durham, Fayetteville, Greensboro, and Raleigh, he'd spent $500 to seek the advice of financial advisers. A group of lawyers and accountants recommended that he file for bankruptcy. "I didn't have a prayer to save the business," Shinn recounted, telling them he simply didn't have the money to even file. Driving down Interstate 85 a few days later, returning home with the specter of unpaid bills on his mind, he turned to prayer. As Shinn tells it, he began to cry, pulling over on the shoulder where he made a covenant with the Lord to share with Him any future wealth, if he could only survive the present.

Shinn says that from that moment he got a handle on the stress that had made him an overeater, drinker, and smoker. He decided to confront his creditors, asking for time, sending a Pittsburg textbook publisher a dollar because that was all he could afford. He began all of his business meetings with a prayer.

But Shinn's books also reveal that George Shinn was a lucky man. He had acquired his business after attending one of the schools because he'd needed to get out of his laborer's job due to a bad back. He had started as a janitor to pay his own tuition, then had moved fortuitously into recruitment. The schools were so badly managed that he soon got the chance to run them himself. He bought others throughout North Carolina on pure intuition, knowing that they too were financially strapped. When the enterprise started to go under, he took a common-sense business approach with his creditors, telling them if they foreclosed everyone would lose.

Shinn's faith and fortunes held long enough for him to meet a rival trade school operator named Jack Jones. Jones, who owned a string of successful trade schools in Florida, showed Shinn how to qualify his schools for government tuition grants, so he could attract Vietnam veterans with funds provided by the G.I. bill. The North Carolina Board of Education gave Shinn another break when it reduced the number of hours veterans had to attend school to twelve, from thirty-five, to be eligible for full benefits. Enrollment boomed and in 1975 Shinn was out of his financial straits.

Shinn was a natural on the church and rotary club circuit. That's where he began taking his dream of landing an NBA franchise, three or four nights a week. On these excursions, he touched on the burgeoning demographics and expanding television markets that made Charlotte a viable NBA entry, but mostly he focused on George Shinn—how a poor boy from Kannapolis had found God and wealth at the same time. After hearing Shinn speak at a gathering sponsored by the Chamber of Commerce in Hickory, a small North Carolina community northwest of Charlotte, one woman stood up to announce, "I don't know much about the NBA, but I like your story. I'll buy tickets to your team."

That he was a practiced public speaker who had become a leader of national sales and motivational conferences, where he pushed his power-of-positive-thinking message, played well in the Bible Belt. He had a fortune—which now included twenty-five business schools, real-estate interests, and car dealerships for an estimated net worth of well over $50 million—and he gave all the credit to God.

The excitement that Shinn generated publicly, however, did not carry over to Charlotte's corridors of power. The rubber-chicken and church-meeting circuit embraced the passionate millionaire's Christian vision of a major-league sports franchise in town, but in the corporate boardrooms and country clubs Shinn wasn't given much of a chance. He was considered an upstart. His string of business schools didn't have much stature in a town whose intertwined business and social strata were ruled by bank chieftains such as NCNB Corporation's Hugh McColl, Jr., the Belks whose department store had been a fixture in Charlotte for generations, and real-estate developers such as Johnny Harris of the Bissell Company.

The powers-that-be listened to his proposal, as did the Chamber of Commerce, but that's about all. No one thought he had a prayer, and he was too much of a wild card for them to stick their neck out for.

Without the clout of Charlotte's old guard, Shinn knew he had to find some way to win the hearts and minds of fellow Charlotteans. But he also needed some expertise, and for that he turned to Max Muhleman. The sports consultant and his staff at Muhleman Marketing used their experience in sports marketing and the information Shinn had gleaned from his visits with Dallas's Norm Sonju and other NBA executives to come up with a five-point plan for securing a team for Charlotte. Shinn only needed to negotiate a favorable lease agreement for the $52-million Coliseum the city was building; make a formal application to the league; presell season tickets; find investors; and lobby among NBA owners to gain support for Charlotte.

The two formed an effective inside-outside team. Muhleman, who'd had the contacts to get inside the NBA loop initially, went to work on the particulars of selling Charlotte's market, while Shinn listened carefully to the briefings before putting his practiced public speaking skills to use. Muhleman shared Shinn's commitment to the Carolinas. He agreed to work for a nominal fee, pushing himself and his sports staff long hours on behalf of Shinn's project.

"There have been only three important events in North Carolina," Muhleman said later. "The founding of the state, the Civil War, and the making of the Charlotte Hornets."

Shinn was conciliatory on January 15, 1986, when he announced his plan for landing an NBA franchise. He had to be because he needed the cooperation of the seven appointed members of the Coliseum Authority to negotiate a lease that would benefit his start-up. It was necessary to establish good-will with city officials, like Mayor Harvey Gantt and the city council, as well as with the local movers-and-shakers. A friendly climate could boost season ticket sales. If Shinn came off in the public eye as a businessman climbing to prominence on the achievements of the good citizens of Charlotte, then Shinn would have more to lose than a chance to become a sports mogul. The chase was on, and Shinn had Sonju in one corner, guiding him through the ins-and-outs of the NBA, and Muhleman in the other, devising a strategy tied closely to Charlotte's hunger for recognition.

Still, Shinn needed help at home. Besides faith and good fortune, Shinn's business success was marked by his ability to persuade influential people to lend him their time and talents. That's how he'd got into the trade school line, kept creditors at bay, and finally, upgraded his schools into money makers.

Mayor Gantt, the architect turned politician, was one of those charmed by the scrappy millionaire. Gantt had never heard of Shinn before the 1985 USFL exhibition games. After Shinn made a visit to the mayor's office asking for the city's help in promoting the event, Gantt asked his staff to check him out. They found no prior civic involvement on Shinn's part. The Chamber of Commerce didn't have a file on him. The best anyone could tell, he wasn't playing golf and talking business on the country club circuit. The mayor concluded that Shinn was "one of those millionaire entrepreneurs in

southeast Charlotte with a big house out on Carmel Road and
a couple of sports cars [thirty-two in fact] who'd quietly made
their money. They usually kept it. The town was full of these
types and even they didn't know who each other were."

But he was impressed when more than 16,000 curiosity-
seekers showed up in a driving rain for one of the USFL
games. They were wrapped in blankets and shielded by plastic
sheets and umbrellas. The raincoats Harvey Gantt and George
Shinn wore barely protected them, but there they were,
making their way around the old grandstands of Memorial
Stadium. Gantt thought it was amazing how those cold, shiv-
ering souls seemed to warm up as Shinn passed through the
crowd, shaking hands and asking folks if they were enjoying
themselves. He really wasn't yet aware of how popular Shinn
was becoming with Charlotteans.

But on that rainy day in 1985, Gantt realized that a
special bonding was occurring between the energetic Shinn
and the people whose hands he was pumping in the crowd.
As the distinguished mayor with the salt-and-pepper hair
strolled after the sports entrepreneur, he sensed that a bond
was forming between them too. When told perfunctorily by
Gantt at their first meeting to call if he needed any help, Shinn
had proceeded to bombard him with ideas and requests. Gantt
had decided that day that he liked Shinn. Shinn embodied
what Gantt thought was the spirit of the city—hard work, a
positive outlook, and no fear of progress.

Charlotte's progressiveness had begun to emerge with
Gantt's election to mayor in 1983. He was a black politician in
a Southern city where four out of five voters were white. When
he ran and beat a white businessman for a second term in
1985, he captured nearly half the white vote. Gantt had
launched his political career in Charlotte as a city councilman
in 1979 when he was chosen to finish the term of a councilman who was leaving for a seat in the North Carolina state
senate. A relative newcomer to the area, Gantt had been a
long shot for that seat. He was appointed when then-Mayor
John Belk, chairman of the local department store chain and
a member of one of Charlotte's oldest families, broke a tie in

Gantt's favor. Gantt was an interesting ally for Shinn. The mayor had been a beneficiary of the town's willingness to reward competence and achievement.

Gantt had been the first black student admitted to South Carolina's Clemson University in January 1963. The product of a Charleston, South Carolina, housing project, he'd been intent on completing architectural studies that he had started at Iowa State University at the state university in rural South Carolina. Four months earlier, when James Meredith enrolled at the University of Mississippi, he'd nearly touched off a civil war. But South Carolina had accepted the inevitable by the time Gantt applied for admission to Clemson and the state's politicians from Washington on down had put out the word that there would be no incidents marring the dawn of integration in South Carolina. Gantt now downplays the drama that accompanied his high-profile journey during one of the nation's darkest periods. The U.S. marshals assigned to him were gone after six weeks, but he did develop the habit of not sitting by windows or with his back to the door. "It's a quirk I brought along with me from my early days of being a pioneer at Clemson. Medgar Evers was shot down in his garage as he drove home one night, at about the same time that I was at Clemson. That wasn't too thrilling. And the dorms we lived in had an all-glass-wall type of construction so I made a habit of always closing my blinds at night."

Gantt had first come to Charlotte heralded as the city's first black architect—though he's quick to point out that history proves there were previous black builders and artisans responsible for several Charlotte buildings. Nevertheless, he was the first college-educated black architect in town. The Charlotte he describes prior to moving on to Boston, where he earned a master's degree in urban planning at Massachusetts Institute of Technology, was one that was yet to develop a coherent character. The downtown square was still something of an employment center, but as a city center it was dying. Talk in architecture and city planning circles, with which he was most familiar, revolved around a great regional mall that was in the works in Southeast Charlotte—the Southpark Mall. It was just minutes from Uptown and had become the impetus for the office building, hotel, residential, and retail development promised in the mid-sixties.

On his return in 1971, Gantt found Charlotte stretching to emulate its neighbor to the southwest, Atlanta—"the city too busy to hate." But Gantt sensed correctly that the town was ready to abandon its envy and settle for "being us." The downtown area was on the threshold of becoming the major employment district. A civic center and a natural science museum were either in the planning stage or being built. There were also plans to restore and rebuild the nearby Third- and Fourth-ward sections—their previous political designations—into a smart, ritzy residential development. Suddenly talk of downtown developing into a cosmopolitan, entertainment and convention center was breaking out in public as well as professional forums.

Though the city was gaining momentum, Gantt thought Charlotte was still insecure about its identity. There were no physical landmarks, mountains, or rivers. "Atlanta had burned down and Charleston was steeped in American history. You couldn't, and to some extent still can't, put your finger on what makes Charlotte tick." What was apparent to Gantt, however—and what he thinks is often overlooked by Charlotteans and outsiders alike—is the energy of Charlotte's people.

He described this intangible thusly: "I came here in 1971 and as a black architect and urban planner was able to play a part in shaping downtown. I got involved in politics and served on the city council. I was elected mayor twelve years later in a city that I was basically new to. That tells you a lot about what kind of place Charlotte is."

With the growing support of Gantt and other city leaders, Shinn was now drawing his own media crowd. Muhleman made sure of that. The would-be owner was appearing on local television stations on a regular basis, with his positive upbeat message of "yes, we can." When Shinn and the Coliseum authority were at a standstill over a viable lease in spring 1986, Norm Sonju, in town on a visit, stepped in to give the city a reality dose. "There is not a chance unless he gets a great lease. People are not thinking of Charlotte. They are not thinking one thing about the NBA here," the highly excitable Sonju told reporters with alarming candor on May 7. "They need a lease that is awesome. This is a small, unique, select group . . . George Shinn and the NBA is the only chance Charlotte has for a major-league franchise in this city."

Gantt, who was getting used to behind-the-scenes wheeling and dealing for Charlotte's NBA bid, was asked to step in. He had been privy to the frequent Sonju, Muhleman, and Shinn skull sessions. He'd also been at a covert spring meeting in 1986 with the owner of the Utah Jazz.

Shinn's expansion machinery was already in gear then, but the NBA didn't know at this point if the league was certain to expand. Shinn was interested in stealing a team for Charlotte, thus circumventing what already was looking like a long, uncertain process, when Sam Battistone of the Utah Jazz put the word out that he was interested in selling. Shinn arranged a secret meeting at his southeast Charlotte home, where Battistone and his Los Angeles attorney, Phil Marantz, stayed the night discussing the viability of bringing the Jazz to Charlotte. The aspiring NBA owner quickly realized, however, that such talk was premature. He didn't have a lease agreement for the Coliseum. There had been no season ticket drive yet, so there was no way to truly judge how much support was building in the area. The financing had also proved to be nettlesome. Shinn's first objective was to persuade Battistone to become his partner. The Jazz owner wasn't interested. The price discussed at that point was $25 million, leaving the still-partnerless Shinn to put up $10 million and finance the rest. It didn't take long for Shinn to realize that the tenor of the talks were exploratory at best. The expansion group in Minneapolis was also feeling the Jazz out, and Battistone was taking his time to assess all his options. When Battistone decided in June to sell his interest to Jazz partner Larry Miller, who vowed to keep the team in Salt Lake, Shinn's plan's were temporarily dashed. The exercise, however, was hardly futile. Shinn earned even greater credibility from NBA insiders who'd viewed his efforts from afar. Shinn appeared eager to make something work, and word that Gantt also was wholeheartedly behind any NBA effort reflected well on Charlotte.

The discussions also underscored how important an attractive lease agreement was to the NBA. Charlotte's planned new facility gave Shinn an edge over the cities so far competing for a franchise. Talk—still speculative at this point because the league had yet to announce expansion—that the first season could be as early as 1987–88, favored the Charlotte and Minneapolis groups. Minneapolis had the Metrodome and Charlotte could play in the existing 11,666-seat Coliseum, then move into the new, 23,500-seat one in spring '88. The other serious contenders, Orlando and Miami, were still building and wouldn't be done before then. Miami's arena wasn't expected to be completed for the '87–'88 season. But if Shinn couldn't get an attractive deal there was no advantage in having a new arena. Sonju had showed up in Charlotte to fire his best shot, as had Shinn and Muhleman. Shinn now turned to the mayor.

The two met one afternoon in Gantt's architecture firm's office on 5th Street, just off Tryon Street. Shinn was agitated about the Coliseum Authority's insistence on a standard eight to ten percent of revenues per-game rental fee, which could amount to as much as $20,000 per night, and a percentage of parking and revenues. They sat down at a conference table in Gantt's second-floor library and began brainstorming, trying to find some arrangement that would sway both the Coliseum Authority and the NBA. Gantt tossed off phrases such as "a buck a game" and "sweetheart deal." Soon the two were conceptualizing what essentially appeared to be a dream deal. Shinn would pay $1 a game, or $41 a year, for the Hornets' home dates, in return for the city getting all parking and concession revenues. The modest rental fee could be more than made up by revenue parking alone. If just a quarter of the 8,000 parking spaces were filled, say at $3 a pop, that would mean $6,000 a night. The Coliseum would be assured an anchor tenant with high visibility, and Shinn would have his eye-catching agreement to lay before the NBA. Everyone

would make money, they thought, while projecting an image
of harmony between public and private interest. Shinn and
Gantt believed they had done a good afternoon's work. The
mayor's staff helped draw up the proposal and approached
the Coliseum Authority in private. Shinn, after being schooled
by the mayor and Muhleman, took his proposal public. Still,
the Coliseum Authority balked. A few weeks later, when the
political arm-twisting wasn't yielding results, Gantt introduced
a resolution asking the Authority to accept George Shinn's
proposal for Coliseum rental with minor modifications, which
the city council passed on May 12, 1986. The resolution was
in itself worthless because the city council did not have the
power to negotiate, but it was an effective reminder of where
most of Charlotte stood on gaining an NBA franchise. Two
weeks later the Authority agreed to accept the proposal for
five years.

The NBA quest was no longer relegated to the sports
segment of television newscasts. It was a local story wanting
to go national. Every step Shinn took was covered by the
news media as if it were of immense importance. Even Gantt
found the cheerleading reaching somewhere between amus-
ing and absurd levels when a contingent of elected officials
accompanied Shinn to New York on June 23, 1986. The
purpose of the trip was to present Stern a check for $100,000,
making Charlotte's application to the NBA official. Rented
limousines were pressed into service for the Charlotte contingent, which included Gantt, North Carolina Governor Jim
Martin, two of his escorts from the state police, and Mecklenburg County Commission Chairperson, Carla DuPuy. As they
rolled up to the NBA offices off Fifth Avenue in the Olympic
Tower, Gantt remembers looking out and seeing a gaggle of
television cameras and reporters, all from North Carolina,
rushing toward the limos ready to capture what they hoped
was a historic moment. "When we stepped out I saw all these
usually indifferent New Yorkers walking by giving us looks like,
'Who the hell are these guys?' "

Nevertheless, Gantt stayed out front with his support for
Shinn and his dream. The mayor recognized that the NBA

campaign had captured the fancy of his city. Wherever he went, his curious constituents asked about the fate of the franchise—could Charlotte pull it off; did Shinn know what he was doing; what was the next step? Gantt thought Shinn was a master at drumming up public support, sending the newspapers and television stations much the same message he was sending to the NBA: that Charlotte was a large enough, fat enough Southeastern city, where basketball was sacred, and pride ran deep. Shinn told both groups that professional basketball in Carolina was to be presented as an old-fashion, family entertainment. No sex or cheesiness would be part of his product.

The momentum building for a basketball team was sufficient enough for Gantt to turn over a city council meeting to Shinn on July 14, 1986, so a season ticket drive could be launched. Shinn was asking that Charlotte demonstrate good faith to the NBA by putting a nonrefundable deposit of $50 to $200 for season tickets for a team no one was sure they could get. Once more the cameras rolled as Shinn presented Gantt with the commemorative first season ticket. The entire city council stood behind them wearing white T-shirts emblazoned with an outline of the state inside a basketball and the slogan "Bring the NBA to Basketball Country."

"Let the world know why they call this basketball country," Shinn declared. "It's time for people in Charlotte to start believing what we can do."

By the end of the day, more than 700 season tickets had been secured with deposits. The crusade was on. Shinn's obstacles were falling one by one as a result of community support. Now only money and moxy stood in the way of a deal.

3

BY THE NUMBERS

T HE Arizona sun wasn't up when Max Muhleman flipped on the lights in a nondescript conference room at the Biltmore Hotel in Phoenix. It was 6:00 A.M. and Muhleman had come down from his room early to check the venue, where in two-and-a-half hours, George Shinn would make Charlotte's case for a professional basketball team before more than twenty-three NBA owners and league representatives. The warm-up period was over. The personal lobbying of NBA officials, the arm twisting of public officials, and the courting of potential season ticket holders at home, all had led to this October 20, 1986, invitation to appear at the NBA league meetings. Charlotte, along with groups from Miami, Orlando, Minneapolis, St. Petersburg, Orange County, and Toronto, would have thirty minutes to explain why their city should be allowed to join the NBA fraternity. Norm Sonju had told Shinn and Muhleman not to worry. This was just a preliminary introduction. "If this was a basketball game, Phoenix'd be the national anthem—you've got to go through it, but the game hasn't started," he'd assured them. In fact, the NBA wouldn't vote on whether or not the league would expand until the next day.

Shinn was about to take his NBA efforts national and he was understandably nervous. While Muhleman was downstairs diagramming the room—noting an aisle halving the auditorium-style seating arrangement, the two television monitors on either side of a raised platform—Shinn was upstairs trying to catch a few hours of fitful sleep. He had been up well past 2:00 A.M., rehearsing his presentation in the bathroom so he wouldn't wake his wife, Carolyn. Shinn and Muhleman were confident they were ready for the meeting. The details of Shinn's presentation had been meticulously attended to— Muhleman's reconnaissance was a final touch to calm Shinn and his partners.

Rick Hendrick and Felix Sabates, two Charlotte businessmen, were in Phoenix along with Shinn. They had signed on as partners three weeks earlier. Their presence in Phoenix was a much needed tonic for Charlotte's presentation. Shinn had been struggling to put an ownership group together for almost a year. The process of acquiring an NBA team was still in its early stages, so Shinn wasn't yet worried about raising the money. But he had been frustrated by the financial doors that had kept slamming at home. Commissioner Stern had made it clear at their first meeting almost a year ago that the price for a franchise was going to start at $20 million. That was a lot of money. Shinn didn't have it, and he wasn't sure of needed financing from the banks without other partners. A potential investor list, with dozens of names, had been drawn up by Shinn, his attorneys, accountants from Arthur Andersen, and Muhleman at one meeting. It included the richest Carolinians north and south of the state line. But the contacts hadn't panned out and the results were disappointing.

Major league sports teams had never been given a chance to succeed in Charlotte. A minor league ice hockey team did well in the old Coliseum for almost twenty years beginning in 1956, but it was small time, as was the Double-A baseball team in Charlotte since 1976. Charlotte's other ventures into

professional sports had been plagued by their leagues' insta-
bility. The American Basketball Association's (ABA) Carolina
Cougars rotated through Charlotte—along with Greensboro
and Raleigh—in the early 1970s before moving on to St.
Louis. The team never quite caught on in Charlotte as it did
in the other two home cities. The Charlotte Hornets got only
one season in before the World Football League folded in
1975. The American Soccer League's Carolina Lightnin'
packed 25,000 people into its championship game in its first
season in 1981, but that league was finished by 1983. The
Gold of Charlotte tried to revive soccer enthusiasm in 1984,
playing in the United States Soccer League, but that lasted
only a season.

     This wasn't to say the town didn't have its sports enthusi-
asts. The PGA's Kemper Open enjoyed a successful tenure in
Charlotte from 1969 to 1979. And the Charlotte Motor Speed-
way draws phenomenal numbers to its two major NASCAR
races. Then the more glamorous of the two, the Kemper
Open, snubbed the town for Washington, D.C., and the
NASCAR circuit isn't quite the city's own because it draws
from a fan base that encompasses the South and Southeast.

     Hendrick and Sabates had in fact been prior players in
Charlotte's spotty sports history. Sabates, who owned an
electronics and consumer goods corporation, had been the
major force behind the short-lived Charlotte Gold soccer
franchise. Shinn had first sounded him out about a USFL
franchise team, but Sabates wasn't interested. He told Shinn,
however, that he'd be interested in a basketball team. When
Shinn arrived at his office a few weeks later with a basketball
plan, he asked if Sabates was willing to be one of thirty-five
limited partners. Sabates didn't want that many coinvestors,
but said he would join if the number was reduced. Sabates
was aware of the trouble Shinn was having enlisting investors.
"He was turned down by every single person he went to until
I came along," Sabates recalled. "Every person he went to
laughed at him." But once Shinn revised his plan in favor of a
smaller group of investors, Sabates joined him.

     The thirty-seven-year-old Hendrick ran one of the nation's largest networks of auto dealerships, and was best known as a Charlotte racing czar of the NASCAR circuit. His four racing teams, running under the Hendrick Motor Sports umbrella, had combined for more than twenty major racing wins including two victories at the Daytona 500—stock car racing's Super Bowl. Shinn had known Hendrick for more than fifteen years and was a minor partner in four of his dealerships. He was more interested in helping out his friend, Shinn, than in owning part of a basketball team.

Hendrick and Sabates had agreed to put up roughly 10 percent of the deal, which amounted to about $1 million each. Hendrick further believed that his more substantial contribution would help sway the current NBA owners. He knew Houston's Charlie Thomas and Utah's Larry Miller from auto dealership circles and was looking to lend a hand.

Sabates and Hendrick's involvement hardly solved Shinn's partnership problems, but it lent some credibility, both at home and in the NBA, to Charlotte's bid. The previous night, while Muhleman was rehearsing the three men in Sabates's room, the group had received an additional boost from Charlotte broadcast magnate, Cy Bahakel. Bahakel had called from Charlotte to tell Shinn that he wanted to join the ownership group. Bahakel, who owned seven television stations—including Charlotte's independent WCCB-18—and thirteen radio stations, was one of the heavy hitters on Shinn's potential investor list. That night on the phone, Bahakel said he was willing to invest an amount comparable to Hendrick and Sabates. Bahakel was a man of substantial net worth (by Shinn's estimation ten or twelve times greater than his own $50 million) and his broadcasting background was invaluable for a made-for-TV sport like professional basketball. "Cy's wanting in really lifted us up," Shinn recalled. "We didn't announce it at the meeting, but it made me feel like things were really coming together."

By morning, Shinn, Sabates, and Hendrick were ready to lay out the Charlotte sales pitch to the gathering of NBA owners. Even a throwaway line in a Phoenix newspaper failed to unnerve them. Muhleman was paging through the morning

paper when he came across an article that handicapped the
various city's chances at wooing the NBA. The sportswriter
placed Charlotte last in the expansion derby, which was hardly
surprising since everyone from Sonju to Stern had been frank
in telling Shinn that he had great deal of selling to do to make
anyone take an unknown city of some 366,000 people seriously. But the sportswriter concluded his capsule analysis of
the Queen City with a stinging summation, saying the only
franchise Charlotte would get "was one with golden arches."
Shinn had asked Muhleman early that morning if there was
anything of note in the paper, but the sports consultant had
shrugged it off and said no. The would-be owner didn't take
his word for it and found the item on his own. "I knew we
were underdogs, but that was ridiculous," Shinn reflected.

It was that perception, however, that Shinn and company
were prepared to dispel when they entered the Biltmore's
conference room to ask the NBA for consideration. Back in
December, when Shinn and Muhleman first sat down with
David Stern, the NBA commissioner had leaned back on his
couch and asked Shinn point blank, "Why Charlotte?"

Muhleman, the sports consultant, recalled, "I made a
note to myself right then, that if we ever got to the presentation
stage, we were going to have some type of display that
answered that."

Shinn, Sabates, and Hendrick were well prepared to
dispel Charlotte's anonymity when they took their places in
front of the members of the elite club they wished to join. The
script called for an all-business, unemotional presentation that
focused on where and what Charlotte was and why it was
going to make money for the NBA. It was an approach that
had been painstakingly plotted by Muhleman after endless
discussions with Sonju and Shinn. Shinn was to do all the
speaking, addressing the NBA owners as the businessmen
they were in a language they wanted to hear. The pitch was
to take twenty-four minutes, leaving six for questions. If it went
as planned, "They will enjoy discovering Charlotte," Muhleman told the trio.

First an eight-minute video was queued featuring the

bank-built skyline of Uptown and the mellifluous voice of local TV news anchor Bob Inman describing Charlotte as the hub of a vibrant region that included both North and South Carolina. NCNB chairman Hugh McColl appeared to discuss the season tickets his bank had bought. The theme of Charlotte as a regional market was underscored by a shot of a map of North and South Carolina with two circles orbiting Charlotte. The first depicted the fifty-mile radius from the new Coliseum, which encompassed 1.8 million people, the second was a one-hundred-mile radius taking in 5.5 million people. Then Shinn moved to the four story boards. True to his word, Muhleman had titled the first one, "Why Charlotte?" Shinn ticked off the bulleted items. "The Heart of Basketball Country, Ready to Play in '87, State-of-the-Art Facility in '88, Extraordinary Lease, Only Show in Town, Local Ownership, Legitimate Season Tickets." Each highlighted point demonstrated that Shinn and Muhleman had listened carefully to David Stern and Norm Sonju. Since Stern took office in 1984, he had been zealous about finding solid hometown owners for each franchise. He wanted businessmen who would live and die by their franchises, not millionaires whose basketball teams were alternative investments. Such management had plagued the NBA in the late 1970s and early 1980s, when the game became mired in sagging attendance and dismal television ratings. By weeding out those types, namely in Cleveland and Indiana, Stern had turned around the league. In 1981, only six of twenty-three teams had operated at a profit. Now better than three quarters of the NBA teams were making money, attendance had grown yearly at an 8-percent rate, and advertisers were lining up to get a piece of NBA telecasts.

As Shinn moved to the other boards, it was apparent to Stern and Sonju, as well as the rest of the league, that he and Charlotte were very serious about capturing a franchise. Once more the state map was shown, with its circles containing five million people. The season ticket board touted $1.6 million of real money collected from Charlotteans, who'd put up nonrefundable deposits of $50 to $250 for specific seats. If they didn't pay the balance after Charlotte won a team, they'd lose their money.

And then there was the lease board. Hendrick, who was on Shinn's flank, facing the owners, watched them come to attention as Shinn recited the five-year, $1-a-game lease for a state-of-the-art, multimillion-dollar arena with a more than 23,000-seat capacity built for basketball. "They sat up in their chairs and I heard one of them say 'Boy, you know what that's worth a year,' " Hendrick related. For a group of businessmen used to paying 10 to 12 percent of their revenues for rent, or easily $1 million a year, the $41-a-year agreement was unfathomable. The second five years addressed in the agreement was still below market rate with Shinn agreeing to pay a graduating four to eight percent of the franchise's revenues.

With Hendrick and Sabates on either side, Shinn spoke to the league gathering about the trio's self-made wealth. They had made their money themselves and knew what it was like not to have something, as well as to achieve a goal. They were Charlotteans who weren't going anywhere else. They would rise and fall in the community on the strength of the franchise. "The message was that we were committed," Shinn said. "Trust us. We're not silver spooners with a casual attitude." Muhleman looked at his watch as Shinn finished up. They had come in at twenty-four-and-a-half minutes, barely off schedule, with plenty of time for questions. One of the owners asked about the Coliseum lease, to make sure he had heard correctly. He had. The NBA was beginning to discover Charlotte.

Shinn and company had taken to heart their underdog role. Their business pitch had served to bring Charlotte out of its obscurity. Orlando had Walt Disney World as a landmark. Miami didn't need to push its image as an international city. Minneapolis at least had the memory of professional basketball's first big man, center George Mikan and the Minneapolis Lakers, along with baseball's Twins and the NFL's Vikings. Shinn and company were buoyed by their Phoenix performance. They'd heard through the grapevine that theirs was the only presentation to come in at thirty minutes, and that the owners were buzzing about "those circles" that illustrated the regional market and the lease arrangement. The following day the NBA named a five-person expansion committee to study the possibility of adding one to three teams to the league. The group included Alan N. Cohen of the Boston Celtics; Charlie Thomas of the Houston Rockets; Herb Simon of the Indiana Pacers; Richard Bloch of Phoenix; and Norm Sonju.

Sonju was pleased with how Charlotte had performed at the Phoenix meetings, and his commitment to help Shinn was firmer than ever. But now he was part of the expansion committee, so his role shifted from friendly consultant to representative of the NBA's interests. It was fine line to walk publicly for a man who was pulling for the underdog. Sonju's visits to Charlotte prior to the Phoenix meetings had made him a familiar sounding board for the local media. The Dallas general manager literally held the key to the city. Mayor Gantt had presented Sonju with a ceremonial key to Charlotte on a visit in May 1986. Afterward, he was rushing through Charlotte–Douglas International Airport with the souvenir in his pocket, trying to make a flight back to Dallas when he was flagged down by metal detectors. The key actually looked like a letter opener, or in security's estimation, a knife. "I told them that it was the very key to their city, that I had just received it from the mayor," Sonju recalled. Still, they wouldn't let him through. Finally, the proclamation from Mayor Gantt was produced, and Sonju made his plane.

The numerous phone calls Sonju and Shinn had shared had cemented a deep friendship between mentor and pupil. The two had talked incessantly about how to fine-tune Charlotte's bid—on car phones, pay phones, even while Sonju skied in Colorado. Shortly after the Phoenix meeting, Sonju made an important call to the owner in hope of heading off a potential problem. Shinn, Sabates, and Hendrick had been restrained in their public assessments of how they'd fared at the league meetings. Privately, the believed they had made a big splash in Phoenix, following the Muhleman plan to the letter and making the NBA take note. But a few newspaper articles Sonju read reported quotes like: "Wow, we really knocked them dead in Phoenix." This wasn't what the NBA needed to hear, so Sonju picked up the phone to warn Shinn.

"George, you've got to stop that," Sonju told him, knowing Shinn wasn't the one who'd said it. "Trust me on this."

He explained that the NBA ownership was sensitive to others making judgments for them. He didn't want him to be perceived as cocky or arrogant. "They were the underdogs," Sonju explained. "They were really getting more and more respect from the committee, just one faux pas and the whole thing could change. I didn't want anything to go wrong."

Shinn knew exactly what Sonju was trying to tell him. Over the course of his quest, Shinn had carefully gauged how his own ego might hold up when surrounded by such select company. Shinn smiled when he described his dance with the USFL's Donald Trump and John Bassett. "I held up just fine. Mr. Trump does things quite a bit different than I do, but, heck, I'm from Kannapolis." Shinn understood that he wouldn't be able to just pay his money and get a franchise. Sonju was his bridge to the big time. He also advised Shinn to stick with business when talking to other owners. The NBA had a history of smiling on smaller, one-sport markets, such as Portland, Sacramento, and Salt Lake City, and the owners were more concerned with proficiency than the personality of its owners.

Besides, Shinn didn't have time for distractions. He was waiting for the decision that would affect his current position— how much an expansion team, if awarded, would cost. The $20 million or so price tag Stern had first mentioned was already rumored to be going up. There were four finalists for expansion: Miami, Orlando, Minneapolis, and Charlotte. Wilt Chamberlain had been part of the Toronto group to speak in Phoenix, but their planning was still in the preliminary stage. Groups from St. Petersburg, Florida, and Orange County, California, had also spoken to the owners, but neither city had an arena to play in. With so many interested cities, Shinn was sure that demand far exceeded supply. The escalating figures just increased the pressure to find additional investors. Shinn was hoping the price would top out at $25 million. "The urge was to call the committee and say, 'Look, what's it going to cost?' " Muhleman recalled.

Instead, the NBA called them. The expansion committee had arrived at an entry fee. They asked Shinn to come to New York for a meeting on January 12, 1987, in the NBA's Fifth Avenue offices. Representatives from Miami, Minneapolis, and Orlando also were asked to New York that day for separate meetings. Sabates wanted to go to the meeting with Shinn. He was a gregarious but straight-talking sort who had heard the price was going to be much higher than the expected $25 million. He was upset, and he wanted a few words with the men who seemed to be adjusting the figures. Shinn knew Sabates wasn't happy about the rising entry fee, and remembering Sonju's warning to avert any missteps, he feared that if his partner lost his temper, Charlotte's chances might be jeopardized. Sabates was in Las Vegas on business the night before the meeting and intended to catch the red-eye to New York in time to make Charlotte's scheduled 1:30 P.M. meeting. Shinn called him there and asked if there was anyway he could be in New York earlier. Sabates said he could not. "So I called the NBA and asked them if we could move up our appointment," Shinn said. "Then I called Felix back and told him that they wanted us there earlier, and not to bother." When Shinn and Muhleman arrived at the league offices that morning and were ushered into a conference room, where the expansion committee was waiting, both men sensed that they were there for a brief business meeting. Phoenix owner Richard Bloch was running the meeting and wasted little time getting right to the point.

"The price is thirty-two million, five hundred thousand dollars," he said.

Shinn didn't respond immediately. The figure was far greater than he'd heard, much, much more than he had expected. No one said a word. Shinn asked if the price was concrete. Bloch told him it was, and asked if it was a problem.

"Are you in or out?" Muhleman remembered Bloch asking straight out.

"We're in," Shinn answered, not yet knowing how he was going to raise the cash. So far he had three partners willing to commit a rough total of $3 to $5 million. But he had come this far, and wasn't about to stumble. He'd figure it out later. Shinn flew back to Charlotte to tell his partners about the price and begin prepping for the final push. Sabates as expected was miffed by the amount, but Shinn didn't tell him about rescheduling the meeting until several months later. "George is the best salesman I know. He has a way of telling you something that you don't want to hear, and he makes you want to hear it," Sabates admitted.

At home, Shinn had the public clamoring for a basketball team. When he attended the NBA All-Star Game in Seattle, he had an entourage of local television and newspaper reporters in tow. Their dispatches back to Charlotte that weekend varied widely, but heightened the city's anticipation of how this hardcourt drama might play out. There were reports that Shinn had approached Los Angeles Clipper owner Donald Sterling about buying the struggling West Coast franchise and moving it to the Queen City. NBA executive vice-president Russ Granik was stalked until he finally conceded that the expansion committee would be visiting Charlotte soon. Shinn was videotaped getting in and out of his private jet, holding up rating placards for Saturday's All-Star Slam Dunk contest, and generally keeping the city's attention focused on his bid for a basketball team.

The weekend was an effective smoke screen for a pivotal event that Shinn knew was right around the corner. The following week, Sonju and Houston Rockets principal owner Charlie Thomas would make an official inspection of Charlotte on behalf of the expansion committee.

The two arrived early February 11 for a full day of meetings, similar to the ones they and other committee members already had conducted in Orlando and Minneapolis. The importance of the meeting was not lost on Shinn and Gantt. These two men would be the ones who would give a firsthand recommendation to the members of the expansion committee and to the rest of the owners. Sonju, by now a familiar face in Charlotte, arrived at Charlotte–Douglas International Airport first, and was greeted with the same question: What were Charlotte's chances to be chosen by the committee? Sonju was diplomatic. "I told Gary Bettman [NBA vice-president and general counsel] that if I had to give any more nonanswers as answers, then I was going to become a politician."

Gantt realized that Sonju was pulling his punches, but he kept looking for some reassurance. "We were pressing at that point because we thought we had a good chance and Norm couldn't tell us if we were in or not. He *was* trying to tell us that there was not a hell of a lot that I could do and he didn't suggest that there was anything else we could do," Gantt recalled.

The day began with a visit to the Coliseum site, about a ten-minute drive from downtown. It was still a year from completion, and not much more than a hole in the ground. Shinn was in negotiations with the Coliseum Authority to make it even more attractive for a professional basketball team, discussing the addition of skyboxes and advertising boards to increase the revenue potential. Sonju had told Shinn to do his best to prevent his visit from turning into a media event. He and Thomas were there on business and had a lot to cover, which would only be hampered if they were accompanied by an entourage. But Sonju, standing near the construction trailer at the Coliseum site, noticed news photographers on a nearby hill zooming in their telephoto lenses on what was at that point an innocuous proceeding. The NBA representatives weren't going to be allowed to slip into town unacknowledged.

Shinn then took the two committee members by the mayor's office, where Gantt once more dazzled them with the city's commitment to bringing a team to Charlotte. Shinn believed things were going well. The trio had a noon lunch meeting with bankers at NCNB, where Shinn was in the process of firming up financing. By now most NBA people knew of Charlotte's stature in the banking world. The city was proud of its banks, which not only slugged it out on Wall

Street, but invested heavily in the community. NCNB was drawing good notices for its aggressive expansion, moving into Florida and Georgia, almost singlehandedly building Charlotte's foundation as a New South city. Hugh McColl, Jr., the bank's chairman of the board, was at the forefront of those efforts. He was characterized by Wall Street as a hard-charging ex-Marine, and at home as Charlotte's kingmaker.

The luncheon meeting was held on the fortieth floor of the NCNB Tower. Sonju and Thomas were expecting to hear about the particulars of the bank's commitment to Shinn and a Charlotte franchise. They met with several bank officers. McColl, who Thomas believed was scheduled for the meeting, was out of town on other business. Sonju was fielding the questions the bankers were firing about the league. But Thomas was having a hard time getting to the heart of what he had come to learn: Was the bank behind Shinn and the basketball team? In fact, both NBA representatives felt that they were being treated as if they were there to borrow money.

"Hey, wait a minute, you've got it all wrong, we're here to ask *you* the questions," Thomas interjected.

The meeting was a disaster. As soon as the trio entered the elevator, Shinn knew that Thomas was upset. Sonju said they'd been under the impression that the bank's commitment was "a tad stronger" than it now appeared.

"They tried to get Norm and Charlie to sell them on why they should loan me the money to get a team, when Norm and Charlie fully expected the bankers to sell *them* on why Charlotte deserved a franchise," Shinn said later. "It got Charlie's water a little warm."

Thomas made it very clear that he was not satisfied with the banking commitment at a meeting following the lunch at Cy Bahakel's WCCB-TV offices. The gathering, which was scheduled to be merely a meet-the-partners affair, turned quickly to what had just transpired at NCNB. Bahakel, who at the time was only a limited partner, tried to head off Sonju and Thomas's concerns. "Cy stood up and said, 'Don't worry about the bank. I'll loan all the money that the team needs,' " Shinn recalled.

Bahakel had the financial muscle to back up his reassurance. The broadcast executive admitted that he was very interested in any television rights that would result from a professional basketball team. But he too had been caught up in the drama of Charlotte's underdog role and scramble for an NBA franchise. Like Shinn, he was a self-made man, an Alabaman with a law degree who, after a short stint practicing law, had decided to take up a friend's offer to buy a radio station. Bahakel had dabbled as a radio announcer while working his way through law school at the University of Alabama. When his friend, a broadcasting engineer, proposed that they each invest $12,500 to set up a station in Kosciusko, Mississippi, Bahakel said good-bye to the law. From those modest beginnings, he had built a broadcast empire throughout the South and Midwest. Bahakel, at sixty-two, was older than his fellow investors. He had served in the North Carolina Legislature in the 1970s, and was better known in Charlotte. Bahakel didn't know Shinn when first approached in September 1986 about becoming involved in the NBA effort. He'd listened to what Shinn had to say, but had taken his time before deciding to buy in for a small share while Shinn, Sabates, and Hendrick were in Phoenix. "I'd be lying if I didn't say I was interested in any potential television rights," Bahakel said. "But after amassing a substantial net worth, as I have, I wanted to give something back to the community. This was all George's wild idea and while I didn't want to be running a basketball team, I wanted to be a part of it."

Bahakel's offer to finance the team was duly noted. But at the time, none of the partners thought it would be necessary.

"I did not have a commitment from the bank then, but it didn't bother me as much as it did Charlie Thomas," Shinn related.

And it bothered Thomas plenty. Sonju flew back with the Rockets' owner on Thomas's private plane. They stopped in Tennessee to pick up Thomas's wife, and then went on to Houston, where Sonju planned on taking a commercial flight back to Dallas. Sonju used the extended trip to discuss Charlotte, Shinn, and the Coliseum. He made no secret that he was a booster. But Thomas kept returning to the bank situation. He was the former chairman of the board of BancTexas Group and understood the nuances of major financing. He was reticent; there didn't seem much enthusiasm on the part of NCNB to get behind the deal. Sonju did what he could to assuage his concerns, but Thomas was a banker, Sonju was not. He knew if the Rockets' owner perceived a problem with financing, there probably was one.

The financial issue seemed to disappear for a few weeks while the expansion committee continued its inspections and assessed the various applicants. The NBA was still talking about adding two teams, so the competition between the four cities intensified. Sonju was on his way to a speaking engagement on Friday, March 13, when Thomas called. "I don't want you blind-sided the next time the committee meets," Sonju recalled Thomas telling him. "I just want you to know that I'm not going to recommend Charlotte."

Sonju was so taken aback, he paused for a minute before asking gingerly, "Now, Charlie, what is it you're concerned about?" He was trying to figure out if it was a personality conflict, or something about the city that had turned Thomas off. Thomas told him simply that he was concerned about the Shinn group's financial backing, specifically the meeting at NCNB.

Sonju said he couldn't disagree, and tried to decide if Thomas could be persuaded. "Still, my heart just sank. All that effort and how strongly I felt that Charlotte was a good place." But there was really no time for despair. He was on his way out, en route to a speaking engagement at Preston Hollow Presbyterian Church in Dallas. It was to be a quick turn before heading back to Reunion for the Mavericks' game with Atlanta. Sonju had to speak with Shinn. He called from his car phone, while negotiating rush-hour traffic on the North Dallas Tollway. But Shinn wasn't in his office. Sonju insisted that Diane Abell, Shinn's secretary, find him. Sonju remained on hold while Abell traced Shinn's whereabouts—first at his accountants, then at the bank, where she finally found him. Shinn went to his car phone and Sonju was patched through.

"The bankers really turned off Charlie," Sonju said, explaining his conversation with Thomas. "He's not going to support the thing. What we need to do is get this particular hitch straightened out. He thinks the world of you and of the city. Once you have Charlie, he'll get the committee to vote for you."

Shinn wasn't wild about how the team's proposed financing was shaking out anyway. Now the guy who had brought him this far was in a church parking lot in Dallas telling him that one of the two members of the NBA expansion committee who had visited Charlotte could not in clear conscience recommend the city for a franchise.

"If he went back with a negative report, that obviously would have hurt us," Shinn recalled. "And that's when I realized how desperate the situation was. I knew I had to get Hugh McColl to call Charlie Thomas." Shinn made several calls shortly after hearing from Sonju. He spoke with his partners, Bahakel, Sabates, and Hendrick. He then called Thomas. He moved quickly to shore up his financial package. Bahakel had spoken up when Thomas had expressed concern after meeting with the bankers. He had the financial clout necessary to impress the NBA and when Shinn asked him to increase his investment, Bahakel had agreed. Still, he needed to reach Hugh McColl.

Shinn explained Thomas's hesitancy to McColl and asked if the bank chairman might call the Houston owner. McColl complied. "I called him and told him I understood that he had some question about whether the bank really was fully behind Mr. Shinn," McColl recounted. "He had concluded from a couple of questions that some of my officers had asked that we were unsure whether we would finance Mr. Shinn. . . . I made it eminently clear that we were behind the team and would finance it, and were behind George and his partners and that it wasn't a problem."

McColl essentially went out on a limb for Charlotte's basketball hopes. A panicked phone call at dusk from Sonju

in Dallas had turned Charlotte's major-league aspirations into
near-major-league reality. Besides swaying Thomas, NCNB's
chairman of the board had indicated to the Shinn group for
the first time that the bank was really behind them.

Shinn believed the bank's commitment and Bahakel's
strong financial sheet had dispelled any doubts among NBA
owners about the strength of their backing. Now if he could
only get the ball in play.

Shinn knew a call was coming from David Stern some-
time on April 1, 1987. The expansion committee's recommen-
dations were due, and soon he would know if the two years
of lobbying and scrambling for an NBA team had paid off. It
also was his wedding anniversary. He started the day off with
his wife, Carolyn, who was in the hospital for a hernia operation. After visiting and comforting her he stayed in his office
on the twenty-sixth floor of Two First Union Plaza. At one
point he flipped through *USA Today* to read that Minneapolis,
Miami, and Orlando were the likely candidates for NBA expansion. Charlotte wasn't even on the list. At about 7:00 P.M.,
he headed home without having heard from Stern. Shinn, for
the first time, began considering failure. What if he hadn't
been able to pull it off? What if he and Charlotte were out of
the running?

As Shinn pulled into his driveway, his son, Chris, was
waiting for him with a message from Stern, asking him to call
as soon as possible. Shinn went into the master bath, where
there was a phone he could use in privacy. He misdialed the
number twice, before finally connecting with Stern.

Max Muhleman had just finished his dinner. At about
9:00 P.M. Shinn called Muhleman at home and asked if he
could stop by on his way to the hospital to see Carolyn.
Muhleman didn't think Shinn sounded right. His voice was
quivering and he was short. About twenty minutes later,
Muhleman heard Shinn's car pull into his driveway. He waited
at the back door and watched Shinn walk slowly toward him.
"Max, I just got a call from David Stern," Shinn told him in a
flat, unemotional voice. He looked like he was about to pass

out. "I was just sure he was going to tell me we weren't going to get a franchise," Mulheman recalled.

Shinn wouldn't sit down. He stood fidgeting and began recounting his conversation with Stern. "This is April Fool's day, George, but I'm not an April Fool." Shinn was on the verge of tears. "Max, they picked us up number one." Both men were crying now. Muhleman managed a smile, but Shinn just continued to weep. They had pulled it off.

The scene was repeated several times through the month of April, in private with allies such as Gantt and in public at a myriad of press conferences. While Shinn wept in relief that he had placed ahead of Charlotte's three bigger rivals, the city was aglow with its sudden rise to prominence. Newscasts inevitably led its segments about the NBA selection by touting the city's newly acquired "major-league status." That Charlotte's NBA selection removed a chip on its shoulder was apparent when local media outlets did round-ups showing how other cities had referred to the news. The town was heartened when *The New York Times* simply referred to the Queen City as Charlotte and forgiving when *USA Today* felt compelled to add "N.C." in parenthesis.

4

ROOKIES

Y OU didn't need to look for a guy with a whistle around
his neck to figure out who was the coach. On this brisk
October morning it was obvious: he was the oldest guy
on the gym floor. He moved quickly among his players,
all of them much larger, working them, leaning up against
them to demonstrate how a pick was set or pulling them by
the arms through the three-second lane to show how to pass
through the offensive patterns he was teaching. Pro coaches
don't wear whistles anyway.

Dick Harter was outfitted in navy sweat pants and a white
golf shirt with a Charlotte Hornets insignia. The team's month-
long training camp was winding down and, along with his
staff, he was winnowing down his basketball talent to the
players who would open the Hornets' 82-game schedule. At
fifty-eight, he was considered old by NBA coaching standards.
Sweat trickled down his temples and a small bald patch on the
crown of his head was shining, betraying his age. The regular
workouts and youthful enthusiasm that kept him fit usually

made him look much younger and hopeful—except during these particularly hard practices.

The regular season was a few weeks away and there was still much for his new charges to learn. Harter had earned a reputation as a defensive-minded coach in stints as an assistant at Detroit and Indiana. But he'd chosen to spend most of the preseason installing an offense so this patched-together group would at least be able to run, pass, and shoot with some proficiency in the early part of the year. The team's number-one draft pick, Rex Chapman, had only been in camp for a little more than a week and still needed extra tutoring in order to grasp his offensive scheme. The coach had waited a long time to take the helm of his first professional team. He had spent five seasons riding shotgun in the NBA after a long, successful, and colorful career at several colleges. But perseverance was a necessary virtue in his profession. After being named the Hornets' new general, he'd quipped; "I knew I was going to get my own team again. If I had to wait until I was eighty-two and get a CYO team in Philadelphia, I was going to do it." That was the way guys from his Philadelphia basketball fraternity talked—to the point, even gruff, but always with some humor.

There wasn't much talent banging around on the practice court before him yet. The NBA had almost assured the two expansion teams—the Miami Heat was the other newcomer—of that on June 23 when they'd conducted what was called a "dispersal draft." No matter how much the league claimed to have bent over backward in adding new teams, the twenty-three owners had taken their $130 million in entry fees and had then proceeded to dump their terrible and troubled on the rookies. Each NBA team had been allowed to protect eight of its veterans from the expansion draft, theoretically leaving their ninth-best player available for a song. That the Hornets and the Heat had had to alternate selections had further diluted the pool. The Dallas Mavericks were the last team to enter the league in 1980 and at least they'd had twenty-two teams from which to draw.

The NBA Player's Association and the Hornets' front

office further undermined the new franchise. A new labor agreement between the league and its players permitted players who had completed five years and signed at least two contracts to become unrestricted free agents. This meant that a player meeting these criteria could sign with any team without his old team receiving any compensation. Thus, Seattle, Washington, and a handful of other teams hadn't had to waste a protected spot on Tom Chambers or Moses Malone, or anyone else who technically was no longer theirs. That might help the Hornets and the Heat down the road when they had the money to sign a big-name player without giving anything up, but it further reduced the already-forgettable talent pool on the initial dispersal day.

Business is business. But what further dismayed those around the league who watched the baseline rather than the bottom line was how Hornets vice-president and general manager, Carl Scheer, player personnel director Gene Littles, and for that matter, Coach Harter, had chosen to paste together Charlotte's first team. They went from small, to smaller, and finally to the smallest in taking 5'3" Tyrone "Muggsy" Bogues from Washington. Seven guards, two small swingmen, and two big guys were what the Hornets had in their stable after a conference call with Miami and the league office in New York. By day's end, there was only 6'11" David Hoppen left in the middle. They had sent their other tree, 6'10" Mike Brown, to the Utah Jazz for Kelly Tripucka. "This looks like a great team for H-O-R-S-E," was Harter's Philly-fashioned comment after the dispersal round was completed.

The Hornets' game plan was based on a mix of veteran and younger players, obtained primarily through the free-agent market. The Hornets had leaned heavily on the advice of Dallas general manager Norm Sonju, and the plan the Mavericks had concocted to become the NBA's "model franchise." Sonju had told the Hornets' front office to bring in scorers and shooters: perimeter players who might keep their team in close games and the hometown fans momentarily happy. Tripucka was a gamble, but Utah was willing to pick up half of his $950,000 salary. Selecting Rex Chapman five days later in the college draft insured further perimeter punch.

The Miami Heat, however, didn't buy into that logic. They too knew what they were after on dispersal day. The Heat was powered by basketball people—Billy Cunningham, Stu Inman, and Lew Schaffell—who felt they could do more for their organization by stockpiling draft picks. They picked up Dallas's number-one college pick for not selecting third-string seven-footer Bill Wennington. They used it instead to pick up DePaul guard Kevin Edwards. They also traded for five second-round picks—two of them also immediately available for foregoing either Kareem Abdul Jabbar, Dennis Johnson, or Seattle's Danny Young. The Lakers, Celtics, and Supersonics offered the charity picks so they could protect younger players on their bench. The Heat then selected Fred Roberts and Darnell Valentine but traded them away to Milwaukee and Cleveland for more number two's.

The Heat was going to ride with youth. They'd go with their rookies, Rony Seikaly, Kevin Edwards, Grant Long, and Sylvester Gray, adding only one or two decent players from the dispersal draft, namely 6'11" Scott Hastings nabbed from Atlanta and second-year Billy Thompson from the Lakers, and take their chances. They'd have to fill the roster with some journeyman selected from the dispersal round, such as guard Jon Sundvold, or retrieved from the waiver wire, but the kids would get the majority of minutes. "Minutes are money" was one NBA maxim. The more the young ball players competed against real NBA stars, the better they'd get. Next year they'd bring in a new bunch of rookies with their surplus picks and clear out the dead wood.

The Hornets, on the other hand, were betting on Chapman to reach his potential as a great player sooner by playing alongside seasoned professionals like Kurt Rambis and Kelly Tripucka. He'd learn the feel of the much more elevated pro game by practicing with them every day, watching them from the bench, and eventually running the floor with them against Magic, Isaih, Michael Jordan, and the best of the superstars in the league. Their second- and third-round picks were less than good. Arizona's Tom Tolbert was too slow and, at 6'8", hardly big enough for the bruising inside game. Auburn's Jeff Moore was overweight, lethargic, and already gone from camp.

Each organization downplayed the wisdom of what they intended to do with their franchise. Neither wished to be rivals—Cunningham, Schaffel, and Inman because they were seasoned basketball practitioners who naturally thought they were right. Cunningham was a North Carolina All-American, NBA All-Star, and coach of the 1983 NBA champion Philadelphia 76ers. Inman had put together the 1977 championship Portland Trail Blazers as player personnel director. Schaffel had been an executive with the New Jersey Nets. The trio was heavy on credentials and basketball knowledge and from the outset, they spoke about building a team. There eyes were set at court level, where the game was played and titles won or lost because of the development of a center, or the key acquisition of a power forward, or because a team had let its young horses run. Miami was a raucous, almost Third-World metropolis, with professional football, horse racing, and burgeoning water sports. It was a bona-fide sports town, even though the ABA's Miami Floridians couldn't make it there in the 1970s. The University of Miami had recently revived its basketball program after lack of fan interest killed it in the late 1970s. The Heat management intended to make money by first building a winner on the court. That's what Cunningham, Inman, and Schaffel knew best.

In contrast, Carl Scheer was a marketeer trying to sell sports entertainment in a white-collar, Bible-Belt town that was still a virgin in the big leagues. He was a showman with a yen for organization and promotion, whose instincts had been finely honed by the innovative, sometimes wacky, always wide-open ABA. Scheer was a skilled executive and administrator who took on problem franchises and successfully filled up the stands. He looked to the arena seats and spoke of building a fan base. The team would bring in perimeter players as if they were merely entertainers. Customer service would be emphasized along with a fun, action-packed atmosphere complete with good-time music that got louder as the game progressed. Hugo, the Hornets' first-rate mascot, would be a clean, down-home cheerleader. This was entertainment and professional basketball was a big-bucks business.

Each organization had readily apparent flaws in its approach to building a franchise.

Charlotte was now loaded with jump shooters; Chapman, Tripucka, and their number-one dispersal pick, Dell Curry, could all put it up. But the trio was in the 6'5" range, had similar games, and couldn't play at the same time. That meant that the inside game was in the hands of the 6'8" Rambis, the quintessential working-class overachiever. His elbows and knees and guts were terrific for clearing out the thugs in the middle so Magic, James Worthy, and Kareem could do as they wished. He could stick any garbage a guy put up back in the hole. But it was doubtful that a player whose second-best shot, after the layup, was by his own admission the "15-foot standstill," (which he'd shot maybe a handful of times over the past six years) could fill the defensive or offensive void in the middle. Earl Cureton might be able to help out on defense and with rebounding. But he too was basically a bench player, having had solid years spelling Moses Malone in Philadelphia thirteen-to-seventeen minutes a game. Despite his nickname, Earl "The Twirl" was certainly no offensive threat. It was an adventure every time he put the ball into play, whether he was 2 feet or 15 feet away from the bucket. Dave Hoppen and Tim Kempton were the only true centers the Hornets had in camp. Both were veterans of Italian basketball and had played only one season in the NBA. Depending on whom you talked to, Hoppen and Kempton were either projects or much needed beef for the hole in the middle. The big question concerning the Hornets' game plan was how much Chapman, Curry, and the few other promising young players were going to improve if they had to share minutes with older, once-great shooters, especially when there was no one underneath to rebound and assure each his fair share of shots.

The weaknesses in Miami's grand scheme were akin to character flaws. Rony Seikaly was 6'10", but many NBA afficionados considered him more of a power forward than a true center. The Hornets certainly did. Charlotte had passed up the former Syracuse star for Chapman. Director of player development Gene Littles spoke for the braintrust when he said, "He's not big enough to play center, he's mechanical and doesn't have a feel for the game." Edwards, Long, and Gray might turn into nice players, but nothing in their backgrounds demonstrated that they had the talent to be superstars or the intangibles to be winners. Edwards was Rod Strickland's backcourt mate at DePaul. Long was the anchor of an Eastern Michigan squad. Gray left Memphis State a year early when it was discovered that he had received money from an agent. In addition, the 1989 draft had been reduced to two rounds because the talent pool coming out of college wasn't felt to be deep enough to justify picking any more college seniors. This perception might change from year to year, but a current survey of the NBA revealed that a small percentage of league players were second-rounders or lower. Basically it was a crap shoot to find a player with any longevity after the first round—even if a team had three chances as Miami might.

The contrast in the Heat and Hornets' styles, and the personalities dictating them, would prove the grist for comparisons as the season wore on. It was a rivalry no one involved really wanted, but it was inevitable that the Hornets and Heat would be assessed side by side. The Minnesota Timberwolves and the Orlando Magic were entering the league in 1989–90 and each would be looking to both for direction.

When the Cleveland Cavaliers joined in 1970, coach Bill Fitch and assistant Jim Lessig had only had forty-eight hours to prepare for the dispersal draft. Computerized scouting systems and videotape were not yet available to teams. So Fitch, as the story goes, took inspiration from Lessig's son who was collecting bubble gum basketball cards. He financed a trip that Lessig made to the corner drugstore, ordering his assistant to buy all the basketball cards he could get his hands on. When Lessig returned to the hotel, they spread all the cards out on their beds and tried to figure out who was available. They were then ready to build a team.

Business principals now guided the game and both the

Hornets and Heat were following five-year plans that they were banking on would bring them a favorable spread sheet in the boardroom and a playoff team on the hardwood. The one strategy the two teams shared was that they didn't want to win immediately. The worse each team finished, the better their draft pick in the draft. It was as simple as that. The better the draft pick, the better the player. As soon as each team got better players, the sooner they would challenge for the play-offs. The expansion teams were planting the seeds of success with every loss. But both organizations also understood that the wait for the harvest five years hence would be easier for the fans to bear—and more profitable for the franchise—if their teams could stay in some games.

Standing on the sidelines at practice, coach Harter surveyed what the Hornets' expansion formula had yielded. He was the commander-in-chief. His job was to take what talent had been given to him and mold it into a winner. It was a simple objective, but one he'd found increasingly difficult to attain as he'd climbed the professional ranks.

There was the game. Then there was the politics of the game. Harter prided himself on being a virtual basketball encyclopedia. He was a gym rat who had been weaned on twenty-five or more doubleheaders a season at the storied old Palestra in Philadelphia. He took in high school and college games whenever his schedule permitted and spent his off-seasons in his car, driving to as many as eighty teaching clinics, where he lectured about the rewards of defense and shot the breeze about basketball with his buddies. His love for the game came from his family. His father was a teacher for forty years, and his older brother coached high schoolers. "I came from a family of teachers and knew by the time I was a sophomore in high school that I wanted to be a coach." He loved talking basketball as much as coaching it. "I used to watch my brother's basketball games when they'd still throw up a jump ball after every bucket. The match-ups would be screwy with tall forwards covering smaller guards because at the time everyone thought that was the way to take advantage of your size."

Harter was learning to network. That's how coaches found out about job openings—constantly calling around the country, asking their buddies what was available and who was tight with the AD or GM. That leads to more phone calls and lobbying by the coach. He seeks out another member of the fraternity who has worked with general manager X in college. He might be available and could you pass that along to the GM? Sometimes coaches just plant an item with a trusted sportswriter who will call whatever college team or professional organization is hiring and ask if they're going to take a look at the coach-on-the prowl. Mr. AD or GM X might say they haven't talked with the coach in question, but might if he's available. Then in the sportswriter's Sunday column, we learn that AD or GM X is interested in the coach-on-the prowl, and the groundwork's been laid for a deal.

Harter had entered the NBA as an assistant to Chuck Daly of the Detroit Pistons. He'd been hired by the Piston's general manager, Jack McCloskey, Harter's mentor and friend. He had served with McCloskey as an assistant before evetually succeeding him in 1966 at the University of Pennsylvania. Daly was then hired to coach the Penn Quakers when Harter moved on to Oregon. That's the way the coaching merry-go-round works.

When McCloskey first called, Harter simply needed a job. He was finishing his eighteenth year in collegiate coaching at Penn State, where in five years he had turned a blue-collar, little-sister program—as he'd done previously at Oregon and Penn—into a major team. He'd decided that he didn't want to live any longer in the shadow of Joe Paterno and the Nittany Lion footballers. Paterno was athletic director, so Harter had only one choice—to leave. He had thought his 315–194 college record and his reputation as a skilled and committed coach would send ADs scurrying to the phone with coaching offers. It didn't. McCloskey was the only one who beckoned and Harter answered.

Once in the NBA, he got hooked on coaching the world's

greatest athletes and most incredibly gifted basketball professionals. He handled the defensive chores at Detroit, while
meticulously observing how Chuck Daly handled his highly
paid athletes and their enormous egos. Harter thought Daly,
another Philly native, was a master at manipulating the overall
performance of his players. Daly was sensitive to their jealousy
over playing time and money and knew on what nights to ask
a well-paid, but perhaps coasting, veteran to put out a little
extra. He also knew on what nights to leave him alone. After
three seasons with the Pistons, Harter felt ready to coach his
own team.

He almost got his wish right there in Detroit when Daly
was set to go to Philadelphia after the 1986 season. But when
the Pistons wanted a number-one pick in exchange for releas-
ing Daly from his contract, the deal crumbled. Harter pursued
and became a finalist for the Cleveland job, only to be nosed
out by Lenny Wilkens. Then he was all set to take over the
Indiana Pacers, but at the last minute the venerable Jack
Ramsay decided he wanted to coach for a few more years.
The Pacers grabbed him. Harter didn't feel too badly about
finishing second to Wilkens or Ramsay. Both had been winners in careers that had spanned almost twenty years, each
had coached NBA champions—Wilkens in 1979 and Ramsay
in 1977. The Pacers offered to bring him in as an assistant,
promising not to interfere if a top job came his way. Harter
joined Ramsay, who was also from Philadelphia, as sort of a
head coach-in-waiting. He gleaned all the x and o knowledge
he could from the dean of Philly coaches, who was much
celebrated for coaxing the sheer beauty out of the game.

Mostly, though, Harter waited.

Coaching circles were tighter in the NBA. Every organization had its own talent pool with specific criteria. Cotton
Fitzsimmons, Gene Shue and Kevin Loughery always seemed
to land on their feet. Harter was in the Philly loop and since
all those jobs seemed secure, he set his sights on the four
expansion teams about to enter the league.

Carl Scheer and the Hornets had their own standards
too. But in addition to Scheer's personal preferences, the

Hornets' head coach would also have to meet George Shinn's qualifications. From the outset, Shinn had said he was going to hire a coach of high moral fiber who would be a contributing member of the community. The owner also didn't want to relinquish the spotlight and lose the momentum the franchise had built during the selection process by sitting idle for a whole season waiting to play ball. So a guessing game was conducted through the newspapers.

It started with an initial groundswell of support for Coach Lefty Driesell. The fallout over Len Bias's death had forced him out of the Maryland job and he was more than available. Lefty had country-boy roots, coached in the area, and was extremely popular for making elite Davidson University's basketball program respectable. A *USA Today* wag had even suggested that fallen evangelist Jim Bakker's PTL should be recast as "Praise the Lefthander." Dick Motta was mentioned as a possibility, of course, for his work in building Dallas's "model franchise" into a Western Conference power. He had finally walked away from the Mavericks in the spring of 1987, disgusted with troublesome star Mark Aguirre and the team's first-round exit from the playoffs. That summer when it was announced that Scheer would be the chief architect of the expansion Hornets, there were cries for former Tarheel and peripatetic coaching genius, Larry Brown, to return to North Carolina. Scheer and Brown were practically inseparable over the seven seasons they'd guided the ABA's Carolina Cougars, and both leagues' versions of the Denver Nuggets.

Shinn at one point even made a run at Duke's "Coach K"—Mike Krzyzewski—a Bobby Knight protege and future Dean Smith rolled into one. He had class, discipline, and had racked up many wins in the ACC. The story goes that Shinn phoned "Coach K" and asked for just ten minutes of his time to make an offer that would change his life. The Duke coach fended off the positive-thinking guru's pitch, according to Shinn, by saying he was very happy in Durham and just didn't want to be tempted.

Serious coach hunting didn't really heat up, however, until the spring 1988. By that time, Driesell had shot himself in the foot with a statement he'd allegedly made at a public function, to the effect that when used properly, cocaine could enhance an athlete's performance. Lefty was either confused, misquoted, or a little of both. The public uproar that followed undercut any support he may have had. Dick Motta also had made it clear that he wasn't interested in going the expansion route again and declined any serious talks. In March, Scheer and Shinn journeyed to Nebraska, where Brown was preparing his soon-to-be NCAA champion Kansas Jayhawks for a tournament game with Xavier. The three men talked. At the time Brown was rumored either to be heading West for a return engagement at UCLA, or to the eventual sweepstakes winner, San Antonio. He was still maintaining that he was going to stay at Kansas. Brown was a longshot for the Hornets' job for a couple of reasons, mainly that he was content to wait to return to North Carolina as Dean Smith's long-talked-about replacement.

Ohio State's Gary Williams, Boston Celtics assistant Jimmy Rodgers, and Philadelphia 76ers interim coach Jim Lynam were unsuccessfully approached. Williams went through the interview motions before finally deciding that he would be unable to take the inevitable losing. Rodgers and Lynam were banking on becoming full-time head men at their respective teams, which they eventually did.

By the time April and May rolled around, the Hornets had either formally interviewed or talked with eight candidates—including Harter. There was the usual cast of familiar faces, all former head coaches: Tom Nissalke, Matt Goukas, Ed Badger, and Bob Hill. The list also included CBA exile Bill Musselman, and assistants Brian Winters and Allan Bistow. Stan Albeck and straddled both the professional and college worlds, and was currently the coach at Bradley University.

Harter sensed he was close to landing the post and was anxious to seal the deal. Shinn had final say and when Harter went in to to see the owner he wasn't bashful. "I'm the guy for this job," both men remembered Harter hammering home. Scheer agreed. Harter was a teacher of the game. Penn, Oregon, and Penn State were hardly basketball schools. Still, the coach had retooled each program, turning losers into winners with discipline and patience. These were two attributes that the maestro of a team that would be lucky to win 15 games needed to endure one, two, three, possibly four dismal seasons. Harter fit most of the Hornets' requirements.

The next obstacle to clear was Shinn himself. The owner trumpeted his formula for management. He had implemented it in his other businesses, sold it to the NBA, and intended to enforce it within his sports organization. Shinn called it managing with love, caring, and reinforcement: the Christian way. What he failed to tout on the lecture circuit and at press gatherings was the ample dose of obedience he demanded. Harter inadvertently met that criteria when he interviewed for the job. Shinn insists that his employees wear white shirts and preferably dark suits. When members of George Shinn & Associates leave their twenty-sixth-floor office, they are required to have suit jacket on and shirt collar buttoned—even if they're only stepping downstairs for some coffee. Shinn doesn't apologize for his dress code. He believes it looks better and signifies something special about his group. Scheer adheres to the code, as would the head coach and his assistants. Harter was a basketball coach, not a clothes horse. He was an Ivy Leaguer and an ex-Marine to boot. A white shirt and dark suit were de rigueur for a conservative guy like Harter. So that's what he wore for the interview, impressing his potential boss mightily. Shinn still comments on Harter's appearance that day, even saying that if his coach was tipped off about his tastes prior to the meeting (as some candidates were), that was all right.

As Shinn promised, there were other criteria his coach would have to meet.

Shinn probed Harter about his faith, and if he was willing to become a fixture in the community. The owner also was concerned that Harter was divorced and that his present wife, Mari, whom he'd met while at Oregon, was more than twenty years his junior. Shinn spelled it out in an upfront agreement. Harter was to join a church in Charlotte as soon as he was settled. He was to be available for community service and as

Shinn himself recounts, "If he ever brought any embarrassment to himself or the team in any way, if he used profanity
and a television camera caught it, or if he threw a chair, he'd
be fired before that chair stopped sliding."

Harter didn't have any problems with Shinn's requirements, though he admitted that twenty years ago such dictates
would have enraged him. Some of it might be overkill, but
Harter was older now and willing to listen to suggestions. The
coach did balk, however, at Shinn's suggestion that they seal
their agreement with a simple handshake, instead of a contract. Much was made of a similar arrangement Motta had with
Mavericks owner Donald Carter. Scheer already was operating
on a handshake. The money Shinn and Harter agreed to was
far below the average an NBA coach was making. It was
basically an assistant's wages. Harter would have liked nothing
better than to believe he would coach the Hornets forever and
Shinn talked as if he would. But Harter knew that this was a
business. Coaching was at best a precarious trade—coaches
came and went as did players. Wins were the only source of
job security and those would be few and far between with an
expansion team. He asked for, and got, a contract, but for two
years only. There already were whispers in the coaching and
basketball-beat writer community that the Hornets were looking for someone to set the table, take the losses, and then they
would hand the reigns over to a big name, Brown maybe, or
perhaps a local hero, like Krzyzewski. Harter didn't let that
bother him. He was a head coach and now the most important
thing before him was his team.

Most of the time a professional training camp doesn't
look that much different than the high school and college
workouts that open in cracker-box gyms and mammoth field
houses late in the fall.

Some things are constant.

One is defensive drills. Harter, or sometimes the tiny
Bogues, would crouch before the assembled players, moving
laterally, as well as forward and backward, making the others
shadow them in a proper crablike defensive stance. When

Harter was the leader, as he was today, he just sort of sidestepped and pointed, barking, "Now this way!"

The lightning-quick Bogues was a darting smile when it was his turn to lead the drills. He shimmied in all directions, breaking the ranks of his taller and more awkward teammates, enjoying the brief moment of dominance he seized in a big man's game. The mandatory weave pattern, or figure eight, was also a staple of practice. Rambis, Kempton, and Hoppen didn't maneuver it with the crispness of a high school team, as they ran their figure-S patterns, taking many steps with the ball as they finished it up with a dunk. There were stretching intervals and lay-up lines, free-throw and jump-shooting exercises.

Then there were the line sprints, hated by ballplayers of all levels, but never more than by the veterans with old legs and battered bodies. All were things they had done by rote for many years, but they still performed them with professionalism and a hint of joy.

This was a competitive training camp. Many of the players recognized that this was their last chance, before being waived and having to cast their lot in with the Continental Basketball Association. Eleven of them had guaranteed contracts, making it difficult for the Hornets to cut them. If they did, they'd still have to pay them, and that simply wasn't good business. Now that Chapman was in camp that made twelve with pocketsful of money. Dell Curry, however, had broken his wrist and would be out for the beginning of the season, opening up one more roster spot.

Tripucka and Rambis were assured starting spots, but they were working hard to buff the rust from their games. Tripucka had languished on the end of the Utah Jazz's bench the previous season, unable to get along with noted comic Frank Layden or to break into a lineup featuring "The Mailman," Karl Malone, whose powerful 6'10", 255-pound frame and supple speed was emerging as the prototype for the NBA number 4. Rambis had averaged only twelve minutes a game the year before with the Lakers. Even in his best season, 1982–83, he'd rarely played more than twenty-three minutes a game. Here he was expected to play thirty-plus hard minutes with little help on the boards. The scrimmages were brutal and spirited, drawing grins and grimaces. Reid, one of those with no money assured, dictated the pace. He dove for loose balls, ran the whole floor, and pushed and shoved inside. It was rookie-type behavior, hustle thirty-three-year-old vets usually didn't have to demonstrate. His unguaranteed contract, however, made him every bit a rookie. Plus he was a pro, taking pride in the game that had been good to him.

So far the Hornets played two preseason exhibition games. The first was a 118–97 loss to the New Jersey Nets at Madison Square Garden. The contest was most notable for the unveiling of Alexander Julian's teal, pinstripe uniforms with pleated pants. Shinn had contracted the Chapel Hill native to come up with a bold new fashion in the summer of 1987. Julian had agreed to the commission in return for a monthly five-pound ration of North Carolina pork barbecue. It was an inexpensive gimmick that had kept the Hornets in the news. *USA Today* reported on the new uniform, as did *Newsweek.* Unfortunately, on game day it was apparent that the dapper new duds needed some additional tailoring. Reid and a couple of others chose to do their stretching exercises in the locker room for fear of revealing more than their game. Poor Bogues's tiny torso was enveloped by his shorts. At halftime, Harter walked into the locker room and found his team standing in their shorts. The uniforms apparently hadn't been washed and were itching his players. Alterations would have to be made.

In their second outing two days later, the Hornets notched a 126–113 victory over the Knicks in Columbia, South Carolina. It was Rex Chapman's debut, the team's number-one pick and by all accounts the Hornets' future. The young Chapman had only arrived in camp four days before the Knicks game. He'd traveled to New York with the team for the New Jersey game, but Harter stuck to his promise that his young guard wouldn't play. Harter, the Philly tough, referred to his new guard as "that other guy" while Chapman was still a no-show, refusing to discuss him in the team equation until he'd signed a contract and reported to camp. He was a rookie, missing valuable practice time, but nobody blamed him for holding out. Business again. Every player in camp, if in Chapman's position, would have held out until the money and terms were right. Still, even on an expansion team a rook underwent some rite of passage. Chapman shot 6 of 11 from the field, with 2 steals and 2 assists over thirteen minutes in his debut. He was a shooter with great leaping ability and an uncanny awareness of the floor. That was his "upside," in coach and scouting parlance. His "downside" was that he was barely twenty-one—having left the University of Kentucky after his sophomore season. His youth made his defense and floor game suspect. He was also a slight 6'5", 185-pounder whose timid, almost choir-boy, demeanor made him look soft by NBA standards. He was, however, a future superstar whom Harter couldn't wait to get into camp.

In the last several practices, the young rookie had been run relentlessly through jolting picks while he learned the offensive patterns. The pick, or screen, was probably the most dramatic difference between the professional and college games. It was the linchpin of virtually all offenses. Bill Lambeer, Kevin McHale, and every other wide body in the league set it stiff and crushing. There was very little switching off in the NBA, as there was in the colleges. The twenty-four-second clock and the superior quickness and passing skills of older, more experienced players made it difficult to execute a switch without getting burned. Each team knew most of its opponents' plays due to extensive scouting and the fact that they played each other as many as six times a season, year after year. A player either got around the wall, went through it, or took a seat on the bench, letting a teammate try to keep the jump-shooters from spotting up to the basket. Chapman tried all three this morning. Reid was running him through the middle, around the edges, and into the rocks Rambis and Tripucka kept setting. After one particular blind-side bashing from Rambis, Harter seemed to simultaneously wince in empathy with his rookie and smile at his veterans' initiative. This

was the game that took place on the hardwood, where everyone was equal.

David Falk arguably didn't have any equals in the agent
game. He was certainly on a roll when he jetted into Charlotte
on Monday, October 11, to try to sign Rex Chapman with the
Charlotte Hornets. It had been a long, profitable weekend for
the chief agent of Donald Dell's ProServ Inc. Falk had started
Friday in Seattle, putting together Dale Ellis's $1.2 million a
year, jetted to Los Angeles on Saturday to sign the overall
number-three pick, Pittsburgh's Charles Smith, to a four-year,
$4-million deal with the Clippers, and then had gone on to
San Francisco on Sunday, where Kansas State's Mitch Richmond, the number-five pick, was signed by Golden State to
$4.5 million over five years. He'd slept very little over the
weekend and was operating on pure adrenaline—his reward
for essentially dictating the market with the three, five, and
eight (Chapman) draft picks.

The high-strung agent was cutting a wide swath in the
basketball world. Among the big names he represented were
Patrick Ewing, James Worthy, and Adrian Dantley. Michael
Jordan's eight-year, $25-million contract with the Chicago
Bulls that Falk had engineered was unprecedented. Slender,
bald, with constantly darting eyes, Falk looked more like a
nervous golf pro than the agent and deal-maker that he was.
His reputation as a tough negotiater was well earned. He had
a hard-line formula, and certainly wasn't afraid to hold players
out—especially rookies. His theory went that it was the team
who was depleting the value of a rookie by not bringing him
in on time to learn the system. Falk believed in the agent's
system. He, and ProServ in particular, shared some of the
credit for having powered the NBA into its current exalted
financial status.

ProServ didn't only win big bucks for players, it also
offered a wide array of marketing, financial, and personal-
service plans. The company had started in the 1970s with
tennis players, promoting them as celebrities and shrewdly
matching them with product endorsements. ProServ had en-

tered the basketball arena with the same game plan—to elevate an individual from team member to the loftier status of the world's greatest athlete and full-blown celebrity. Some owners and general managers thought Falk was simply a bandit, while many league officials groused that his ego outpaced those of his clients. They didn't agree with Falk's assessment that his role was two-fold: he was an agent of the principal, in this case Chapman, as well as a principal himself due to the nature of the negotiating process and ProServ's commitment to cultivating the client's earning potential to the maximum. Falk also didn't mind talking about how deals were done. He believed the public was as fascinated as he was with the inside maneuvering of deal-making—especially when he could dispel the image of an agent as a seedy, backdoor confidence man.

Like him or not, Falk, and others of his ilk, had revolutionized professional basketball's image. Michael Jordan was as renowned for the "Air Jordan" basketball shoe he pushed in the sweeping, back-lit dunks with sidekick avante garde film director Spike Lee in Nike commercials as he was for taking it down the middle with a midair pirouette before ramming the ball down Moses Malone's throat. He was paid almost as handsomely for his endorsement work after Falk signed him to a seven-year, $19-million contract with the athletic shoe manufacturer.

Falk enjoyed the give-and-take of contract negotiating. He was in Charlotte intending to finish his rookie "hat trick" with an old friend and familiar nemesis, Carl Scheer. Falk and Scheer first went head-to-head back in 1977 when Falk was representing North Carolina's Tom LaGarde in his dealings with Scheer and the Denver Nuggets. The agent had made his first big splash the year before while representing Dantley, Wally Walker, and John Lucas. The two men hit it off during the LaGarde negotiations and a friendship had blossomed over the years. GMs and agents regard each other as necessary evils, but after so many bouts, there's often mutual respect, if not friendship. Falk and Scheer were closer than most. The agent had been a houseguest at Scheer's home, and the previous summer ProServ had arranged to fly Scheer's wife, Marsha, to the Wimbledon finals on her birthday. The two men trusted each other and shared a track record of deals well done. Both men were lawyers, and both were fastidous control freaks.

The Chapman deal proved troublesome for their relationship. Each knew at the start where the other was coming from. The Falk pitch started with what he called "defining the economic value of a player." The agent was notorious for pumping up the virtues and star qualities of his client. Scheer met Falk in August at the Charlotte–Douglas International airport for a three-hour-plus meeting. A salary figure never came up. Instead, Falk made a case for Chapman's value based on a five-point argument. One, that Chapman was young and represented longevity for an expansion team that was building. Two, that it would take some time for the Hornets to create any chemistry, so the team would want the young guard around for a long time to establish consistency. Three, that Chapman already displayed resiliency, growing up as an icon in basketball-crazy Kentucky. This quality would be needed on a team that was expected to lose often in the beginning. Four, that Chapman was a multidimensional player, which would prove vital on a team with a dearth of talent. Five, that Chapman liked Charlotte and was willing to become involved in the community.

Falk was preempting any argument Scheer might make about Chapman's age. Scheer, Littles, and Harter believed it would take time to develop the rookie. They felt he was physically and emotionally immature, and they were prepared to bring him along slowly. What Falk dubs "The GM game"— also known as "slotting"—was also at play. Chapman was the number-eight pick. He couldn't make more than the seven guys selected ahead of him, according to the "game," and the previous year's seven, eight, and nine picks were paid in the $200,000 to $500,000 range per year. The parameters, though slightly skewed, were set in both Falk's and Scheer's minds. Still, they were unable to reach an agreement. Scheer

and Falk had hammered away at each other by phone but
had still come up empty.

Now Falk was back in Charlotte. Both he and Scheer
were anxious to get it done. They went at it for most of the
day at the Hornets' offices at First Union Plaza with Shinn
occasionally dropping in to see how it was going. They were
at an impasse, however. The two friends were growing impatient with each other, the discussion escalating into what Falk
characterized as "two reasonable men disagreeing loudly."
The situation was becoming impossible and by nightfall Shinn
suggested that the negotiations move to his home. Falk wanted
Scheer to make the deal, but it was clear that Shinn was about
to take over. He was the owner and it was his money. Falk
believed that Shinn felt he had to set the tone for how his
organization would deal with contract disputes.

The principals arrived at the owner's twenty-five-room,
$1.7-million estate off Carmel Road in an understated, but
affluent, southeast district of the city at about 6:30 P.M. Spencer Stolpen, Shinn's attorney, was there, as was Scheer and
Andrew Brandt, an associate of Falk who represented Muggsy
Bogues. Chapman and his father, Wayne, also were there. On
their way to the basement where they were to meet, the
Chapman team passed a piece of artwork that hinted at the
Hornets' owner's deal-making philosophy. It was a glass box
with a replica of the coyote of Roadrunner fame inside. This
time, however, the coyote was standing tall and grinning as he
gripped his feathery adversary by the neck. The caption below
read: "Gotyerass." Shinn had bought it himself in Mexico and
claimed it was the only item he ever really had to have in his
house.

For about two hours, the Chapmans held the floor. Father
and son said they were anxious to get the deal done and get
Rex to camp. Charlotte was the place he wanted to be. Soft
drinks, peanuts, and M & Ms were on the tables, but the two
sides were too tense to reach for them. The Chapmans were
then asked to leave the room, while the hard-core negotiations
continued. At 10:30 P.M., negotiations got so bogged down
that those in the room thought Chapman might not sign for

weeks. Falk had kept the Chapmans away from the negotiations intentionally. He believed a player might get jaded if he
was a party to contract haggling—either he'd get an inflated
ego or become angry at ownership's arguments for less favorable terms and money.

About 1:00 A.M., Brandt, hoping to break the stalemate,
suggested that Shinn and Chapman go off and speak in
private. The owner had asked repeatedly through the course
of the day and evening sessions what the rookie was like.

"He didn't ask about money or about terms. All George
wanted to know was what kind of person Rex was," Brandt
recalled.

Chapman and his father knew about Shinn's demand for
social responsibility from his players. They had read the books
Shinn had written, which Falk had given to them prior to the
meeting.

Shinn, for his part, believed it was time to get involved in
the process. The discussions were dragging on too long. The
public was getting antsy for their new player. The impression
he believed they were getting was that either he was too
cheap, or Chapman was too greedy.

The owner was ready to probe Chapman about his faith
and personal habits, as well as verse him on his now-notorious
"Hornet-as-role-model" expectations. When the two men returned nearly three hours later, Shinn seemed satisfied: "I
think Rex is a good boy and he appreciated me asking him
about his faith and character." Chapman seemed relieved that
a deal seemed near, but he was unsettled by what had just
occurred. He'd stood his ground with Shinn, but it had left a
bad taste in his mouth. He told Brandt, "I don't know if I'm
playing for a basketball team or a church."

The next day, he signed a four-year, $650,000 package.
The "boy king" made a poignant public comment that perhaps foreshadowed his first year in the NBA. "Watching men
going back and forth like that, not arguing, but taking either
side of the issue . . . well, I'd rather be out playing basketball.
. . . But that's business and you can't take it personally."

5

FIRST WIN

THERE are too many firsts to celebrate for an expansion team. At least that's what Robert Reid was thinking as he stretched out on the couch of his southeast Charlotte apartment, watching late-afternoon cartoons. Tom and Jerry, Ghostbusters, Bugs Bunny, and the Roadrunner had all been incorporated into his pregame ritual—the product of spending afternoons with his two young children. Strangely enough, no media pundits, or for that matter members of the Hornets, had mentioned anything about when the team might get its first regular-season victory. They had won two exhibition games, but they were just tune-ups for the players and previews for the fans. Opening night had already come and gone, capped by a 40-point drubbing at the hands of the Cavaliers. Two nights later, the first road game was equally ugly as the Detroit Pistons handed the Hornets a 94–85 loss.

Reid believed the team's first victory was at hand. They were to play their third game against the Los Angeles Clippers this evening, and the veteran felt they were going to win. After all, the Clippers were the NBA's perennial doormat. They had improved themselves with three number-one draft picks, taking Danny Manning of Kansas, Gary Grant of Michigan, and Charles Smith of Pittsburgh. But Manning, the number-one overall pick, was still a holdout, demanding $10 million from the Clippers for his services. A price the team was willing to pay, but the Clippers had hoped that they could have a portion deferred. Manning, however, wanted it all. The other two might become nice NBA players, but as a team the Clippers were young and too inexperienced—even with Manning—to make much noise in the league. Reid, however, was worried about himself first. He had played with rookie abandon in camp, pushed by the younger guys. It had been fun. But his unguaranteed contract made him vulnerable. No one had expected him to start the season with the Hornets—in fact the newspapers had him teetering on the waiver wire. He believed Scheer had included the option of guaranteed money if Reid made it impossible for the team to get rid of him. His camp had been outstanding and he was a starter, but nobody was talking about contracts. Reid had figured as much. The NBA ruled contracts binding for a season for players still on team rosters as of December 27. It didn't make sense for the Hornets to promise anything until the spring, he reasoned. There might be injuries or new acquisitions that might make Reid tradable or expendable before then. Plus, Reid was old. He probably wouldn't be around for the four or five years it would take the Hornets to become a contender; why not use his slot for a younger player who could develop with the team?

Reid was reminded of his uncertain status every day. He had just moved out of a hotel and into a furnished apartment, but his family was still in Houston. Since before camp. Harter had made it known that the Hornets needed, and were looking for, a big man. Maybe he was just keeping that yet-to-materialize inside player's spot warm. The veteran didn't want to be cut for the first time in his career, so he'd resolved to keep his head down and do whatever was asked.

At one time, Reid would have been shocked at how much a Danny Manning—as potentially great as he was—wanted to play the game. No more. Ten seasons later, Reid was now a business man. The progression of his career—from first signing with the Rockets to his current stint in Charlotte—had shown him how necessary it was to be savvy these days in the NBA.

In his heart, Reid thought the game on the floor was what would determine where he landed after the next 82 games. In his head, he knew better.

Reid was no Manning. Coming out of San Antonio's St. Mary's University, he was a fast and erratic 6'8" swingman with a wild afro, sometimes framed by a red bandana. "Bobby Joe" as he was known in those days, was an NAIA All-American—along with a skinny 6'11" center for Illinois Wesleyan named Jack Sikma—who twice led his team to Kansas City for the annual national championship. "March Madness" for the small-college championship only lasts a week in Kansas City. Thirty-two teams converge in the Midwest for a day-and-night round robin, which requires the champion to win five games in five days to claim the crown. It was a talent-filled tournament. Bob Dandridge, Lloyd Free, Detorit's Rick Mahorn, and the Bulls' Scottie Pippen are a smattering of players who went on to the NBA after a week in Kansas City. It was also notorious for its wide-open brand of playground ball, and for allowing twenty-three-year-old freshmen, fresh from military stints, to wear the colors of Drury College, Central Washington, or St. Mary's. Also legendary were the colorful nicknames of some of its stars: "Slick" Watts, "Foots" Walker, and Travis "Machine Gun" Grant lasted for a while in NBA programs.

When he entered St. Mary's, Reid was a 6'1" point guard who intended to take his game to the recreational leagues and his bachelor's degree into the workplace after four years. He was an Air Force brat from a close family that prized education. He was brought to St. Mary's almost as an afterthought when Buddy Meyer—an assistant coach and an old Navy guy who greased the armed-services pipeline for the South Texas school—crapped out in recruiting a Texas schoolboy named Dennis Teeler. Meyer was in Schertz, Texas, watching Teeler's team play Samuel Clemens High School when he first noticed Reid. The kid was small and still shooting a two-handed jump shot, but he handled the ball well and seemed smarter than the others on the court. It also turned out that Reid's godfather was a friend of Meyer's from the Navy. When Teeler and a couple of other recruits St. Mary's was counting on went elsewhere, the South Texas school needed players. Nobody on campus harbored any NBA illusions. The majority of Reid's teammates were at the small Catholic college after stints in the military. They were mostly married, trying to raise families while nailing down an education. Then the summer following his junior year, some of the San Antonio Spurs showed up at St. Mary's gym to work out and play pickup games. George Gervin, Larry Kenon, James Silas, and Coby Dietrich would run the floor with Reid and whatever other Rattlers were around. Gradually, Reid found he could compete with the pros better than some of his teammates. Gervin, "The Iceman," took a special liking to Reid. The two were about the same size—Gervin's a willowy 6'8", Reid, thanks to a late six-inch growth spurt, an inch smaller. They matched up well in one-on-one games. Gervin, with his twisting moves and agile, behind-the-head jumper, often schooled Reid well into the night. He liked the way he kept coming after him, asking for another rematch. Finally, after a long night that saw Reid close Gervin out in back-to-back games, the pro told the college kid he could play, and that he should definitely take a shot at the NBA.

It wasn't that easy. No one outside of South Texas had really ever seen Reid play. NBA superscout Marty Blake had compiled a dossier on the NAIA All-American prior to the draft that complimented Reid's athleticism, but concluded that he didn't have enough basketball skills to make it in the pros. Reid, however, was determined to try.

The St. Mary's coaching staff was willing to make a strong push on behalf of their star. Assistant coach Rudy Davalos initiated something of a grass-roots campaign to get Reid selected in the draft. Davalos then put together a brochure featuring pictures of Reid in action and highlighting his collegiate stats. He quoted Gervin's assessment of Reid, as well as some kind words uttered by University of Houston coach Guy V. Lewis. The Rattlers had played Lewis's Houston Cougars three times while Reid was at St. Mary's. They'd upset the nationally ranked Cougars in 1975 in Houston. The other two were narrow defeats, but Reid had held his own in shootouts with All-American guard, Otis Birdsong. The venerable Guy V. was the John Wooden of East Texas. When he drawled that a guy was "a helluva play'r," scouts usually listened.

The brochure was a crude promo, but it got the word out on Reid. On draft day, Davalos continued lobbying NBA teams. He was a one-time assistant of Houston coach Tom Nissalke and knew the Rockets were a lumbering, mediocre team in search of speed. He stayed on the phone all day pleading with Nissalke to take Reid. Finally, Nissalke acquiesced, selecting Reid as the fortieth overall pick. The Rockets didn't have a number-one selection that year, but had picked University of Nevada Las Vegas's Larry Moffet earlier in the second round. The UNLV star arrived in Houston that afternoon in a limousine. Reid rushed to Houston from San Antonio, coming up six dollars short on his cab fare from the airport. The cabbie reluctantly took his word that he was the Rockets' second-round draft pick, and drove off.

The circumstances under which he signed his first contract were even more humbling. That summer before camp, Nissalke had called Reid from a pay phone and asked to meet him at a truckstop on highway 10 outside of San Antonio. The coach was in town and the two needed to discuss a contract. They chatted briefly over milkshakes, before Reid signed a $30,000-a-year contract—the minimum—on the hood of Nissalke's car. No agents, no guarantees, just a signature from Reid and a handshake from Nissalke. Before the coach hit the highway for Houston, Reid told him, "As long as I have a practice uniform I think I have a chance."

Reid excelled immediately in the NBA. He moved into the starting lineup in his second year, and by the 1980–81 season he was in full stride. He averaged 15.9 points, led the team in steals, and trailed only Moses Malone in team rebounds and Allan Leavell in assists. With Malone, Leavell, Calvin Murphy, and Rudy Tomjanovich, the Rockets made a run at the NBA championship. Reid played brilliantly in the playoffs, averaging 16.1 points and 4 assists a game. The Boston Celtics, however, led by second-year phenom Larry Bird and the newly acquired Robert Parish at center, proved too much for Rockets and closed them out four games to two in the finals.

That season was especially satisfying for Reid. He was firmly established as one of the top ten forwards in the league and was getting paid accordingly—about $325,000 a year. The NBA named him as their "Humanitarian of the Year" for the work he undertook on behalf of dozens of charities. He was in his prime at twenty-five, and the Rockets looked like they might be contenders for a while after trading two second-round picks to the Bullets for Elvin Hayes in the off-season. They seemed poised for another title campaign.

Hayes was a legend in Houston, largely for his role as the losing half of the Lew Alcindor–"Big E" duels while at the University of Houston. He was credited with bringing a championship to the Washington Bullets in 1978, and was expected to do the same for the Rockets. Then everything fell apart. The Big E was a couple of steps slower and was unable to match the quicker pace ignited by Malone and sustained by Murphy, Reid, and Leavell. He still wanted the ball, thus forcing the Rockets to play more halfcourt offense. The Rockets finished second in their division with a 46–36 record, but were knocked out by the Supersonics in the first round. In Reid's view, the Rockets had gone from wannabees, to a pretty good team, to a contender, to also-rans.

The game held little joy for Reid that season. He cited religious reasons for his sudden disenchantment at the peak of his career, so the next season he quit. The Pentecostal Church, of which he was a member, had always frowned on the worldly nature of the game. Reid wanted to reestablish his slightly waning faith by working at his grandmother's church in Miami. Other factors influenced his decision. He was finding it harder to get in shape for a game he was getting sick of. There were lackluster attempts at his usual strict off-season regime of running and weightlighting. His heart just wasn't in it.

One afternoon he overheard some of his teammates bad-mouthing him in the locker room. The Rockets' organization was apparently contemplating a publicity push centered on Reid, Terry Teagle, Wally Walker, and some of the other younger Rockets for the upcoming season. The vets didn't like the idea. They felt Reid was a self-promoter. A good-looking guy with soft features, an easy smile, and curlicue bangs that make him very telegenic, Reid likes talking, which he does very well, with just about everyone—especially the press. It isn't that Reid is cocky. He is perhaps one of the most popular players in the league. But he had, and still has sometimes, the tendency to assume the leadership role and speak for his teammates.

This characteristic proved to be a relief for the younger Hornets, who didn't have much desire to step in front of the cameras. They needed a team spokesman. Reid was thought presumptious by the older Rockets for telling the television cameras what the team needed to do. When he overheard his teammates—guys he had been "skinning and grinning" with for a couple seasons—unloading on him, he decided that it was time to get out.

The lure of another shot at a championship ring proved too much. When Houston GM Ray Patterson asked him to rejoin the Rockets for the following season, a recharged Reid jumped at the offer. After only one year away, Reid came back more cognizant of how the character of the players had changed. Reid's early Rocket teams harkened back to a simpler time. Guys like Major Jones, Kevin Kunnert, Tom Owens, and "Easy" Ed Ratliff might tape the doors of a teammate's hotel room shut as a prank, or go out and carouse as a team. Ego confrontations were left on the court, and revolved around who was going to take the shots. Things were different in this new Rocket incarnation. Houston was just beginning to build its "Twin Tower" dynasty with Ralph Sampson. Two other talented rookies, Rodney McCray and Lewis Lloyd were also on board. Each was getting pretty good money (Sampson had already broken the bank), each seemed to be coddled by management.

Reid himself was also different than he had been in his first go-round with the Rockets. He was starting his own advertising agency and courier service, cementing his already-deep roots in the community at large. He was becoming Robert Reid, business man and community servant, and not just Bobby Joe Reid, Houston Rocket.

His second season back, the Rockets added Akeem Olajuwon—the Nigerian soccer player turned dominating basketball center for the Houston Cougars. He was another hometown hero. Olajuwon was young and gifted and under the tutelage of volatile coach Bill Fitch, the Twin Towers—Sampson and Olajuwon—were powering the Rockets into a major force. Reid believed Fitch to be a great coach. He hated losing and anyone who seemed to accept defeat. Reid liked the way he drove the young, talented team. He was a championship coach, winning it all in Boston in 1981, and took no guff from his team. The Rockets got knocked out in the first round of the playoffs, but they went out satisfied that they'd be a better team in the 1985–86 season.

They were. The Rockets were awesome. Sampson was averaging 18 points and 11 rebounds a game and Olajuwon was scoring nearly 24 points and swatting away more than three shots an outing. The Twin Towers pushed the Rockets to a 51–31 Midwest division title, winning 36 or 41 games at home. Houston was into their team and everyone—especially Reid—was having a great time on the floor. Off the court, however, the Rockets were showing chinks in their armor—chinks that would quickly snuff out any hope of a Twin Tower dynasty, as well as set up Reid's ignominious departure from the Rockets. During the March stretch drive, John Lucas was suspended because of drug use. The left-handed guard was an exceptional athlete who'd supplemented his income early in his career by playing professional tennis—a congenial leader on and off the floor. But his career had become plagued again and again by the acknowledgment of his drug use. Lucas's suspension greatly upset the young Olajuwon. The young star didn't understand why the league and the Rockets didn't wait for the season to end before suspending Lucas. At a team meeting, Reid, who was the Rockets' NBA player representative, tried to explain to him that Lucas needed help immediately—his family was counting on him, and in the long run it would be better for the team. Olajuwon was still upset—with the league, with the Rockets, and with Reid. Reid didn't believe Olajuwon's reaction was insensitive or selfish, just immature. That left Reid and old friend Leavell to anchor the explosive team. The Rockets steamrolled through the Western Conference playoffs, shutting out Sacramento in three games, beating Denver in six, and totally dismantling the defending champion Lakers. After losing the opening playoff game in Los Angeles, Sampson and Olajuwon ruled the inside, allowing the Rockets to have their way with the Lakers for the next four games. After that string of victories, though, the Rockets crashed into the Boston Celtics in the finals. Boston was too rough, too mature, and too good for the Rockets' young superstars and dispatched them four games to two. Despite averaging almost 15 points a game in the playoffs, Reid was again denied the coveted championship ring.

The team's fabric began unraveling at once the following season. Lloyd and guard Mitchell Wiggins tested positive for drugs after 32 games. They were banned from the league, but not before triggering news reports that insinuated drug use was rife among Rocket players. Off the court, Reid already had distanced himself from "skinning and grinning" with his teammates. He was working hard in the community, contributing his time and efforts to mayoral committees and charities such as fighting AIDS, leukemia, and muscular dystrophy. Reid was attaching more than his name to his various civic endeavors. He commissioned a sculpture for a new arts center, became involved in several local political campaigns, and crusaded against drugs and teenage pregnancy. Reid was digging in in Houston, prepping for a life beyond the game and the city took note. He was named the final torch bearer when the city hosted the 1986 U.S. Olympic Festival. There was talk among local Democrats of pushing the player for a city council spot.

Reid turned in one more good season amid all the on-court turmoil and off-court activity, before undergoing arthroscopic surgery on his knee prior to the 1987–88 season. He came back slow, working his way into the starting lineup in midseason and turning in only about half of his career numbers. The Rockets believed he was getting too old. Then a confrontation with Olajuwon in the fall added fuel to the fire.

Unsubstantiated drug rumors had surrounded Akeem Olajuwon ever since the Lloyd–Wiggins suspensions. Olajuwon blamed them, at least partly, on Reid. Reid was a part-owner of a Houston nightclub at the time the drug rumors surrounding the Rockets had first surfaced. Through his club he'd met several Houston police officers, who moonlighted for him as secuirty guards. A couple of them approached Reid and told him that the word on the street was that Olajuwon might be involved. "They didn't know if it was true or not, but they told me to pull on Akeem's coat and let him know some things were being said," Reid recalled. He apparently told one of the Rockets' television announcers, McCoy McLemore, who was a friend of Akeem's, what he'd heard and what the police had asked him to do. By the time McLemore passed on the message, the young center believed that Reid was pointing the finger at him. At a shoot-around the day after talking to McLemore, Akeem charged Reid, delivering a hook that grazed his cheek. Reid believes the incident was blown out of proportion. He and Olajuwon settled their differences in a closed-door meeting soon after, but there were some lingering bad feelings. Reid knew his pink slip was drawing nearer. A new coach was coming in, Don Chaney, with a new system, and the Rockets were cleaning house. Reid knew Patterson was looking to deal him. The veteran thought he had struck a deal, sealed with a handshake, for his money to be guaranteed. The four-year deal he'd signed after coming off knee surgery called for guaranteed money if he played a thousand minutes that season. He'd worked hard at rehabilitation and came back after missing the first 20 games. But the Rockets had worked him into the lineup slowly and erratically—not, he thought, coincidentally—and he finished the year with only 980 minutes.

A ten-year career in Houston that had begun with Reid signing a contract on the hood of a car, had ended with him being dumped like a used car. The deal that sent Reid to the Hornets was a work of art on paper. Houston was trying to sign free agent Mike Woodson, a shooting guard three years younger than Reid. If the Rockets were to sign Woodson, they needed to cut their payroll substantially below the $7.232-million salary cap each team was allowed for player payroll. By cutting Reid, the Rockets would lower their cap by half of Reid's $450,000 salary, or $225,000. By trading for Bernard Thompson, who was making about $150,000 a year, Houston exchanged contracts and gained $300,000 in leeway. Thompson didn't figure in the Hornets' plans, or in the Rockets'. But when Houston eventually cut him a month into the season, they gained another $75,000, or half Thompson's salary, in usable funds. That left $375,000 in cash to use in acquiring Woodson. Economics dictated that Thompson never had a chance in Houston. Reid didn't have much more hope to make it in Charlotte.

Scheer had basically picked up a future number-two draft choice by exchanging warm bodies in training camp. Reid was a proven player. Thompson was a journeyman who in four seasons had averaged 5 points a game. At best, Reid was inexpensive insurance. No one needed to twist his arm to fit Shinn's role-model criteria. He was an explosive scorer who'd keep Charlotte in some games, and he had a pretty good track record for working with younger players. At worst, Reid was a cheap training-camp look-see with no contractual strings. Bring him in, suit him up, and as long as they needed him, pay him. He was a rarity in the ledger books—a truly disposable player.

There was just a little over four minutes left to play in the game when Reid returned for what was beginning to look like Charlotte's first regular-season win. The Hornets were up by eight, 103–95, and Harter had four thirty-plus-year-olds on the floor. He was taking no chances. Chapman, Bogues, and Kempton—the kids—had played well off the bench, keying what had started as a 14-point, fourth-quarter lead. When the Clippers scored three unanswered baskets, Harter called time-out and inserted Reid and Rambis back in the lineup to join Tripucka and Cureton.

The crowd also sensed a win was near. They were on their feet now, giving their team a standing ovation as the Hornets returned to the floor. The game wasn't sold out. This was a wet, overcast Election Day. The 18,865 fans who'd showed up couldn't conceal the patches of teal in the cavern-ous arena, revealing the empty seats. For much of the game, they were subdued. The occasional roars for a Chapman three-pointer or a Bogues-triggered fast break weren't nearly as crisp as they had been at the season opener. The plain-old regular-season game seemed anticlimatic after the raucous atmosphere of the opening-night gala. The back-to-back thrashings of their team by Cleveland and Detroit had perhaps contributed to the crowd's collective emotional hangover. Even the team's mascot, Hugo the Hornet, seemed tentative during his break-dance routines.

Harter was surprised that there was even this big a crowd on hand. The Clippers weren't much of a draw, especially since Manning wasn't signed. Besides, win or lose there would be a new President-elect in the morning. Hopefully, there also would be $100 million in bond money approved to unsnarl Charlotte's abysmal road system. Like most newcomers, Harter was amazed that for all its jaycee ambitions, the town didn't have a beltway or any navigable transportation system.

The Hornets were closing in on a win. It would be a dramatic one if they managed to just hold on. Moments before tip-off, Scheer had informed the coach that Shinn had suffered a stroke earlier in the afternoon. The owner had become ill after a luncheon speech before the Charlotte area radio man-agers at a downtown hotel. He was a little wobbly and disoriented when he returned to his office, but was reluctant to see a doctor. Shinn kept a wicked pace of public speaking engagements, wedging the talks in over the course of sixty-hour work weeks. He was also an avid jogger and clean liver. He honestly didn't believe it was anything but fatigue. After he had rested on an office couch intermittently through the afternoon, Scheer and Hornets trainer, Terry Kofler, finally talked him into seeing a doctor. After an office visit, Shinn was taken by ambulance to Charlotte Memorial Hospital where he was admitted to the intensive-care unit in serious condition. A blood vessel had burst in the right frontal lobe of his brain, causing a mild stroke.

Harter elected not to tell his team before the game. There was no win-one-for-the-owner speech. His players were professionals who knew that it was their job to play hard and win. Word had filtered down, however, from the fans, who had seen the news reports on television. The secret was revealed during pregame ceremonies when the public address announcer asked for a moment of silent prayer for Shinn.

As hardhearted as it sounds, none of this mattered when the Hornets broke their huddle and returned for the final minutes of the game. They were closing in on the only "first" that mattered—a win. In the middle of it all was Robert Reid. The cocaptain was suffering through a dismal shooting night, having hit just 4 of 15 shots from the floor. This was crunch time now. He hit a 21-footer from the baseline with 1:34 left, pumping the Hornets' lead to 8. He grabbed his ninth rebound on the defensive end, started the break, finishing it on a pass from Tripucka at the other end for a lay-up to give Charlotte an insurmountable 10-point lead. The Clippers raced back to throw up a few desperate shots before the buzzer went off signaling the club's first regular-season win.

The crowd wouldn't leave. Fans were pushing toward the floor, barely able to contain their joy. All of a sudden the election results that sporadically flashed on the scoreboard, prompting applause from the obviously Republican crowd, who cheered Vice President Bush's commanding lead over Mike Dukakis, didn't matter. Rambis, clutching the game ball, threw his arm around a smiling Harter at halfcourt. Chapman was smiling as he wandered aimlessly at halfcourt. Reid and

Cureton slapped high fives and exchanged congratulatory scowls under one basket. The two vets then disappeared into the tunnel, heading for the locker room, where they would await the box score. That left Tripucka at halfcourt, first making the thumbs-up sign to those in the arena. Finally, he began applauding the fans who'd stayed in their seats to hail him and his teammates.

This was a grander moment than opening night had been for the players on the expansion team. They had won in only their third time out. Each knew the team wasn't expected to win more than 15 or 20 games this inaugural season. Those numbers had been arrived at on a spread sheet, distilled from past performances of expansion teams and based on data that suggested the team's talent was suspect. Harter had coached this game—like he would the rest—to win. Rambis, Reid, Cureton, and Tripucka had played it like they had played every game since boys—to win. The Hornets were professional athletes. Older men playing a kids' game. They were entertainers making money for their owner and their league. On nights they won, though, their athleticism preempted their professionalism. The fun was in competing. The joy was in winning. No agent, general manager, fan, or sportswriter could share in their sense of accomplishment. They ultimately won or lost on the court. Nowhere else.

Reid and Cureton slipped through the showers and into the training room to look over the box score. The Reid line read 9 rebounds and 16 points—10 in the fourth quarter, 7 of them in the last four minutes. Outside, Harter was crediting Reid with the win. He'd hit the big shots down the stretch, the veteran shots. Two chairs down from Reid's, Tripucka was sitting in his, surrounded by television cameras and newspaper reporters. "This one is for you, George," the star forward was addressing the stricken owner. "This was a win for the fans."

6

WIN STREAK

THERE is nothing sweeter than a winning streak. The Hornets had one going early on—a two-gamer after the season's thirteenth and fourteenth outings. A pretty modest accomplishment, considering the team hadn't won in ten days and there was already two four-game losing streaks in the record book. In this the year of the Charlotte Hornets, a 99–84 thumping of the beleaguered Miami Heat and a 109–107 victory over Charles Barkley's Atlantic Division–leading Philadelphia 76ers, was big, big news in the Piedmont burg. The following morning, *The Charlotte Observer* chose to trumpet the occasion with a front-page banner headline. Beneath it, sports columnist Ron Green waxed eloquently about how Charlotte had "got a glimpse into its future as an NBA franchise. . . . Gosh, is it gonna be fun." Below were two pretty big stories: the first concerning how a New York investment firm was about to break up RJR Nabisco, the tobacco-and-food conglomerate with hallowed origins in neighboring Winston–Salem as part of the nation's most expensive takeover. The second reported that President Reagan under no circumstances intended to pardon Colonel Oliver North for his participation in the Iran–Contra affair.

Charlotte was used to having the Hornets splashed across the front page. The Pulitzer–prize winning newspaper had been instrumental in fueling Shinn's, as well as the city's, dream of gaining major league status through the acquisition of a sports franchise. While the banks and the town bigwigs were dismissing his quest as quixotic, *The Observer* had chronicled Shinn's every move, breathlessly reporting his small triumphs, such as landing a meeting with the NBA, as well as the slights. The now-famous "the only franchise Charlotte will land is one with the Golden Arches" dig in Phoenix became a rallying cry for the city. Over the course of the three years it took Shinn to join the NBA, the newspaper became both a tool and a participant in Shinn's crusade. Gantt believes that the clammoring of sportswriters for the city to support Shinn's effort cleared the way for him to intercede on Shinn's behalf in the Coliseum Authority's lease negotiations. The Coliseum Authority was characterized as the villain who was throwing up obstacles for Shinn, as well as the city, by demanding that a profitable lease be worked out with its potential tenant. Gantt thought that the would-be owner was a master at building public support for an effective effort for the professional league. Shinn developed such a close relationship with the managing editor, Mark Ethridge—who has since resigned—that he hired him as the Hornets' publishing consultant. He is also helping Shinn with his autobiography.

Shinn's seeming lock on the hometown newspaper would continue to frustrate disgruntled general partner, Cy Bahakel. Bahakel felt that by reflecting Shinn's point of view, the newspaper conveyed a skewed, Shinn-serving version of how the NBA franchise came to be and was operating in Charlotte.

Green's front-pager following the win streak was almost prophetic. He asserted in print that in three, four, or five years the Hornets would be waging war with the "big boys" on a nightly basis, and more often than not, winning. He closed his argument with a comment from Philly center and former Duke

star, Mike Gminski. The eight-year veteran apparently forgot
for a moment that he was an ACC homeboy and responded
candidly when asked if there was any significance to the 76ers
losing to an expansion team. Not really, he answered. "Nobody will remember this tomorrow." The columnist's response? "Don't bet on it."

The Observer wasn't about to let Charlotte forget. The
next day's headline made it official: "Hornets Mania!" and
"Piedmont Is Abuzz With Pride." Seven reporters dispatched
across the metropolitan area had dug up a series of vignettes
that illustrated how smitten the town had become with their
new major-league franchise. There were the four monks at
Belmont Abbey who, despite having to miss home games in
lieu of evening prayers and reflection, hung on every newspaper account and radio report about the travails of the town's
new basketballers. "I was edified last night when they won,
because I'm from Philly," admitted the Reverend Martin Hays
in the newspaper. "It was great to see the Hornets come
through with such great style." One Charlotte couple, it was
reported, interrupted their viewing of "Sherlock Holmes" on
public television to listen to the final minutes of the Philadelphia victory. There were tales of diehard Tarheel fans already
switching their allegiance (blasphemy!) to the new mutt of an
NBA team. At Rick Steamboat's Mid-Atlantic Gym, thirty-five
body-building enthusiasts reportedly halted their workouts to
listen to how the Hornets brought home the victory before
wildly celebrating the occasion, presumably by hitting the juice
bar.

Most impressive, however, was a brief sidebar prepared
by Hornets' beat writer Rick Bonnell. Bonnell checked with
Las Vegas bookmakers, finding that if a person bet $10
double-or-nothing and let it ride that the Hornets would cover
the point spread over the past thirteen games (excluding the
Cleveland debacle), multiplied exponentially that original few
bucks would now total $81,920. The point was that the
Hornets were much better than expected. They had beat the
betting line twelve times as underdogs. They'd won the only
game in which they were favored, over Miami, by more than

the eight-and-a-half points they were giving away. This was sports talk for basketball fans, not mania mongering for civic boosters.

The truth was that Charlotte was starting to turn the corner. What had started as a civic crusade three years before had culminated in a celebration on opening night and was now passing into a more personal and essential phase. The city was beginning to identify with its sports heros.

Sitting in a chair in front of his dressing stall, half-clothed, swaddled in tape and braces, Kelly Tripucka was holding court for the media after hitting the winning lay-up with four seconds left that had sealed the 109–107 victory over the 76ers. Working the press was as important as playing the game these days and one of the masters was at work.

Most of his teammates were filtering out of the locker room, their contributions to the postgame commentary long finished. Assistant coach Ed Badger was needling Tim Kempton, another after-game dawdler. The rugged center was trying to claim credit, as well as the $10 the coach had promised, for picking up the charge against the 265-pound Charles Barkley that had ended the game. Before tip-off Coach Badger had posted a $10 bounty for any player who stepped in the path of the so-called "Round Mound of Rebound," thus successfully drawing an offensive foul. Ironically, that is what happened in the final seconds when Barkley went down the middle to hit what appeared to be the tying bucket. Lee Jones's whistle, however, nullified the basket and sent the man-mountain in pursuit of the referee, but not until he'd first fired the ball into the scorers' table.

No one ever has accused Barkley of being well mannered. The 76er acted more like an overgrown kid both on and off the court. He smiled when he monster-dunked, laughed when admonished for committing a cheap foul, exploded in anger when he felt that he'd been done wrong—like tonight.

Rex Chapman was the player who'd actually picked up the charge, sacrificing his body, then ricocheting into Kempton. But as he did after most games, Chapman showered

quickly, pulled his clothes on over his wet body, grabbed his
tennis shoes, and headed out a back door of the Coliseum,
where he could avoid the kids staked out for his autograph.
The Boy King wasn't much for postgame chatter, with the
press or anyone else. Badger ended up paying $10 to each of
the five players on the floor at the time. All of them had tried
to get in Barkley's way. Winning can make a big spender out
of anyone.

Tripucka always remained behind to relive the game
highlights. The 6'6" forward was establishing himself as the
Hornets "go-to guy." His 25 points had paced the expansion
team most of the night. A three-point play with 1:29 left,
capping a comeback, had put the Hornets ahead by one at
105–104. Then he'd hit the game-winner. Tripucka also was
becoming the "go-to guy" for the throng of television and
newspaper reporters who flocked to the Hornets' dressing
room. As Shinn had promised the NBA, the team was getting
radio, television, and newspaper coverage from as far away as
Columbia, South Carolina, to the south, Greensboro and
Raleigh 100 miles to the north. *The Observer,* the *Winston–
Salem Journal,* and *Gastonia Gazette* all had full-time beat
writers traveling with the team. The attention Tripucka currently enjoyed was a far cry from the past two years he'd spent
languishing on the end of the Utah Jazz's bench. He was now
Charlotte's leading scorer with a 20.2 average and was playing
almost thirty-five minutes a game. So far he had been the only
constant Harter could count on.

Tripucka was finding redemption in the expansion franchise. Once more he was the poster boy, winning fans and
influencing sportswriters with his play on the court. He was
the team's leading scorer in nine of the thirteen games he
played. Tripucka was popular with the fans. The star bought a
block of twenty tickets for each home game and in a classy
gesture made them available to underprivileged kids. He called
them "Kelly's Heroes."

The Notre Dame graduate was adept at the postgame
interview. He welcomed the microphones and television cameras, playing directly to them while effortlessly tossing off a

string of cliches. Teammate Michael Holton, an articulate communications major from UCLA, termed the whole post-game exercise "generic locker room rap." At a summer press conference introducing the Hornets' newly acquired fading superstar, Tripucka had asserted that one way he might lend stability to the expansion franchise was by handling the press, "keeping you guys off the younger players." Tripucka was glib, charming, and immensely quotable. Before season's end, he would have uttered all the old standards from his postgame throne—how five seconds was a long time in the NBA, etc.—most appearing in the next day's newspaper.

It was a curious situation for a man who'd blamed much of his troubles in the NBA on sports writers who didn't understand him. It was almost as curious as the Hornets' plan to build its team around an enigmatic scorer they'd hoped to salvage from the junk heap.

Harter was the one responsible for catching Tripucka's falling star. Most coaches around the league had written him off after his 1987–88 season in Utah. He was thought to be tempermental, whiny, and—at almost $1 million a year through 1991—too expensive a headache by most NBA executives. The Jazz management was kicking themselves for not pulling the trigger on anything that had resembled a trade sooner. For two years, Tripucka and Frank Layden, the clown prince of NBA coaches, had tolerated each other in an uneasy truce that had frustrated both men. By the dispersal draft, it was obvious that the Jazz were willing to bend over backward to get rid of him. Here was yet another castoff, though a pricey one, that suited the Hornets well.

Tripucka fit the Hornets' perimeter needs. He was twenty-nine, a former NBA All-Star, and though the neon flickered, he was still something of a marquee name. Scheer and Littles were leery, but Harter, who'd been an assistant in Detroit while Tripucka was posting his best numbers, was pushing for him. Barring a total erosion of skills, there was little question about Tripucka's talent. His game was like a flawed gem, sparkling in some aspects, so rough in others that it depleted the overall value. Tripucka's shooting touch was golden from beyond the three-point line. He was crafty on offense, going to the hole with what looked like forced drives, but somehow getting the ball to fall, or getting fouled—a lot of times both. He passed pretty well when he wanted to. Most of all, Harter believed Tripucka to be a competitor—a guy who did whatever was necessary to win on the floor. Harter conceded the downside of Tripucka's game: he was lousy defensively and wasn't much good on the boards. He was too small to be a true number three, or small forward (though that's where he'd play), and too slow for the number two, or shooting-guard position.

Still, Harter believed Tripucka could win some close games for the Hornets. He was counting on him to step in immediately and shoulder the scoring load. He envisioned Tripucka's play reflecting the aggressive, gutsy brand of ball Harter hoped to coach.

Besides, the coach and the player were buddies from their shared Detroit days. "Buddy" was a term Harter liked to use for guys who were as well versed, or respectful of the history of the game, as he was. They ranged from Indiana coach Bobby Knight, whom Harter knew since his Philadelphia days when "The General" was commanding West Point, to an Indianapolis businessman named Bobby Plump.

According to Harter, Plump was the player who sank the winning shot in the 1950s that had catapulted tiny Milan High School over South Bend Central in the Indiana State High School Championship. That was the game immortalized in basketball lore by the film *Hoosiers*. The coach beams when remembering how his buddy Plump continues to carry bundles of newspapers recording that dramatic event in the trunk of his car, ready to show to those who do not believe his role in the victory.

Harter later winced, however, when Tripucka made a lighthearted reference at his introductory press conference to another passion the two shared. "I like to get a tan and he likes to get a tan," Tripucka told reporters when asked about the two's reunion. "Maybe I can get discount tickets to his tanning booth."

Ultimately, Harter was able to win over Scheer and Littles on the idea of pursuing Tripucka. The Jazz were more than willing to deal. The original plan, hatched between the two clubs on the eve of the dispersal, was for the Hornets to select Jon Sundvold from San Antonio and then trade him for Tripucka. The Jazz needed backcourt help, and the dependable Sundvold could play either point or shooting guard. But Miami foiled that by taking Sundvold as their number-nine overall pick. Layden became miffed and canceled the trade that morning after the Hornets gave him a choice of Clint Wheeler, Ralph Lewis, and Sedric Toney. They were guards, but also free agents. The Jazz wasn't prepared to cut any new contracts. Finally, NBA general counsel Gary Bettman was called on to arbitrate the deal, requiring that Charlotte offer players who had contracts. That left draftees Bernard Thompson of Phoenix, Michael Holton of Portland, and beefy big man, Mike Brown of Chicago. Layden went with Brown. The Hornets now had Tripucka, plus an agreement that Utah would pay roughly half of his salary. In the process they lost the only other big guy, besides Dave Hoppen, they'd selected. Scheer and especially Littles were none too happy.

Tripucka's reaction to the day's transaction was to tell Salt Lake's *Deseret News*, "It doesn't matter how they make the deal as long as I get my money. I'm sure the Jazz wanted to get something for me, but they don't deserve it for the way they treated me for the last two years."

There lies the reason for Tripucka's fallen star. The league, the business of basketball, has its share of prima donnas, outlaws, and flakes who are amply rewarded with long-term, big-money contracts as long as they practice and perform forty-eight minutes a game, 82 games a season as professionals. Over the course of his eight seasons, Tripucka had developed a reputation for such annoying behavior that even the most seasoned NBA handlers didn't want to touch him. His ego was thought to be irrepressible. The chip on his shoulder was so enormous that his misfortunes or setbacks always seemed to be someone else's fault.

Tripucka, through little fault of his own, had been cast as the villain almost from day one. He was a workmanlike All-American when he came out of Notre Dame in 1981, graduating as the Irish's fourth all-time leading scorer. His skills were not particularly flashy, yet he gobbled up the scenery on the court with his petulant, brooding, and pouting reactions to a referee's whistle, a skinned knee, or a missed shot. The brawny New Jersey kid with the football player's jaw and disco-coiffed bushy hair, was a guy fans loved to hate—especially since he was playing for Notre Dame.

His much-touted bloodlines proved for many even more irksome. Tripucka often recounted, the Golden Domers liked to hear, how he and his five brothers shoveled snow off their suburban driveway, donning gloves to wage basketball battles that always ended in fights. He told about the New Year's Eve he stood outside with a wristwatch, counting down the minutes so he could make the first basket of the New Year. There were tales of how his older brothers beat up on him so much in pickup games that he'd end up running inside the house crying. The Tripucka boys were all athletes. The oldest, Tracy, played basketball at Lafayette; Mark, football at Massachusetts; Todd, basketball at Lafayette; T. K., hoops at Fordham; Chris, the youngest, football at Boston College. Family competition was so routine and so raucous, according to Kelly, that their patriarchal father, Frank Tripucka—a former Notre Dame and pro quarterback—often ended up emerging from the house with a bat or rake ready to waylay whichever son had started the scrap. These were colorful anecdotes of which Tripucka was very proud. Once dished out to sports pundits and disseminated to the fans, they sometimes conjured up an unflattering portrait of Tripucka. Everybody's All-American tended to sound like a brat.

This was especially true after the college draft. Tripucka was dismayed that he didn't go higher than number twelve in the first round. He was vocal about being a two-time All-American and the MVP of the showcase Pizza Hut All-Star

Game. He thought he was better than the majority of the eleven guys chosen before him. It was the skeptics and scouts who said he was either too small or too slow and that was what had kept Washington, Dallas, or his home-state team, New Jersey, from picking him sooner. He joined the Pistons as a number twelve determined to make his detractors pay for the snub. He had a brilliant rookie-year campaign, posting career highs in rebounds and assists, averaging better than 21 points a game, and making the NBA rookie team. Isaih Thomas, the Pistons' first first-round pick, and Tripucka improved Detroit to an almost .500 club from the 21–61 team it had been the previous year. Thomas, who had left Indiana early, also made the NBA rookie team. He was quieter than Tripucka the first year—in numbers, as well as in personality. Thomas was childlike and shy around the media. Tripucka swaggered into Detroit, declaring the dirty-fingernail Motor City his kind of town. He was the Pistons' poster boy—tough, talented, and white. Seldom has an NBA team ever resisted pushing such a talented white player into the limelight.

The rookie didn't need much of a shove. He initiated the love affair with his new city and the people of Detroit responded. Even though he transferred his whiny, collegiate court demeanor to the pros, the fans still loved him. The most poignant illustration of Tripucka's crazed competitiveness occurred during this rookie campaign. Near the end of a sterling 36-point, 10-rebound night, Tripucka had an opportunity to close out the Knicks with two last-second free throws. He missed them both. The Pistons ended up losing the game in overtime. Afterward the rookie retreated into the trainers' room, buried his face in towels and cried. Trainer Mike Abdenour found the player so disconsolate that he finally called Tripucka's mother in New Jersey, asking her to calm her twenty-two-year-old son.

The first couple of years in Detroit, the tale of a crestfallen rookie was told as a homage to Tripucka. Then head coach Chuck Daly came to town in Tripucka's third season. There was a shootout of sorts that, much to Tripucka's surprise, Daly won. By the time he was shipped to Utah in 1986 the

Tripucka-as-crestfallen-rookie story was recounted with a snicker. It was perceived as just one more example of how self-absorbed the scorer was. Daly is a burly, raspy-voiced, tough, whose ability to harness head cases and runaway egos into championship teams is widely hailed. He's proved time and again that he'll tolerate the off-court antics of his players as long as they show up as professionals on game days. If a guy wants to play and he can help Daly's club, the coach will take him on. Adrian Dantley, the problem player the Pistons obtained for Tripucka, proved an integral part of the 1987–88 near-championship Pistons. Later in the 1988–89 season, when Dantley no longer struck the Daly balance of wanting to play vs. helping his club, he was dumped on Dallas for another player of questionable character, Mark Aguirre.

But Tripucka got his shot with Daly. The groundwork for today's Central Division–leading bruisers was being laid by Daly. Vinnie Johnson came to the Pistons from Seattle. Bill Lambier started taking up space in the middle and Thomas was emerging as the offensive focal point. Tripucka held his own—at least numberswise. He was used to having things his own way, and he was slow to embrace Daly's hard-nosed defensive schemes and desire for a more evenly distributed offense. Both men had tempers too. There were flare-ups and heated discussions. Tripucka, however, was more prone to pout than shout. When he did, it made Daly more resolved to push the superstar he'd inherited. Tripucka has always been a charming and engaging gentleman off the floor. But troubles on the job inevitably affect his attitude. During his fourth season, when he missed 38 games with an injury and was embroiled in what he called "philosophical differences" with Daly, his sensitive, wounded superstar act began wearing thin with fellow Pistons. The scorer had never been much of a team leader.

Tripucka was a thirty–twenty man. He wanted his thirty-plus minutes a game, so he could take his twenty shots. That's the way it'd been when he was an All-American at Notre Dame. The same formula had produced playoff teams for Detroit, and two NBA All-Star selections for Tripucka while with the Pistons. The simmering Daly–Tripucka scraps were hammering it home to his teammates that Tripucka put his concerns ahead of the team's. Lambeer groused to reporters that Tripucka was dogging it instead of trying to come back strong from an injury. And Daly's passion for defense was now taking hold of his team.

Tripucka still grimaces at the criticism of his defensive prowess. It's garbage, he'll say. He argues that, at 6'6" and admittedly slow, he is the last of this breed of small forward. His defensive and rebounding liabilities, though overrated, are the product of being outmanned physically by the taller, quicker athletes who now play small forward, like Atlanta's Dominique Wilkins. They can post him up at will—besides, he point out, in today's league no one can consistently stop an NBA player from scoring. Tripucka concedes that he is not the greatest defender, but claims to work hard at it.

Daly, the Pistons, and for that matter no one in the league buys Tripucka's logic. After the trade to Utah was completed, Daly went out of his way to downplay the problems that he and Tripucka had had. He was outwardly pleased with the deal. He admitted that Tripucka wasn't an easy player to deal with because of his temper, but asserted that he had been a model citizen his final season in Detroit. Plus Daly said he liked him. The deal was intended to make the team better, that's all. The coach, however, did strongly point out that in the eighteen play-off games the Pistons had participated in during his tenure, the small forwards for the opposing team had averaged 30 points a game. Tripucka hadn't played that position solely, Daly added, sugarcoating his implied criticism, and his size had made it tough, but four small forwards had had career highs against the Pistons in those games. One of those was Atlanta's Wilkins, who, later in the 1988–89 season when the Hawks faced the Hornets, would grin with all the subtlety of a fox and say, "It's always nice to see Kelly out there."

Nevertheless, Tripucka was once more dismayed and appalled when it was announced the summer following his fifth season that he and Kent Benson were going to Utah for

Adrian Dantley and some draft picks. He blasted the Pistons. They were obviously panicked, he charged, making the trade for the sake of change. The Pistons had been nowhere before he got there, he claimed. He'd helped build them into a playoff team, and, according to Kelly, the fans were turning out because he was part of the town. He and his wife, Janice, had recently bought a condominium there. Tripucka insisted that the fans were upset, as were some of his teammates, about the transaction. By this point, he wasn't speaking to the Detroit media. Tripucka blamed them for writing that he was selfish, with his eye on his own stats instead of his team's standing. Then he was crying again, this time off the court, to a lone Detroit television reporter and members of the New Jersey press. He was beside himself, justifiably so, about how Detroit had notified him of the trade. Piston GM Jack McCloskey admitted it should have been handled better. Tripucka was finishing up in the locker room after a charity golf tournament when a kid came charging through repeating a radio report that Tripucka had been dealt to Utah for Dantley. McCloskey claimed he had been unable to raise anyone at the Tripucka household, so he'd called the Tripucka family home in New Jersey, relaying the word to one of his brothers. This was demeaning, according to Tripucka.

What was worse was that Tripucka immediately starting lobbying grenades from his own glass house at Dantley. Wounded, he blasted away at Dantley in the newspapers: wondering why the Pistons wanted a guy three years older than he was; a guy whose stint with four teams had each been rife with rumors about Dantley's inability to get along with his teammates; a guy with a bad attitude, whom of course Tripucka knew and liked (he'd finished behind him in scoring at Notre Dame) and didn't really want to malign, but why Detroit? Why trade your leading scorer and the city's favorite player for a troublemaker?

There are very few people in the NBA who have nice things to say about Dantley the person. His ego is mammoth, and invariably poses many prickly dilemmas for the chemistry of a clubhouse. But Dantley is admired, even praised, in the

NBA for the professionalism that has characterized his game over thirteen seasons. He always came to camp in shape. He had played through nagging injuries. On the floor, he was a gentleman who was strictly business. Later in the season, when Dantley was sulking about his trade to Dallas, refusing to report until his contract was renegotiated, even his harshest critics were surprised. "It was an asshole-for-asshole trade," one league official in New York said of the Dantley–Aguirre deal. "It's sadder, though, because AD is the one acting unprofessionally. He had his professionalism going for him all these years, but this is what everyone will remember."

No one will ever accuse Tripucka of sterling professionalism. He breached that in a big way by badmouthing Dantley. Cureton and Reid are probably the most eloquent spokesmen for the NBA's player code. Each believed management was fair game for venting frustrations. They were too many layers removed from the game, mired in contract and attendance figures, too performance-conscious because that's what drove the numbers. GMs and owners also were image-conscious, so when charges were leveled publicly, they reacted quickly. Coaches less so. They were in the trenches, aware of when an ego was out of whack, or when an injury was slowing a player down. At least the good ones were. They could become a player's ally. Besides, it didn't do much good to go after a coach. The coach was at the controls. He didn't have to react. If he could win without you, the player looked foolish. If he couldn't, all he needed to do was slightly adjust your minutes. If a player missed a couple of shots after entering the game, the coach could pull him and tell the player, as well as reporters after the game, that Bobby Joe, Earl, Ralph, Barney, or whoever didn't seem to be in the flow tonight. Again the player would look foolish. It just didn't pay to become publicly disgruntled. But under no circumstances was it ever correct for one NBA player to go after another. Everyone was in the same players' union. There was also the possibility that someday you might be teammates. Circumstances and personalities were different at every NBA stop. No one ever really knew what a player might be dealing with at each. Most important

was the fact that you were in the same fraternity, usually had
the same bitches (money and security) and obstacles (coaches
and management), and it was unthinkable to publicly beat up
on your own. That's what the locker room and practice floor
were for.

Cynics around the Detroit team pointed out that never in
Tripucka's posttrade tirade did the forward mention that he'd
gone out and signed a $6.3-million offer sheet with Cleveland
two years earlier, ready to leave the goodwill of Detroit behind
for greener pastures. When Detroit matched the offer at the
time, making Tripucka one of the highest-paid forwards in the
league, they thought that that should count for something. It
apparently didn't to Tripucka.

The forward's stay in Utah was shorter, but probably
stormier. By training camp, Tripucka had overcome his "jilting" enough to say publicly how he was looking forward to
playing for Frank Layden. The Utah coach was a 240-plus-
pound New York Irishman best known for his keen wit. The
humor, however, didn't mask the basketball purist inside the
coach. He had cut his teeth on the East Coast with Niagara
University. He'd never had prima donnas there, and he
wouldn't tolerate them in the pro ranks. The trade for Tripucka
perhaps had come under less than ideal circumstances. Layden primarily was trying to get rid of Dantley. "Murder" is the
word he used to describe his relationship with the powerful
and complicated forward. The Jazz were becoming perennial
Midwest Division contenders around young, at the time little-
known stars, such as Karl Malone, point guard John Stockton,
and svelte forward Thurl Bailey. Dantley, and his nearly 30-
point scoring average, had taken the Jazz to the playoffs for
three straight years, but except for the 1983–84 season when
Utah won the Midwest and made it to the Western Conference
semifinals, the team had always been disappointed early in
each of their playoffs. Like Tripucka, Dantley wanted his thirty-
plus minutes and twenty shots a game. It was no longer
enough to get in the playoffs on the shoulders of a scorer.
Like Detroit, Utah was ready to assemble better players with a
variety of skills to make a championship run.

Besides getting rid of a major headache, Layden believed perhaps wistfully that he might cajole Tripucka into modifying his scorer's game into one more suitable to team play. It never happened. There are two theories, one less flattering to Tripucka than the other, about what happened in Salt Lake. Tripucka again swaggered into town, causing a mild stir by laying claim to Dantley's jersey, number 4. It was his wife's favorite number, he explained, and besides, his choice, number 7, was already retired in honor of the late Pistol Pete Maravich. Those close to the Jazz say Tripucka came to camp in less than playing shape. He was still reeling from the Detroit spurning. He was an Eastern boy trying to relocate in the vast expanse of the Far West. The rouge-tipped Wasatch Mountains had replaced the gray-black smokestacks of Detroit. The fresh air and fresh faces of the predominately Mormon population were discombobulating for a guy used to walking down the street, bundled up in winter clothes, returning the rough greetings of frost-breathed Motor City residents.

Twenty games into the season, Tripucka was playing more than twenty minutes a game, scoring about 10 points, but wasn't looking very sharp. The newspapers began asking why. Layden kept up an optimistic front, praising his new acquisition for his better-than-expected passing and defensive skills, saying that Tripucka just needed to relax and take some time after making the transition to a new team. Tripucka began whining immediately—in typical Tripucka fashion. He said he knew he was between a rock and a hard place and didn't want to sound selfish, but he just wasn't getting the minutes he wanted. The in-and-out rotation was a tough adjustment for a guy used to being out there all the time. This talk irritated Layden and the Jazz, however, because some say the coach felt he was doing Tripucka a favor initially by easing him into the rotation. The forward wasn't in any kind of shape to carry the workload he was being weaned on. Layden didn't want to embarrass an out-of-shape, struggling Tripucka. The forward had labored to get his shooting percentage slightly above forty percent.

Also, after going round and round with Dantley, Layden

thought he had made it clear to Tripucka that playing for the Jazz was going to be different than the good old days. Malone and Bailey were developing nicely and there weren't going to be many thirty-five-minute games in the offing. By midseason, the Jazz, as well as Tripucka, knew the situation was becoming impossible. The highest-paid player on the team was playing spottily, stewing about it, and making life miserable for his coach. The "trade-me-or-play-me" blues were starting. Tripucka finished the season playing barely a fourth of the 2,000-plus minutes he'd logged the previous season in Detroit and taking about half the shots. The Jazz tried to accommodate his trade wishes after the season, but made the mistake of thinking they could get something of value in return. A handful of teams, New Jersey and Philadelphia among them, made half-hearted queries about obtaining Tripucka. But the Jazz weren't ready to concede that they'd made a big enough mistake to give the high-priced enigma away for nothing. After spending the first 24 games as the Jazz's twelfth man the following season, Utah owner Larry Miller convinced Layden to play Tripucka more, hoping to showcase his skills and set up a trade. He had a couple of decent outings as a starter for 21 games, even returning to form one night to score 25 against Milwaukee. Tripucka complained about being yo-yoed between the starting lineup and bench. Darrell Griffith and Bob Hansen were even more disgruntled because Tripucka was cutting into their minutes. Griffith now was openly asking for a trade. The Jazz got some peace in late February and March when Tripucka missed 19 games with a calf injury. Layden by now was admitting his mistake, calling the forward a disruption that had to go. The only hope was the expansion draft, and the coach was forecasting that only as a remote possibility. The Jazz needed to sweeten the pot.

"I'd like to thank Carl Scheer, the coaching staff, and Mr. Shinn for posting my bail to get me out of the jail I was in for two years. It was not that hefty a sum, but it was enough."

That's how the fallen star chose to introduce himself to his new town and his new team on June 27, 1988. He was half right about the price tag. The Jazz would pick up a substantial portion of his salary. The graceless shots he took at Utah that day demonstrated that little in the star's makeup had changed. When asked if anything positive had come out of his Jazz experience, the superstar on the comeback trail responded, "Yes, not to answer the door when they [Mormons] ask you to convert. I believe it's pretty much public knowledge. Probably the Russians know how I feel. They really put me through the grind out there."

Again it hadn't been Kelly Tripucka's fault.

7

A CAROLINA

CHRISTMAS

MICHAEL Jordan was coming to town. So was Christmas. But Michael was arriving in Charlotte first, two days before December 25th, along with his eleven mere mortal Chicago Bull teammates—count coach Doug Collins, and it was an apostolic twelve. Michael Jordan. Air Jordan. The classiest, most talented 6'6" forward, guard, player in the NBA was coming home to North Carolina, and Charlotte stopped just short of greeting him in the street with palm branches. Symptoms of hysteria always appeared in the NBA towns Jordan visited. The first signs were usually at the box office. Jordan drew crowds, the kind that began crackling as soon as they spied him in his pregame warm-up, gliding toward the bucket, springing skyward, and, almost as an afterthought, dropping the ball with one hand softly through the net.

Nobody knew better what Jordan meant to the business of basketball than the man pacing the sidelines, wheeling on his heels in midstep to rush off in every which direction. The

Charlotte Coliseum was Carl Scheer's arena. At least it provided the venue for the Hornets' general manager to view the final product of his twelve-hour days. It was the place where the marketing strategies, the ambience managing, and, finally, the twelve guys in Charlotte uniforms, would be judged. This ultimately was what building a fan base was all about.

There was such an elegance about the former Tarheel. Jordan never seemed to make bad choices on or off the floor. Atlantic Coast Conference aficionados had recognized this knack early in Jordan's career at North Carolina. The slight kid from Wilmington, North Carolina, had been able to sublimate his awesome talents while playing for Dean Smith from 1981–84. As a freshman he'd scored 13.5 points a game, melding with a talented Tarheel team that won the National Championship. Jordan's play hinted at his athleticism without upstaging his coach, Smith's beloved seniors, or the Carolina blue. He was a winner who was willing to learn for the good and glory of the Tarheels. Even when he decided to forego his senior year in favor the NBA, where his talents would be better showcased, he did it in a quiet, deliberate manner that had catapulted him into his position as basketball's current preeminent professional.

There was little doubt that Jordan would become a rookie sensation. He was the college player of the year in his sophomore and junior seasons, as well as a U.S. Olympian. Jordan is a gifted jumper who is breathlessly creative with the ball. His game was grounded in "God's conference," the ACC, where poise supercedes ego and individual accomplishments. He also was one of Smith's precision-practiced players, grounded in the fundamentals who pro coaches covet. Still, he was the third overall selection in the NBA draft, perhaps the most magic ever to come out of a number-three NBA draft selection.

There will always be arguments about who are, or were, the greatest basketball players of all time. Kareem vs. Wilt. Dr. J vs. Elgin Baylor. Magic vs. Larry Bird. The "Big O," Oscar Robertson, and Jerry West. Bob Cousy and Bill Russell. Walt Frazier, Earl Monroe, Rick Barry, Jerry Lucas, John

Havlicek. The NBA has always had its superstars, each with his fair share of well-schooled, or merely opinionated, supporters. Heated arguments have broken out in barrooms, newspaper columns, magazine articles, and books about how each brought an explosive talent or refined subtlety that has revolutionized the game. There is no doubt that when Jordan's career is finished that his legendary dunks, 63-point outings, and perhaps, the yet-to-be-realized championship will add grist to such discussions.

But Jordan's most substantial accomplishment—one none of the others can claim—has been to elevate pro basketballers from mere athletes to full-blown celebrities. He is a star who cuts across all basketball lines—that of business, player, and fan—and turns a kid's game into lucrative entertainment.

Carl Scheer is an intense, moody man, who bares an uncanny resemblance to failed presidential candidate Michael Dukakis. He always seems distracted. Scheer can be either expansive—even magnanimous when a broad smile cracks his weathered face—as quickly as he can become brooding, standoffish, and arrogant.

Scheer was excruciating to watch or deal with on game nights. Before tip-off, he was like a fly flitting everywhere, never in one place long enough to pin down. Sometimes he'd blow through the press room to ask the beat writers if they needed anything, but rarely broke stride long enough to wait for an answer. Then he was off to courtside to meet with almost a dozen of his marketing and publicity charges—most armed with a two-way radios and a precisely scripted schedule of the night's program.

Scheer personally made sure the curtain rose and fell on time for his productions. Game operation staff meetings were held in the morning, so everyone was familiar with the script. There was no ad-libbing allowed from the public address announcer, the performance of the national anthem was allotted exactly two minutes, and the army of salesman-turned-stage hands knew when the various pre- or postgame presenters needed to be in their places. There was nothing left

to chance, no serendipity. Scheer believed precision was the
key to manipulating 23,000-plus basketball fans into a raucous
and fun-loving crowd. It was induced spontaneity. Even the
music was selected and choreographed based on what works
in other NBA arenas. The Charlotte Coliseum staples,
"Shout" and "Old Time Rock 'n' Roll," had been lifted from
the Dallas Mavericks' playlist. The Hornets added a wrinkle by
hiring a local deejay who was assigned the task of program-
ming the beach or "shag music" as danced by Carolinians.
The twenty-eight sponsors who paid to have their wares sold
to the arena crowd were relegated to four silent message
boards that ring the Coliseum's mezzanine—so their pitches
did not interrupt the ever-pumping music.

Charlotte fans had already demonstrated that they were
verbose, energetic, and knowledgeable, but Scheer was fearful
that his basketball-crazy constituents might lose interest in a
team that probably would lose more than 60 games.

Once that huddle broke, he was back on the prowl, glad-
handing the visiting general managers or league officials he
had cultivated relationships with over his twenty years in
professional basketball management. He greeted the civic
leaders and Charlotte luminaries he had met on his mission to
spread Hornets mania.

Of the three men who dictated what the Hornets were to
become—Shinn, Scheer, and Harter—Scheer perhaps had
the most pivotal role. He was the professional paid to bridge
the worlds Harter and Shinn represented. The hierarchy was
such that the players were on the lowest rung, with Harter a
step up, then Scheer, and finally Shinn. There was little direct
interaction between each level. The players steered clear of
the general manager, with the most contact coming at contract
time, but then only with their agent as intermediary.

Harter was the coach. He was hard-nosed and straight-
talking, the kind of guy you'd enjoy having a beer with even if
it meant having some kind of an argument. The game was
what mattered to Harter and he would lie awake at night
thinking about how his twelve guys were going to beat somebody else's twelve. Basketball talk sandwiched Harter's rela-

tionship with his players and Scheer. He strategized and
x-and-oed with his team, while prodding, pleading, and cajol-
ing Scheer to find bigger and better players through trades so
that the Hornets could win more games. His most joyful nights
were spent winning games. Next closest to his heart were
experiences like the "great night" spent in a Boise, Idaho,
hotel room, where he and two other coaches wiled away the
hours in a bathroom, diagramming lob-pass plays on a mirror
with a bar of soap.

"My predecessor at Oregon, Steve Belko, and Ladell
Andersen of BYU got in an argument about how many plays
could set up a lob pass. At the time I thought I knew a dozen
or so. The next thing we're in the bathroom drawing 'em up
and as soon as one finished, another would grab the soap and
start another play," Harter recounted, clearly excited by the
memory. "It was great. If I could have a buck for each of those
plays I'd be a rich man."

Shinn the owner, with his humble country-boy manner
and his rags-to-riches resume that he wore on his sleeve, was
at the other end of the spectrum. He was an autocratic
crusader who believed his management-by-love and well-
intended, if not flexible, motivational techniques could be
applied to a culture he himself knew little about. Shinn was at
the top of the pyramid, reachable only through Scheer, who,
for the most part, was left to run the basketball operations.
The owner was content to be the chief executive and standard
bearer—the final word on taste and morals. The scrap between the rookie owner and the NBA illustrated Shinn's iron-
willed commitment to do things his way. Along with a pregame
worship service arranged at Shinn's behest for Hornets and
visiting NBA-ers, a brief invocation was installed as part of the
Coliseum's program. Several area ministers, rabbis, and
priests were to take turns giving an ecumenical thirty-second
blessing before the national anthem. When the league office
heard of the arrangement, officials asked the Hornets not to
go ahead with the public prayer. No other team in the NBA
had such a practice, and such an arrangement was against an
informal NBA policy. Shinn flinched at first. Letters were

written to the pastors who'd volunteered, notifying them that their services would not be needed and thanking them for their offer.

Then he had a change of heart. The more Shinn thought about it, the more irritated he got. It was *his* franchise and he could do whatever he wanted with it. The prayer would be a part of his formula because Charlotte was a Bible-Belt town and he personally was grateful for all the Lord had done for him. Charlotteans were going to pray, and so they did.

Scheer ruled his middle ground with a cagey devotion to his owner that inspired an us-against-them loyalty. That loyalty seemed to grip virtually the whole business organization. The general manager circled his wagons around the owner who'd returned him to the NBA after two years in the minor leagues. Granted, Scheer had reigned over the minors in a productive tenure as the commissioner of the Continental Basketball Association. But as Denver coach Doug Moe, a friend and former employee of Scheer, put it, "Nobody goes to the CBA because they want to. There are a limited number of jobs for players, coaches, and front office people up here. When those are filled, you go where you can."

Scheer was Shinn's only candidate for the Hornets' general manager's job. The owner had found a twin in Scheer when it came to drive, commitment, and irrepressibility. According to Shinn, Scheer was the only front office executive he spoke with who had believed in his quest to land a franchise. Even during the dark days when it appeared the deal might crumble, Scheer told Shinn to keep the faith, that he was going to get his team and when he did, he wanted to run his basketball operations. The owner heard from plenty of executives after it was announced that Charlotte had bested the others in the expansion hunt, but noted that none of them had paid him much attention when he was just a North Carolina entrepreneur whistling "Dixie" with his proposal. Scheer, in turn, was extremely protective of his boss. He pointed out Shinn's naivete in pro sports management, spoke his sensitivity, and gentle, trusting nature and told the newspapers that he didn't want Shinn to get hurt when and if criticism hailed on his operation. Scheer made his message clear: nobody was going to rock Shinn's dreamboat, if there was anything he could do about it.

After the owner's stroke, Scheer consolidated even more of his far-reaching powers. Shinn was in the hospital fifteen days after the November 4 stroke, rested for longer at home, and only recently (and against doctors' orders) had started going to the office. He was far from the effervescent figure who'd bounded about the offices alternating hugs and instructions to his staffers. The medicine he had been taking made him sluggish and, not surprisingly, he moved more tentatively. Meanwhile Scheer's devotion to Shinn, and his dominating, arrogant manner was alienating Cy Bahakel. The general partner and the Hornets' top employee had gotten off to a rocky start after Scheer had failed to include Bahakel or limited partners, Rick Hendrick and Felix Sabates, in the Coliseum for season-opening ceremonies. Bahakel had called the slight a "rank discourtesy" and believed Scheer's sales and marketing staff were also being discourteous to his own employees at WCCB-TV, who were trying to coordinate promotions with the station's game broadcasts. Scheer never seemed to be available for Bahakel. No one seemed to want to cooperate with or brief Bahakel about the Hornets' operations that his money had helped establish. Bahakel knew his disagreement was with Shinn, but he was further frustrated by the obstacles his partner's good soldier seemed to be putting up.

Scheer's showmanship concept of professional entertainment went hand in hand with Shinn's mandate for establishing a model corporate citizen as a season ticket holder. The 15,500 season ticket holders who had come through in the town's hour of need were showered with premiums before the historic first tipoff. They were given a free subscription to the team newsletter, STING, invited to a preseason players' autograph party, given a Christmas gift and preferred parking. The highest-priced ticket holders were invited to join the arena's Crown Club, where, for an additional fee, they could purchase drinks or enjoy a buffet before or after each game. Crown

Club members were also guaranteed gifts in any promotional children's giveaway.

When Scheer spoke of the game-time product, he sounded more like a Broadway impresario than a basketball executive. Sound bites such as, "We think we provide the cleanest, most exciting atmosphere in the NBA. Everything we do is calculated for our fans' enjoyment," were staples of the Scheer sell. He unleased them with enthusiasm on out-of-town reporters assigned to find out why nearly 23,388 people a night had been gripped by Hornets mania.

Two days after officially landing the franchise in 1987, Shinn declared that Charlotte's goal was to lead the NBA in attendance. That's exactly what the fans were doing. Game nights at the Coliseum were always an event. The crowd was predominately white, well heeled, and dressed either for pin-stripe success or outfitted in Charlotte Hornets sportswear. "Spike," "Blind Eddie," and "Lurch," as they called them-selves, were the only brief exception to the rule. The trio spiked and tie-dyed their hair, donned dog collars and new-wave attire, to lead cheers and initiate the wave. They were a hit on opening night, but were soon asked by Hornet manage-ment to cease their impromptu displays of mania because it didn't jibe with Shinn's image of clean, wholesome entertain-ment.

What was most impressive about Charlotte fans was that they spent money. After Christmas, the Chamber of Com-merce issued a press release that showed Charlotteans had bought more than $1 million in T-shirts, caps, jerseys, and foam-rubber "Hugo the Hornet" hands through the holidays. The ever-vigilant NBA marketing and properties division fur-ther validated this claim with calculations, showing that the Hornet fans' ratio of money spent on novelties to tickets sold for each game was far outpacing the league average. The average NBA team sells 39 cents in licensed properties per ticket sold, while the Hornets were ringing in a phenomenal $1.25 per ticket sold.

The great Jordan's homecoming made the December 23 game an assured sellout as soon as it was scheduled. The

Hornets' staff spent most of their day disappointing last-minute callers, long-lost friends and such, with the news that there was nary a ticket or pass, complimentary or otherwise, available for tonight's game. Scheer himself had turned down requests from South Carolina governor Carroll Campbell's office and the great one himself, Jordan. The Bulls forward had called that afternoon looking for thirteen more tickets in addition to the forty-two he had previously acquired for family and friends. No luck. Scheer would later recount the awkward phone conversation with the NBA's star attraction with wonder, amazement, and more than a hint of glee. This was the expansion team's seventh sellout in twelve home dates and the front office was giddy about the box office success they felt partly responsible for.

Scheer, however, remained every wary. He was a seasoned front office hand who at various times of his career had been tagged the NBA's fair-haired boy wonder, the game's shrewdest and most ambitious innovator, and now returning exile. When he drove his staff extra hours, sometimes rattling them with his temper and impatience, he told them that they had to perform every minute like it was the franchise's last: "It can turn on you any day." At least, that had been his experience.

The marriage of Scheer to Shinn and the Charlotte Hornets' franchise was one that had been brokered by NBA commissioner David Stern. Stern had first sent the would-be owner Scheer's way during the fall of 1985 while Shinn was on a whirlwind tour of NBA teams in hopes of obtaining a feel for the pro sports league and any management tips. Stern recommended that Shinn see Scheer in Los Angeles, where he at the time was trying to breathe some life into the floundering Clippers' organization. It turned out to be a fateful meeting.

The Clippers franchise epitomized the buffoon era of management Stern was fighting fiercely to replace with financially sound ownership and responsible business practices. The Clippers had become something of an embarrassment with their ineptitude on and off the floor, unpaid bills, and a meddling owner, Donald Sterling, who'd moved the team to Los Angeles from San Diego in 1984 without the NBA's permission.

The commissioner had pleaded with Scheer, whom he considered a friend and talented executive, not to take the Clippers' post. He didn't need the headache of trying to sort out a troubled franchise, or the sure-fire disappointment of a team trying to fill the dilapidated L.A. Sports Arena in the shadow of the deep-pocketed, talent-laden Lakers. Scheer didn't listen to Stern, his wife, Marsha, and countless others who'd counseled him not to take the Clippers job. Scheer told himself at the time that the challenge of revitalizing the troubled franchise was too attractive. He had worked miracles in the ABA, first with the Carolina Cougars, then with the Denver Nuggets. After helping to force the ABA–NBA merger, he'd managed to peacefully coexist with Denver's Bronco Maniacs, which had enabled him to turn the Nuggets into one of the NBA's most admired franchises. Scheer is a supremely confident man who has amassed a successful track record under less than ideal circumstances. He decided the Clipper job wouldn't be much different. He believed, perhaps naively, that he could communicate with Sterling. He convinced himself that it was going to be a tough task, but that he was the man capable of turning things around.

Scheer was already frustrated by his Clipper stint on the fall morning he met Shinn at a Los Angeles eatery for breakfast. The nay-sayers had been correct about the hopelessness of the Clippers' plight. Scheer had made the wrong move going West. He'd been a basketball executive without a team for only a few months after a new ownership group ended his ten-year stint in Denver. But he had jumped too quickly at the Clipper opportunity because, as he explained, his "romance with the game was on the rebound."

The Clippers' general manager listened intently to Shinn's seemingly quixotic commitment to bringing a franchise to Charlotte. He was aware that Shinn's success was a longshot at best, but Scheer was encouraged about what he perceived as Stern's earnest interest in the Charlotte proposal. Shinn also proved to be a delightful guy. That night Scheer told his wife that the Carolinian had "a special twinkle in his eye. If anyone can pull off this miracle, George Shinn can." Scheer was immediately interested in hitching his wagon to Shinn's star. Besides the obvious challenge to Scheer the builder of putting together an expansion team, there were more practical reasons for the basketball executive to pull for Shinn's success. His wife, Marsha, was from Greensboro, North Carolina, and the Scheers had spent more than six years in the area. They considered it almost home.

Not long after Scheer's breakfast meeting with Shinn, his interest in Charlotte became more firm. Scheer and the Clippers had parted ways just a few days after the 1986 season. Scheer claimed he was tired of fighting with management, was burned out, and simply walked away. The Clippers indicated that they'd asked Scheer to walk away after a mutual agreement was reached. At any rate, it was a messy exit that left Scheer once again without a job. This time, he didn't panic. Scheer and David Stern discussed potential expansion, but since that was a year or two away, he returned to Denver, where he'd persuaded the CBA to move its headquarters as part of the deal under which he'd assumed the commissioner's post. Sober contemplation and anticipation marked Scheer's time in the minors. Professionally, the post offered Scheer a new perspective on the game. "My family and I had been very happy in Denver. I needed to step back and reassess my family life and career. Plus, it allowed me to stay close to the game," he said almost morosely of this humbling tenure. "I kept in touch with the NBA, looking for opportunities. But I was monitoring George's progress and hoping to return to North Carolina."

The Tarheel state was in fact the first place Scheer had combined his promotional skill with his passion for basketball, and where he'd launched his quick rise through the professional league's ranks. Scheer's love for the game came honestly. Like many in sports management, he'd played basketball pretty well, first as an All-State schoolboy in Springfield,

Massachusetts, and then as a collegiate at Middlebury College in Vermont. His natural talent, however, didn't equal his competitive fires, so it wasn't much of a letdown when he settled on pursuing a law degree at the University of Miami. Scheer still tried to remain at courtside as much as he could. At Miami, when he wasn't in the library he was providing radio color commentary for the basketball team. After law school he ended up back in Greensboro, where he had married and lived briefly after finishing his undergraduate work. It was as a good as place as any to practice law. His wife had family there and Scheer's mother was living there too. His parents had moved to Greensboro after Carl had married, so they could be close to their son. His father, however, was struck by a car while Carl was finishing law school and Scheer had found it necessary to return and look after some of the family's business interests.

Scheer found an outlet for his basketball interests at nearby Guilford College. He talked the small NAIA school, which was emerging as a sports power, into letting him put together radio broadcasts for the football and basketball teams. From 1965 to 1967, the sports shows helped create a broadcast network and gradually became more involved in the athletic program. Scheer the Guilford booster became Scheer the one-time sports agent when one of the school's best athletes, Bob Kauffman, found himself in the midst of a bidding war. Kauffman, a husky forward and ex-Marine, was picked in the first round by the Seattle Supersonics in the 1968 draft after Wes Unseld and Elvin Hayes. The ABA's Oakland Oaks also had made Kauffman their selection, complicating the young forward's move into the pros. Kauffman knew Scheer was a lawyer and asked him to field the offers and negotiate the contract. This provided Scheer with an unlikely entree into the NBA, but he took advantage of it. Sam Schulman, the former owner of the Supersonics, liked the way the young lawyer handled himself at the negotiations. Scheer obviously loved the game and in the early days of the NBA, that was the most important prerequisite for joining the clubby, but still financially unsophisticated, circle of basketball professionals. Schulman told Scheer there was an opening for an administrative assistant in the NBA office and asked him to talk to commissioner Walter Kennedy. He was flattered, but didn't put much stock in the offer. He had two small children, a home and law practice in North Carolina. He didn't see any harm in traveling to New York twice and talking with Kennedy though. When the commissioner called to say that he had done well in the interviews, but that the league was going to hire an assistant from the National Hockey League because he had more experience and, frankly, he could type, Scheer was relieved. His chance at pro ball thwarted, he was ready to go back and enjoy Greensboro. Kennedy called back, however, to say that the other candidate had turned the NBA offer down and could Scheer be ready for work in December 1968? The NBA offices then bore little resemblance to the sleek, efficient publicity and profit machine of today. Scheer joined Kennedy and former NBA great Dolph Schayes, who was supervisor of officials, in a cramped midtown office supported by maybe four or five secretaries. Eddie Gottlieb, the former Philadelphia Warriors' owner who'd signed Wilt Chamberlain to a then-astronomical $30,000 contract in 1959, served as a consultant, taking the train to New York a couple of days a week to school Scheer on the vagaries of the NBA. There was plenty for this small office to handle. Buffalo, Cleveland, and Portland were preparing to enter the league as expansion franchises. The constitution and bylaws of NBA Properties were on the drawing board and in need of polishing. Someone needed to act as a liaison with the game officials, review the tapes, rule on protests, and levy fines. There were lists to keep and statistics to be updated. In short, Scheer was quickly immersed in all aspects of running a professional sports league.

The most pressing issue was the impact the upstart ABA was having on NBA player salaries and league competition. The ABA was stealing players and the NBA owners didn't like it. Scheer and Gottlieb decided to fight back in the NBA's tight-fisted way, adding player contract signing to their already overful plate. Scheer and his mentor crisscrossed the country to find basketball talent, sign them to a deal, and then divvy them up to NBA teams before the ABA had a chance. It was crazy, disorganized, and ill conceived. Scheer not only loved it, but was able to bring some semblance of organization to the league and the game he clearly loved.

Calvin Murphy, Bob Lanier, Rudy Tomjanovich, and Jo Jo White were just some of the players Scheer earmarked for long and fruitful NBA careers. The signing of White for the Boston Celtics was handled with the abandon that would come to typify Scheer's deal-making ability. Scheer made his pitch to the guard and then Kansas University coach, Ted Owens, in a Kansas City hotel room. There were two factors gumming up the works. The Celtics were experiencing some lean times and Red Auerbach didn't know much about the smooth-shooting guard from the Midwest's hinterlands. To complicate matters, White, who wanted to sign, was holding a 1a draft classification and it looked as though he would be drafted. Scheer was undaunted. These were simpler times. He worked on the legendary Auerbach, touting the Kansan's basketball virtues, while he scrambled to find a reserve unit willing to take White. Scheer was living in Connecticut at the time. White borrowed his address long enough to finish a six-month reserve stint before reporting to a now-thoroughly convinced Auerbach for training camp.

Scheer's tireless work in the NBA office was rewarded swiftly in 1970 when he was asked to join the expansion Buffalo Braves as team president. He was on the job just four months when the investment group behind the Braves started to fall apart. The ownership situation was so uncertain that when the ABA's Carolina Cougars dangled the key job in front of him, Scheer bolted for familiar terrain. His defection to the enemy was not appreciated by Commissioner Kennedy and other NBA stalwarts. Their boy wonder was gone.

What the ABA lacked in funding and prestige, it made up for in brass and outlandishness. The red, white, and blue basketball, the three-point line, and twenty-year-old acrobats who'd jumped before completing college, such as one Julius Erving, typified the renegade league. The ABA Carolina Cougars were at the cutting edge of redefining marketing concepts. Scheer believed that the Cougars were an idea ahead of its time; a sports team trying to infiltrate a regional market. The Cougars were a traveling road show, splitting home dates between Greensboro, Raleigh, and Charlotte in an attempt to capture an even-broader fan base. But in addition to the logistical nightmare of transporting players and promotional staff and material, the idea never really grabbed hold of Carolinians. No one city felt the team was its own, and in Raleigh and Charlotte the Cougars were perceived as carpet-baggers. Still, Scheer managed to boost attendance forty percent during his four-year stay in the Carolinas, while the Cougars fielded some pretty good teams. Billy Cunningham, Tom Owens, Steve Jones, Joe Caldwell, Mack Calvin, and Hornets player personnel director, Gene Littles, were just a couple of the players who made the Cougars decent. The gregarious Littles still reminds anyone in earshot that the Cougars beat the Kareem Abdul Jabbar-Lucious Allen–led Milwaukee Bucks and the Walt Frazier–era New York Knicks in exhibition games.

By 1974, when the Cougars moved on to St. Louis to become the Spirits, Scheer's reputation as a front office maes-tro was on the rise. The ABA's Denver Rockets were waiting for Scheer with an offer. They'd take the executive along with some valuable baggage—Cougars head coach Larry Brown, and his assistant, Doug Moe. Brown had turned the Cougars into winners in the past two seasons after Scheer had gambled and given him his first coaching job. The two men were mirror images of each other, intense, passionate about basketball, and hungry to climb the professional ladder. Brown was a former Tarheel who'd kicked around the backcourts of the ABA. The irascible Moe also had Carolina ties—he'd spent one year as a Tarheel before flunking out and heading to the state's smaller Elon College, a year as a Carolina Cougar, and he was also well traveled in the ABA. Brown was young and flamboyant, Moe his trusty sidekick, and Scheer the front office whiz who mined the wealth of their basketball talents. Moe, who is starting his tenth season as the Nuggets' head man (the longest active reign in the NBA), says he and Brown commissioned Scheer to get them all a job. The trio couldn't stand the prospect of being split up.

Scheer blew into Denver a confident executive ready to display his myriad talents that exceeded finding and signing players. He was sure that Brown and Moe were going to take care of the forty-eight minutes of game time, so he focused on stabilizing the franchise financially and generating interest in his team—no small task, since Denver had very little basic basketball orientation. In his first year, he put together a group of local investors that bought a percentage of the team from its San Diego–based owners and then, within a year, purchased the remaining interest. He changed the team name to the Nuggets, redesigned its colors and logo, and set out to market his hand-sculpted product to a booming Western city with a younger, affluent citizenry fat on oil and real estate money. Scheer hit the Rotary and Elks club circuit, touting the signing of North Carolina All-American Bobby Jones, talking up "Nugget ball" as an event, and McNichols Arena as the hippest "in place" to be seen.

Scheer's courting of the people of Denver was similar to what his new boss had just done in Charlotte. The elbow grease and financial toe dancing paid off. The Nuggets went 65–19 and played before twenty-nine sellouts in the 7,000-seat auditorium arena. The following year talk in Denver turned toward either forcing or praying for a merger with the more established NBA. The NBA had been able to keep its rival at little-brother status with deep, if not narrow, pockets, where the coins could be fished out when needed—say, to sign a particularly high profile draft choice. Scheer challenged this premise by signing the 1974 college player of the year, David Thompson, and The Human Eraser, Marvin Webster, out from under the Atlanta Hawks. It was a major coup that rocked what until that point was a complacent NBA. The older league pointed at Scheer for escalating the size of player contracts with the highjacking, but it forced the issue of the merger. The NBA was either going to take unification overtures seriously or dig deep in its coffers for an all out war. That year the Nuggets moved into the 17,022-seat McNichols Arena, where they set an attendance record of 730,624, and won the ABA regular season championship.

Scheer had set the table for the merger with the Thompson–Webster coup, then finished it off as a member of the merger committee in 1976. Scheer concedes that the NBA absorption of the flashy league was not actually negotiated. The NBA told what was then the New York Nets, Indiana Pacers, San Antonio Spurs, and Denver that if they each paid $3.2 million each, gave up television money for three years, and didn't mind sitting out the dispersal draft, they would be allowed in. The new teams also were required to indemnify the NBA and settle the lawsuits and debts, which were substantial, that the ABA had incurred. But they were in and Scheer made sure the Nuggets looked like they belonged; more than 17,000 of Denver's beautiful people, NBA attendance leaders, packed McNichols Arena to watch Brown conduct a talented Thompson, Dan Issel, Bobby Jones–led Nugget team to a Midwest Division title with a league-leading 50 wins.

The Nuggets' transition to the NBA looked effortless and Scheer was widely hailed as the savior of basketball in Denver and other ABA cities. He was a local hero in the Rockies, once voted one of the ten most influential men in Denver. He was as hip as the product he was pedalling, with his longish, salt-and-pepper hair and thick sideburns. Stories of the intense, driven man and his single-minded, almost eccentric behavior, became fodder for newspaper articles and admiring cocktail chat. He was said to be so preoccupied with the Nuggets that those who knew him well rode in his car only reluctantly because of his habit of choosing the wrong way on one-way streets. His wife, Marsha, had relegated him to standing out on their lawn when the Nuggets were on the road so that he wouldn't break anything while listening to their broadcasts. After one tough Denver loss, he ate so much ice cream that his body temperature dropped so precipitously that he needed medical attention. "Nugget anxiety" not only induced Scheer to devour copious amounts of ice cream, but triggered Chunky and Pepsi and corn muffin binges as well.

Sometimes in Charlotte Scheer hits the potato chip bowl with vigor after a loss, but for the most part he seems better tempered than in Denver. The long days and relentless driving of his people remain, though. As do the barely concealed, wincing, slamming, and muttering sideline antics that Scheer would break into during game time. Like Denver's McNichols Arena, the Charlotte Coliseum has a court-level corridor behind the Hornets' bench, where a totally immersed Scheer could live and die at game time. In Denver, fans reveled in tales of Scheer getting bound up in a curtain after swirling in agony over a bad call, or leaving the game with bruised or paint-smeared hands from beating on a nearby rail. There was too much decorum for that in Charlotte. It wasn't part of the script.

What unfolded before a pacing Scheer and a house full of product consumers two days before Christmas wasn't scripted either. After the Michael Jordan posters were given away at the door, as soon as the Bulls' superstar was awarded his well-earned standing ovation, the Charlotte crowd turned on their favorite son. And so did the Hornets. Reid and Holton took turns leaning on Jordan, and their physical play was earning the fans' approval. This was Charlotte's first nationally televised game and viewers of Ted Turner's WTBS superstation were getting a vivid introduction to the rowdy Charlotte crowd. The wave was a staple as well as the team mascot, Hugo, who was whipping it up on roller skates during the entire game. Those watching on TV also got a surprise from those castoffs in designer duds. The game was nip and tuck all the way down to the wire. Jordan gave his people their money's worth with a fourth-quarter sprint of effortless drives and string-singing jumpers. When he stepped to the free-throw line with time running out, he was roundly booed by the Coliseum crowd who sensed an upset being stuffed in their Christmas stocking.

With the score tied at 101–101, the Hornets had the ball

for the final shot. They ran the clock down to four seconds before Reid put up a 16-footer. It was partially blocked, wobbling toward the bucket where Rambis grabbed it and tossed it up. His shot was rushed, but the ball got caught on the rim long enough for him to follow it, tipping it left-handed off the glass. The ball fell through at the horn, sending Rambis running back toward the Hornets' bench pumping his fists. Tripucka and Reid soon followed, wrapping themselves around Rambis, together jumping up and down. The crowd provided a thundering soundtract to the moment. No one in the arena was thinking about the canned music, the cute mascot or orchestrated spontaneity. The next day at the office, in fact, Scheer would be deluged with phone calls from angry fans wondering why the hell the Hornets were giving away Michael Jordan posters.

8

MIDSEASON

BLUES

THE last tall figure in a long leather coat to shuffle into the Salt Lake Marriott was Dell Curry. Italian suits, along with spread-collar dress shirts with bolos and thin silk ties (or simply buttoned to the top) were de rigueur for the well-heeled, off-court Hornets. Their style went hand in hand with their designer uniforms, they all looked good— except for Rambis, whose tan corduroy sport jacket and knit pants made sportswriters feel better about their own wardrobes. Someone had left a rose at the front desk for the soft-spoken Curry, but the smile he mustered at the gift didn't thaw the late-January cold. Curry was in a funk frostier than Salt Lake's ten-degree weather. Talk that any day now he was on his way to Indiana as part of Charlotte's first major trade was getting him down. He was only half-joking when he told Tucker Mitchell, the beat writer from Winston–Salem, that he'd asked the desk clerk not to put any calls through to his room. Like that would really stop the trade from happening.

Things weren't going well for the Hornets. They had lost

four in a row—three of them blowouts, before losing by three points the night before in Phoenix. Tripucka and his 23 points a game had missed the last two outings with a head cold. Dave Hoppen also wasn't playing because of a cold. There'd been a circuslike atmosphere on the trip. It was the Hornets' first extended road show and nine newspaper and television reporters were traveling with the team to chronicle "life on the road" with their hometown hoopsters. Harter got a bit miffed with the journalism contingent after a picture of him soaking up rays at poolside and one of Muggsy Bogues smiling as he ripped a peewee basket with a dunk at a practice in Phoenix were beamed back to Charlotte and splashed across the Sports section. The coach didn't want the fans at home getting the wrong idea that road trips were all fun and games.

Harter was concerned. The team's last win had been ten days ago in Philadelphia. It was a satisfying victory in the coach's hometown, where Harter'd admitted getting "a little senile." After holding practice in his cherished Palestra, Harter related, "I started rattling off some of the things that I had seen—Jerry West stealing the ball three times in the last thirty-five seconds so West Virginia could tie up a game with Villanova. I saw Wilt score fifty. I watched Oscar Robertson held to twelve points and get so mad that he threw the ball at the referee and got a technical. I wanted the guys—especially Rex—to appreciate these things." He concluded: "To play or coach this game, well, you've got to know its history and love it." He even had the bus driver stop at the famed steps of the Philadelphia Art Museum, where film hero Rocky Balboa had triumphantly ended his workouts. Harter had a photographer snap a picture of his team so each could have a keepsake from this historic first season.

The thrill of directing his first pro team may have taken the edge off of some of the early-season losses, but now almost half way through the year, Harter was finding little solace in good efforts. The Hornets were 10–30. That had already meant thirty sleepless nights for Harter, reliving the lowlights and miscues of his team, thinking about the "if only's" he might have done to get a few more points and a few more games. The coach rarely slept after a loss. For that matter, he was a reluctant sleeper on nights he won—too excited, or perhaps unwilling to give up the rare moments of triumph. Harter didn't lose well. After a loss, he would rumble into the press room as was his duty, shoulders slumped, eyes glued to the floor, before mumbling a brief statement to the awaiting sportswriters. His postgame comments usually hit three major themes: that the other team, the Knicks, for example, were very strong, and that Patrick Ewing was a great player; that nobody on the Hornets played anything resembling defense, or on nights when his team played hard and still lost; that the Hornets had given it all they had, but his team just didn't have enough talented big people. That said, he'd bark out "questions," wait until someone broke the silence, then grimace and shake his head while answering, making it clear that he detested the whole drill and was dying to be someplace else. These sessions were usually brief and merciful for Harter and the fidgeting media. Nobody blamed him for his abrupt behavior. He hated to lose, got paid not to, and essentially wasn't doing his job when he did. Or at least that was the attitude fostered by the owners, the coaches, and the media. It was the one place in professional basketball where "entertainment value" had no significance. The next day at practice, you could always count on Harter to be upbeat, engaging, and willing to take on all basketball chatter. "The day I can sleep after a loss is the day I'll quit coaching. I'll do the same the day I bring the night before's loss to practice. It just isn't professional."

Being on the road deepened the malaise of losing. NBA coaches and players are numbed by the dizzying whirl of wake-up calls, bus rides, and airport terminals that make travel a strictly sleep-and-eat affair. Baseballers at least get to stay in one city for a couple days. The NFL asks only that its hulks fly in for a single night before the game. These long road trips only left Harter time to agonize about when or how his team was going to get its next win. The pessimist in him said it was doubtful that it would come on this trip. The Hornets were 2–18 on the road. The Hawks had already blown them out.

They would have had a shot at the Suns if they stayed healthy. The Jazz, whom they were playing tomorrow, were atop the Midwest Division with a 15–2 home record. It was really hard to win on the road, Utah was just 9–13 away from home. The Lakers were next. No go. They finished up with the Portland Trail Blazers and their 14–4 home record. But Harter was coaching to win. His players were playing to win.

Then there was the trade. Since July, Harter had been pushing Scheer to peddle one of their surplus guards to Indiana for Stuart Gray—a third-string, 7-foot center who in four pro seasons had averaged 2.4 points a game. The deal they were now closing in on—Dell Curry and Rickey Green for Gray and eleven-year veteran guard John Long—looked astonishing on paper. The Hornets were willing to give up on Curry, their number-one expansion pick and a former number-one college pick, who in just his third season was arguably the best pure shooter on the team, for a 7-foot reserve center with limited or no talent. Harter was convinced Gray was the answer to the Hornets' soft middle. They were getting killed on the boards. Earl Cureton was starting at center and doing yeoman work, but at 6'9" he was consistently overmatched to the point that Harter feared his crafty, hustling veteran was getting worn down much too early in the season. Harter ascribed to the big-man-in-the-middle theory. Seven-footers made teams adjust to all phases of their game. On offense, a scorer couldn't just waltz down the middle as they did now, knowing that there was no one inside to swat away shots. The opposing teams' big men would not be allowed to slough off on defense to double-team, or get in easy position for rebounds. Gray would clog up the middle and hit people, freeing up Tripucka, Chapman, and Reid to spot up for jump shots. Finally, Harter had coached Gray at Indiana, liked him, and thought he was tough. It was amazing how often this last criterion is cited in NBA personnel moves. Perhaps it's the coaches' confidence in their ability to teach and motivate, or their knack for recognizing talent and character. Gene Littles, who didn't like the Gray deal, was pushing at the same time to sign former Duke star Gene Banks—a free agent fresh from

Europe. Littles recited his reasons much the same as Harter did, inevitably ending his soliloquy with "I had'm in Chicago. He can play." Just like the guy on the barstool, in the newspaper, or in the boardroom, NBA coaches are human enough to abandon sound logic and rely on their instinct—even emotion—about a player.

At 6'5" Curry was the Hornets' only tradeable commodity. Any high hopes the Hornets had harbored for him were dashed in training camp when he broke his wrist, prompting him to miss the first 19 games of the season. By the time he returned to the roster, Reid was playing well at the number-two slot and Chapman, though struggling with a thirty percent shooting average, had showed flashes of brilliance that validated the plan to bring him along. There just weren't enough minutes to go around. Harter also had some problems with Curry's game. He could flat-out shoot the most supple, two-wristed jump shot that bottomed out nets from beyond 23 feet, but his on-court demeanor looked as effortless as his jumper. Curry was cool, expressionless, and silky smooth. Harter believed his defense made Tripucka look like a stopper. Curry often lost his man. Some of that may have been due to rust, but Harter was too impatient to stick with another suspect defender who didn't look like he was giving one-hundred percent. Chapman was a defensive liability because he was a rookie. Tripucka's deficits were well documented. Harter didn't have anyone in the middle to match up with solid backup centers, let alone with the likes of Parish and Malone. Rambis played tough. So did Reid, but inconsistently. To hear the coach talk about his beloved defense, it was a wonder that Charlotte stopped anybody. Besides, Harter had his heart set on Gray.

Green and Long were tossed in for the ride. After pulling a groin on opening night, Green disappeared from Harter's rotation. Bogues was set at backup point guard for his ability to shake up the tempo of a game, and Holton had proved that he was a dependable, almost prototype, NBA guard. He didn't do anything particularly well, but his floor game and defense were solid. The age game was thwarting Green. At thirty-four, it didn't make sense to play him ahead of a twenty-four- and twenty-six-year-old, especially when three senior citizens already were cutting into the younger players' minutes. Indiana was trying to dump the troublesome Long. Harter had also had him in Detroit and Indiana and was willing to take the hard-nosed veteran on to shake up the practice sessions a bit.

It looked like a done deal the night before the Jazz game. Harter was relying on the word of the sportswriters who had been in phone contact with Scheer back in Charlotte. Rick Bonnell of *The Charlotte Observer* told the coach that the trade looked imminent. Gray was reportedly giving farewell interviews to Pacer sportswriters that night after a game with Boston. The following morning the *Observer* ran a statistics box, comparing the careers of the two principals, Gray and Curry. The stats were jarring. The Hornets looked ready to trade a former college All-American, who'd averaged more than 24 points his senior year at Virginia Tech, and 10 points in his second pro season with the Cleveland Cavaliers, for an unknown center who, in his senior year at UCLA, had averaged 9.9 points and 8 rebounds a game, with his best NBA average only 3 points and 3 rebounds a game.

Almost as soon as the paper hit the streets, the transaction crumbled. Scheer was pushing it, though he was reluctant, as a show of support for his coach. This time the business of the NBA tripped up the Hornets' deal-makers. The salary cap—created to keep maverick owners level-headed and assure the players an interest in the NBA money-machine—made the deal impossible. The only way to finagle the two-for-two deal was for John Long to take a reported $100,000 pay cut. Even then, he would've had to clear the waiver wires before the Hornets could have signed him to a reduced salary. Long exercised his contractural right to nix the deal. Since the December 27 guaranteed money date had passed, he was assured his salary through the rest of the year. If he was waived, which he was a couple weeks later, his money would keep coming in full. The veteran apparently decided to take his chances getting picked up at full pay, rather than sitting at the end of the bench in a financial style to which he was not accustomed in Charlotte.

The obviously disappointed Harter resigned himself to finishing the western swing with all the players he had. There was still three weeks left until the trading deadline, he reasoned, perhaps something could be done. The phlegmatic Curry reassumed his seat on the bench, somewhat disappointed that after all the anticipation he wasn't bound for a team that wanted him. So far in Charlotte, it had been the same old story for the twenty-four-year-old guard: too many bodies in the backcourt, not enough balls, and a dearth of minutes. This was his third team in three years and he was ready for a fourth.

The trade talk, though, provided a rallying point for Curry's teammates. Most felt bad for the guard and were a little perturbed at how Harter was handling the rumors in his eagerness for the deal. Switching cities and uniforms in midseason was a part of the game. Green, who knew he was part of the package, acted as if the prospect didn't upset him. He knew it was a matter of time before Charlotte gave the last seat on its bench to somebody else. That's the way he'd ended his career in Utah—a seat down from Tripucka, which might as well have been in the upper deck. The frustration of not playing had torn him up the past season, and he wasn't ready to give into that anxiety again. Still, he and Reid and some of the other veterans believed that he and Curry should have received some counsel about the trade from the coach. If he wanted his 7-footer fine, but Harter might at least have told the two players that a deal was in the works and that, though he was in the dark about the details, he'd let them know as soon as he knew something. Instead, Curry and Green were fending off questions from sportswriters who sidled up and in low voices asked them what they thought about going to Indiana. They thought they were owed at least that professional courtesy from Harter.

Most felt that the West Coast junket was an important trip for the team's chemistry. Harter took his team to Phoenix from Atlanta on Super Bowl Sunday, even though the game with the Suns wasn't until Tuesday. The hype of the inaugural season, the steady diet of community service work, and the players' coronation as Charlotte heroes had been perhaps too much for a team that didn't yet know one another. The players weren't getting used to losing either. Expansion ball was something those guys down in Miami were playing. This was an important distinction for veterans like Rambis, Reid, and Cureton. They were professionals who'd cut their teeth on championship-caliber teams. Expansion was no excuse for losing. If they played hard and smart and together, they were going to win. That trio rarely cited the team's newness as an excuse. Reid choked on the word "expansion" as if it suggested the Keystone cops. Rambis preferred to talk about the development of the young guys. Cureton just shook his head with his big easy smile and said, "Naaah, we haven't got it together yet." The older Hornets preferred being known as a lousy, veteran NBA team than a group of bumbling neophytes.

At practice, there was a good bit of collegiality among the team, but by game time, it was all business. Off the court, the players were forming awkward friendships and alliances. The rowdiest clique was a curious mix of veterans Green and Cureton, twelfth man Ralph Lewis, Muggsy Bogues, Curry and Chapman. Cureton and Green were the ringleaders, fueling the chatter in the back of the bus where the crew chose to sit en route to airports and hotels. The easygoing Cureton was at once a big brother and practical joker. He kept the whole team loose at practices, maintaining a deadpan face in the huddle while reaching around to snap Rambis's shorts or jock strap as he listened to the coaches. The 6'9" Cureton and the 5'3" Bogues were especially tight. When the two wandered through the hotels or hit town together it was like a father with his semigrown son. At some point Cureton would usually put his hand on top of Muggsy's head or on his shoulder and point at something while his little buddy beamed and giggled. Green seemed to be in charge of Lewis and Chapman. The three lived near each other in a southeast Charlotte apartment complex, shared rides to practice, and holed up together to watch other basketball games. Lewis was a little older than Chapman, but looked every bit a rookie at 23. The sheepish, wizened vet bounded around the court during warm-ups with the two laughing youngsters trying to steal the ball or block his shots.

The organization was worried enough about Chapman at Christmastime for Scheer to have a sit-down with the rookie, asking him to loosen up a bit. Chapman was frustrating media members with his disappearing act after practice and games. When he did stick around for questions, he appeared to be reading from Tripucka-written scripts, but he delivered the cliches in lifeless monotones. Chapman simply wasn't living up to Falk's assurance that the Kentucky icon was better equipped to deal with adulation and criticism than your average twenty-one-year-old.

The pressure on Chapman at Kentucky was more than any teenage phenom could handle. At the traditional midnight practice when he was a freshman, a banner was unveiled before the thousands at Adolph Rupp arena proclaiming the dawn of the "Chapman Era" as soon as he stepped on the court. Littles tells a story about watching Chapman show up at a prominent Louisville playground, where games stopped at the sight of the Kentucky hero and chants for "Rex, Rex" broke out. Some of his Charlotte teammates believed that Chapman was just burned out on the Kentucky limelight. The rookie himself admitted to Andrew Brandt, Falk's associate, that the constant scrutiny at Kentucky had worn thin. There were furtive glances and snide comments from classmates, pleas from fathers for Chapman to take their daughters out, and persistent curiosity on how, and with whom, he spent his hours away from the court. It was as if Chapman wanted his own terms when he chose to reveal that he was more than a basketball player. In fact he was a better-than-3.0 student at Kentucky, and by all accounts a fun-loving guy. But he was very distrustful of the press, partly because it had intruded so much on his adolescence and partly because of the circumstances under which he left Kentucky. The NBA was only mildly surprised when he came out after his sophomore year. Wildcat coach Eddie Sutton's program was under a swarming NCAA investigation for a variety of alleged serious violations. Most knew that tough sanctions were around the corner, and many bet that Chapman's father, Wayne, would encourage Chapman to jump to the pros. Wayne Chapman was a long-time coach and currently the head man at Kentucky Wesleyan. He thought a great deal of his son's talents and was very involved in his career. The elder Chapman was on the phone daily with Falk and ProServ on the days leading up to the draft and Chapman's signing with Charlotte. He also was causing some consternation among Scheer, Shinn, and Harter for a series of letters he'd been writing to the trio, criticizing their decision not to put Rex in the starting line-up. His boy was the future and they were playing too many old guys was the theme of the correspondence.

As promised, Falk had landed the rookie several lucrative endorsements with area sponsors Wendy's and Coca-Cola, which if they went as projected would escalate into regional and national platforms as the rookie's star rose. Still, Shinn and Scheer wanted more. The control they wanted was illustrated by Chapman's current attempt at growing a beard. It wasn't much more than a spotty goatee, but its presence was irritating the Hornets' owner. Shinn asked Scheer and Harter to say something to him about it. Both declined, however, telling their boss it really wasn't appropriate for them to do so. Shinn told them if they didn't he would. Sure enough Shinn called Chapman a week later and told him, "Son, I just wanted you to know my eleven-year-old daughter thinks the world of you. But that stuff you're growing on your face is just spoiling the All-American image. I wouldn't want you to do anything for her to fall out of love with you now," Shinn recounts. "And you know after I explained that to him, Rex went out and shaved."

Harter also was worried that Chapman wasn't enjoying his teammates or the game enough. His pasty face and bug-eyes made his typical rookie miscues look even more painful. Rookies don't get any calls in the NBA. They are bounced, hacked, and whistled at for charges on a referee's whim. Chapman aggravated the situation by appearing timid, sometimes even lost, on the floor. The coach and the veterans were patient with him, but when Chapman began coming from the outside and launching shots, without squaring up or even knowing where he was on the floor, the head shaking and sheer looks of exasperation of his teammates showed. Harter, unlike the owner and management, didn't care what the rookie did on his own time. All he wanted was the kid to have some fun; to enjoy his teammates, to enjoy playing basketball, and to lighten up a bit on the court.

Chapman perhaps was fooling everyone. He was getting along well with his teammates. He got in the swing of team silliness in Phoenix, buying a fake rat at a mall and tossing it into Cureton's room, startling the big guy. The team didn't hold it against him that he was quiet—that's the way rookies usually are. The veterans especially admired the way he put off Shinn's and, to a lesser extent, Scheer's overtures that he should raise his profile and become community property. The Boy King had been held up for public consumption in Kentucky. He chose anonymity in Charlotte.

The dry wit of Rambis also had its followers. The two other big white guys, Tim Kempton and Dave Hoppen, stuck close to their adopted mentor. They were primarily a sleep-and-eat crew, gathering in hotel restaurants for huge meals before returning to their respective rooms for some power lounging. Kempton had a prodigious appetite that was immortalized on this road trip after *The Charlotte Observer*'s Tom Sorensen sat in on a breakfast feast with the trio and reported in the hometown paper that the stout redhead had claimed to the disbelieving Hoppen and Rambis that he could put a whole Burger King Whopper in his mouth. Doug Rorbarchek, the paper's humor columnist, took this tidbit and for weeks baited Kempton to prove it. When the showdown finally took place at a local eatery, Kempton's eating prowess was so awesome that the columnist wrote that the center still had room for Muggsy Bogues. The horseplay was rougher—on and off the court—between Kempton the redheaded New

Yorker, Hoppen the lean Nebraskan, and the goofy Californian, Rambis. Even shooting exercises usually deteriorated
into bump fests with Kempton banging Hoppen whenever he
felt he was too close. For Rambis, the excessive contact on the
court was quite enough. He appointed himself floor leader for
the big men, and believed that the jostling was a tribute to his
own style of play. He had learned the inside game in much
the same way at Los Angeles at the elbows and knees of Mitch
Kupchak. Rambis needled the two on a regular basis. He once
interrupted an interview Hoppen was conducting to ask the
reporter why he wanted to know anything about the center.
Not waiting for an answer, he said, "Oh, you must be from
one of those free weeklies that they give away in shoe stores."

With Kempton, Rambis was usually dishing out mock
discipline. One morning in Salt Lake, Kempton greeted Rambis by slapping him on the back of the head. "Tim, don't you
know that physical humor isn't funny anymore?" Kurt said
with a sidelong glance. "Now, if you were to fall down that
escalator, that might be funny. But don't ever hit me again."

Michael Holton was one of the loners on the team, along
with Reid and Tripucka. He prided himself on his ability to talk
the big men's "Mork and Mindy" stuff. Holton flitted between
the team's two cliques, bantered with reporters and ball boys,
but mostly stayed to himself. He was a student of the business
of the game, and in many ways his varied, modest career had
shaped his perception of the team. The Hornets were his fifth
professional team in four years, the last being Portland. There
had been two CBA stops in Puerto Rico and Tampa Bay,
along with a few months as a basketball hero in the Phillipines.
To Holton, the NBA was nothing less than a "cold, cold
business," interested only in numbers and money. Holton
believed that of the 300 NBA players, 30 were superstars and
paid like it, another 30 were important enough to their teams
for them to offer the players security, and the rest were all
interchangeable. These could be traded, waived, or released
without making much of a difference, except to the financial
quotient of a team. Holton desperately wanted to find his way
into the second tier. He wanted to put the days of trying out

for five teams in a six-week period, as he'd done after his stint in San Juan, behind him for good. He never again wanted to wangle an invitation to join a general manager for jogging— like he'd once done with Scheer, who at the time was heading the Clippers—so he could ask for a job. Eight miles later he was still unemployed.

Holton was playing well enough to make Green expendable and keep Bogues in a backup role, but he was nervous about showing the slightest chink in his professional armor. He was excited about the possibility of making real money at the end of the year when his contract was up. He longed for security after too many uncertain years in the minors sharing a house with three other players, scrimping by on the $17-a-day in meal money, and dropping in and out of towns such as Grand Rapids, Albany, and Bradenton. His wife, LaShell, liked Charlotte and she was finding plenty of work as a model. It was fortunate that she liked the town because they'd had to leave a house they'd built in Portland, upsetting them both. He also enjoyed the celebrity Charlotteans bestowed on him. Lunch and dinner checks were rarely delivered to the table. The silver Mercedes he drove had been made affordable by racing czar Rick Hendrick, who owned a small share of the team. Things were how he'd imagined they should be when he dreamed of becoming a pro athlete as a youngster in Los Angeles.

Still, Holton was guarded around his teammates. In Portland, he was secure as the team's third guard, satisfied with this fifteen minutes a game. The camaraderie was genuine because everyone in Portland knew their role. The Hornets were players simply trying to cut a bigger piece of the pie for themselves in the league. The chemistry was slow in coming because each looked at expansion as a way of getting back on track, of showing they belonged. They liked each other, but with the exception of Rambis, Tripucka, and Chapman, who were firmly rooted in the franchise, everyone was looking for an edge. Holton sensed the competition early on, deciding that his time and energy would be better spent on his game.

Robert Reid's "skinning-and-grinning" days were behind

him. As a rookie, he'd carried Calvin Murphy's bags, tolerated Moses Malone's habit of pulling his hair, and hit the NBA ports hard with his buddy Leavell. At thirty-three, Reid recognized his back-of-the-bus days were over. He got along well with everyone on the Hornets, but now during the downtime there were phone calls to be made to his businesses in Houston. He was preparing for life after basketball, diligently keeping abreast of how his advertising and courier services were doing. He also had to take better care of his body than the younger guys did. Reid attributed his eleven years in the league to his physical conditioning. During the off-seasons, he had worked out with several of the Houston Oilers, sprinting up a man made hill and hitting the weights. He'd cut back once the season began, but he was aware that he needed more rest. Reid didn't mind the travel. He knew people in every town after so many years on the road. After the game, he always had somebody lined up for dinner. At a game earlier in Milwaukee, Reid and Bucks center Jack Sikma had stood at center court, trying to figure out which of their contemporaries were still in the league. After coming up with Alex English, Walter Davis, and Green, the two veterans were stumped. They stood there for a minute shaking their heads, trying to remember more, but couldn't. For Reid, it was a bittersweet moment, wondering how many years had passed him by, remembering the players he had outlasted, and for the first time sensing that the end of his career was drawing near.

Tripucka was the one guy who appeared to be orbiting in his own universe. The locker room's Dick Cavett was remarkably quiet in street clothes. Tripucka usually sat by himself in the front of the bus with his head buried in the newspaper. At airports, he'd go stand by himself while everyone else circled the luggage carousel awaiting their bags. When he did fraternize, it was usually with the Hornets' radio play-by-play man, Steve Martin, or Harter. His relationship with the latter alienated some of his teammates. The social culture of the NBA allowed a certain amount of banter and joking with assistant coaches, but players weren't supposed to be too tight with the head guy. Most understood that Tripucka and Harter had a history together, but an incident during the preseason had cast the friendship in a different light. After an exhibition game in Richmond, Virginia, the team was making the long bus ride back to Charlotte. Most everyone had joined the back of the bus crew, where the music and storytelling was becoming spirited. Tripucka, who had been sitting up front with the coaching staff, moved to the back to join the party. When someone suggested that Tripucka ask Harter if the team could go ahead and practice as soon as they arrived in Charlotte, which would be about 2 A.M. instead of the following morning, the star forward responded quickly, "We talked about that." It brought a roar from his teammates, but they were stunned that Tripucka took his relationship with the coach that seriously.

The front office was pushing Tripucka as its star and Harter's offense revolved around his one proven scorer, so naturally it put him at odds with the rest of the team. That he wasn't elected by the players as team captain was telling. For most pro teams keeping the various egos in check is part of the game. The expansion Hornets were no different—that they could keep any conflict in the locker room and off the playing floor was to their credit. Tripucka was at the center of the storm. He was the star and knew it. His game had fully returned and he rarely failed to mention in his postgame addresses that he always knew he was one of the better players in the league. Already, he'd had two 40-point outings. As much as he was a joy to watch, shuffling to his spots unleashing rimless 23-footers, or lumbering through the middle getting bullied and pushed to the floor while still touching the ball off the glass and through the net, the never-my-fault head shakes when he booted the ball out of bounds and his self-serving pronouncements in front of the cameras were just as disturbing. His teammates were usually diplomatic when speaking of Tripucka, but the losses and the road trip had tried their patience. Holton was flat-out tired of reading Tripucka's comments in the morning newspaper. The team was working hard together. Chapman was finally coming around. Cureton was making big plays. But the focus was still on Tripucka, who

rarely deferred to, or even complimented, his teammates for
bailing him out the many times he lost his man on defense.
Reid had publicly taken the whole team to task prior to the
road trip for not playing hard. Now he was wondering why
Tripucka had even made the road trip with his head cold. So
far he'd spent a couple days at poolside in Phoenix.

The Salt Palace, the Jazz's home floor, is a cozy, intimate
arena with 12,444 seats. The brown earth tones with hints of
cheerful purple, green, and gold that swath the Salt Palace's
innards belie its crowd's inhospitable nature. For such a good-
looking, healthy, fresh-off-the-Utah-ski-slopes bunch, the Jazz
fans are awfully bloodthirsty. Tonight, they were lying in wait
for Tripucka, who, besides making disparaging remarks about
the environs of Salt Lake City during his involuntary exile,
had offended the team's star forward, Karl Malone, with a
stunt he'd pulled in Charlotte.

The powerful Malone had read a newspaper article in
Charlotte a few weeks back, on January 9, when the Jazz
were in town to play the Hornets, in which Tripucka ripped
Coach Frank Layden with a couple of "fat" jokes. Layden,
Tripucka's old nemesis, had quit coaching the previous month
to become the Jazz's president. The NBA's funniest man was
no longer having fun in a job that had become increasingly
plagued by "too much pressure." Malone felt beholden to the
robust coach, who'd drafted him in 1985 as Utah's first pick,
which at the time was considered gambling on the raw, little-
known forward out of Louisiana Tech. Layden stood by his
man, however, and developed the explosive Malone into an
NBA All-Star. In tribute, Malone had printed "Frank" on the
back of his game sneakers. Already irate at Tripucka's published comments, Malone was further enraged at tip-off of that
January 9 contest, when Tripucka showed up at center court
with "Dick" presumably in mock honor of Harter, printed on
the back of his shoes. The ploy backfired. Malone had terrorized the Hornets with a 38-point, 19-rebound display in a
114–92 thrashing, and then he'd blasted Tripucka for his lack
of class. "They were unprofessional," Malone said of his

former teammate's remarks. "That's typical Kelly. There are just some things you don't say. When Kelly does as much for the game of basketball as Frank Layden, then he can talk." After the game, when Malone was asked about Tripucka's shoe scrawlings, it was clear he'd taken Tripucka's gag more personally than suspected. "Who's Dick?" he glowered, apparently not aware of the name of the Hornets' coach. After one of the waiters told him Dick Harter was the Hornets' coach, Malone was still not convinced and snapped, "I don't even know who Dick Harter is."

Tripucka's poolside convalesence had apparently zapped his flu long enough for him to be in uniform for the game with the Jazz in Utah. The scattered boos began as soon as he emerged from the players' tunnel, building into a chorus as he made his way to a basket for warmups. Tripucka had tried desperately to douse the simmering feud immediately. Tripucka once more blamed the press for the controversy, telling *The Salt Lake Tribune,* "The writer was wrong, dead wrong, I never said that. I hardly ever talk to that guy." He was speaking of *The Observer's* Rick Bonnell, who had written the initial story and covered the Hornets every day. "He was very wrong and I apologize for what happened." Tripucka's jokes had hardly been knee-slappers—the best one alluded to a Layden-sized Thanksgiving dinner (two turkeys instead of one). Finally he conceded that they'd been made, not for publication, but as offhanded quips uttered after a game to no one in particular on a visit to the Charlotte Coliseum's press-room. He said the shoe gimmick was just his way of trying to be funny, as well as showing gratitude to Harter for rescuing him from a frustrating situation.

An unwitting participant in the fued, the Hornets' coach didn't care one way or another. He had his game face on, intent on trying to steal a win for his team. Mike Mathis, one of the officials assigned to the game, needled him about placing eighteenth in the *USA Today's* recently released best-dressed rankings of NBA coaches, but Harter proferred only a weak smile and headed for the bench. Even with owner Shinn's conservative makeover, Harter had little chance to

crack the top of the NBA's best-dressed list, where Los Angeles's Pat Riley, Detroit's Chuck Daly, and Seattle's Bernie
Bickerstaff reigned. He often tried to highlight his white shirts
and gray, off-the-rack suits with a teal, or sometimes spray-
colored, test-patterned ties with matching handkerchiefs, but
still couldn't compete with the Italian double-breasted, silk
threads of those on the leader board. But for Harter to finish
in the bottom third with such polyester and fly-away-collar
kings as Denver's Doug Moe and Washington's Wes Unseld,
seemed hardly fair.

On the court, the Hornets–Jazz match-up quickly disinte-
grated into an ugly brawl of a basketball game. Both teams
looked barely interested in playing for the first five minutes.
The Hornets made only four of its first fourteen shots. The
usual calamities were plaguing them: Chapman came off a
devastating Rambis pick of Darrell Griffith and instead of
spotting up, spun to launch a three-point effort that caroomed
off the back of the rim, Cureton twirled inside with a beautiful
drop-step move only to lose the handle in midair, squirting the
ball to the top of the backboard, and Holton was passing up
wide-open 18-footers, still too tentative to launch his modest
left-handed jumper.

They should have been buried right then, but the usually
swift-footed Jazz were playing plodding, sloppy basketball,
turning the ball over five times, with the usually sleek and agile
Malone looking like he was going out of his way to run over
people. After Malone stole a pass with about 3:00 left in the
first quarter and raced his 255-pound frame up the floor for a
monster dunk over the stationary Reid, Harter got hot on the
sidelines. He wasn't upset with his team, who, despite their
ineptitude, were digging out rebounds and getting bounced all
over the floor of the Salt Palace much to the delight of the
crowd. He was upset with the officials.

Working the small guys in navy sansabelts and pullover,
dusty-blue jerseys was part of the game. Coaches always
jawed at the refs, trying to get that edge, making sure the
officials heard their objections, that they watched the injustices
being inflicted on ricocheting 250-pounders by opposing sharp

knees and elbows. But now Harter was genuinely indignant, as if Mike Mathis and Bruce Alexander—the official who'd missed Malone's charging violation—were conspiring with the Jazz, the Suns, the salary cap, the league's better dressers— everyone and everything denying his team wins. Reid was getting up slowly underneath the bucket, propping his hands up behind him, trying to lift his thirty-three-year-old body off the floor after Malone's thirty-two-inch thigh had caught his chest at full speed, raising him off the floor before spilling him over like he'd just kicked one of those cheap tin garbage cans.

Harter's trademark balled fists were pumping at his sides, his foot stomped the floor once, then again.

"Come on, Bruce. You gonna let him beat on us all night? He can't run over us because we're new. What you afraid of? Make the call."

Just behind the bench, a fat guy who had been mercilessly riding Tripucka while he was on the bench, turned on Harter.

"Quit crying, Dick. Get off your knees. You guys are lousy."

The coach turned his back to the floor, but wasn't really looking for the heckler. He threw up his hands, exasperated, but then thought about it, and called a time-out.

As his team approached the bench, the coach clapped his hands hard. "We're okay, we're okay." He gave Reid kind of a one-armed hug, Holton a smack on the rear, before marching down the sideline toward Alexander. "That's four you gave him, Bruce. He's an All-Star, but he can't beat on us."

The ref stood with his arms crossed over his chest, looking away. "I don't want to hear any more about it, Dick," he said out of the corner of his mouth, as if he was bored with the coach's routine.

When the buzzer sounded for halftime, Harter was on the heels of the referees all the way to the locker room. The Hornets were down by 13, 55–42, and the coach was pleading his case. Stu Jackson, an assistant coach and scout for the New York Knicks, watched Harter pass from a table behind press row, where the other vagabonds of his ilk diagrammed future opponent's plays.

"Dick really likes these kind of games. He might pull it out," Jackson observed. The Knicks' coach knew of what he spoke. Jackson had been one Harter's "kamikaze kids" at Oregon in the 1970s. In those days, Harter was a crazed disciplinarian who heaped a host of physically demanding drills on his players in practices that far surpassed any possible game-time contact. One of his favorites, according to Jackson, resembled the play in which Malone had decked Reid. Harter had his players take turns under the bucket eagerly awaiting charges. The whole team would run at the helpless defender, one after another, from all angles, knocking the man down, then forcing him to spring to his feet to collect yet another charge. The coach shrugged off most reminders of those rough-and-tumble collegiate days, acting almost embarrassed that he'd asked his kids to do that. He could never ask a professional player to submit to something like that, and wouldn't, but his sly smile and bright eyes revealed his prefer- ence for pro games where "it's almost like a wrestling match out there." That was aggressive, hard-nosed "Harter ball."

That's what was happening in Utah. The thuggery contin- ued into the third quarter and instead of rolling over, Harter's team was pushing back. The usually peerless Malone was struggling through a dismal shooting night. The more frus- trated he became, the looser his elbows began to swing. With a little over six minutes left in the third quarter, Malone was thundering under the basket for what looked like a dunk when Holton came rushing down from the weak side and jumped into him. The two got tangled up on the way down with Malone trying to forcefully toss Holton off. Surprising every- one, especially The Mailman, the 6'4" guard shoved back. Holton wasn't exactly committed to scrapping with the much- larger Jazz man, but he faced him off until Thurl Bailey and Rambis could step between them. That was the down-in-the- trenches stuff Holton believed players like he had to master to keep their precarious place in the league: "I'm no super talent so I got be ready to give everything back." The next trip down

With a capacity of 23,388, the Charlotte Coliseum holds the largest number of fans in any NBA arena. With a cost of just over $55 million, the Hornets' nest is nestled between the North Carolinian woods and the dominating Charlotte skyline.

A flurry of hopeful tryouts run sprints for the coach during a pre-season practice.

(Below) Four Hornets at summer training camp take instruction from head coach Dick Harter. Before the end of the season, Ricky Green and Larry Spriggs were gone. *Left to right:* Tyrone Bogues, Ricky Green, Larry Spriggs, and Michael Holtom.

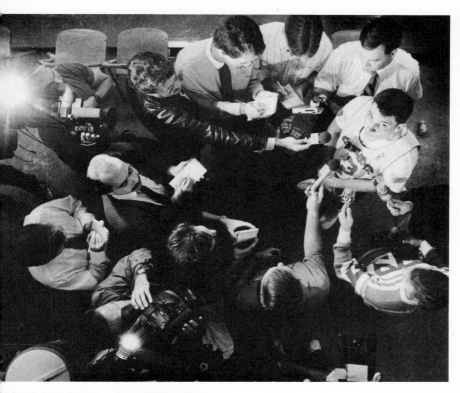

(Above) Swarmed by reporters, first-round draft pick Rex Chapman arrives to play for the Hornets.

(Left) First pick in the expansion draft, Dell Curry was sidelined well into the beginning of the season with a broken wrist.

Opening night in the Charlotte Coliseum, November 4, 1988.

The first and worst loss of the year (133–93) came hard. The indomitable Cleveland Cavaliers squashed the Hornets' hopes of starting the season with a victory. Here, ex-Laker and now co-captain, Kurt Rambis battles Mark Price for a loose ball.

NBA veteran and co-captain, Robert Reid had played 762 games in the league when he came to play for Charlotte.

For the tiny Tyrone Bogues, down and under is the easiest route to an open basket. At 5′3″, Bogues is the smallest player in the NBA.

First win: Head coach Dick Harter and Kurt Rambis celebrate after the Hornets stung the LA Clippers 117–105.

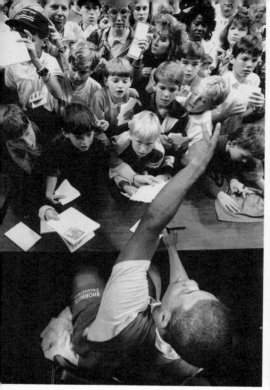

Autograph seekers, young and old, are the only crowd that can hold Tyrone Bogues in one place.

The leading scorer for the Hornets, Kelly Tripucka, goes for the hoop.

Rookie Rex Chapman was the second highest scorer for Charlotte during the 1988—89 season.

Charlotte Hornets' owner George Shinn (*right*) congratulates assistant coach, Gene Littles, at the final home game of their first season.

(Below) After the season ended, a procession of Corvettes carried the Hornets through downtown Charlotte. 30,000 fans showed up to cheer the players, coaches, and the Charlotte Hornets organization for a season well done.

The Charlotte Hornets became the first expansion team to lead the NBA in attendance. The Charlotte Coliseum proudly displayed this banner at the final home game.

the floor, Malone again went head-hunting, this time finding Rambis. But the referees called a block foul on the Hornets' forward.

"That's his sixth, Bruce. Give us a break, will you?" Harter was yelling in Alexander's ear.

The second-half melee was hurting the Jazz far more than it was the Hornets. Chapman and Reid were keying a rally far from the inside brawl with 22-foot jumpers. When Reid nailed an 18-footer to end the third quarter, he pumped his fist and let out a "yeahhhhhh" that startled a now-silent Salt Palace crowd. The Hornets had outscored the Jazz 26–13 for the quarter, tying the score at 68. With the score tied at 79–79 halfway through the fourth quarter, Harter watched in near silence as his team held the Jazz scoreless for five straight exchanges. There wasn't much he could say. His team was digging in. The Jazz had a one-point lead and the ball twice in the final minute, but the undersized Rambis, Cureton, and Reid clogged up the middle enough to force Darrell Griffith to launch an ill-advised three-pointer, and Stockton to barely beat the twenty-four second clock with an off-balance 17-footer. There were now nine seconds left in the game and Charlotte had the opportunity for the final shot. Harter called a time-out. The ball would go to wing and Tripucka, who at best would take it to the hoop for a shot, a foul, or both. Harter was to the point in sketching the play out. When the buzzer sounded and his team got up to return to the floor, he stopped them.

"This is ours, guys. You've killed yourselves to get in this position," he said, abandoning his matter-of-fact coaching cadence. "Let's get it down and steal one. Come on."

The play appeared to be unfolding as intended. Tripucka got the ball on the wing, stepping pass Bailey in decent shape, but then kicked the ball to the corner where Holton was standing all alone for an 18-footer. Holton put the ball on the floor and headed for the basket. As he went up, three Jazz players converged on him, knocking him to the floor. One of them got a piece of the ball. Everyone seemed to stop, anticipating either a foul or the game-ending-buzzer—except

for Rambis. He snapped up the ball from the floor on a short
bounce underneath the bucket and in a single motion tossed
it up off the glass. He was all alone as the ball ripped through
the net, barely beating the buzzer. Harter, who was skipping
sideways down the sidelines watching the final seconds, was
as near to sprinting as a fifty-eight-year-old coach is capable
of being. He was slapping backs, giving hugs, and beaming as
he herded his team off the court. This was the second time
Rambis had one won at the buzzer and in the Salt Palace's
cramped dressing quarters, his teammates were tapping on
the metal folding chairs chanting, "Rambo, Rambo."

"Wonder how Hot Rod described that one?" Holton
asked out loud, referring to the Jazz's colorful commentator,
Hot Rod Hundley.

"Bring on L.A.!" Kempton exhorted.

Just outside the door, Harter was meeting with reporters.
His team had won ugly and he was loving it. They'd snatched
one from the road, from a losing streak, and had done it with
their backs to the wall.

"It's the first time we didn't back down. I like that," said
a chattier-than-usual Harter. "We'll come back here in two or
three years and it'll be our bodies crushing *them* to the floor."

When Gil McGregor, the team's radio color commentator, asked him about the Jazz's poor shooting night, pointing
out that Karl Malone was a dismal 8–29 from the floor, the
Hornets' coach paused for a moment with a look of great
confusion.

"Karl who?" he deadpanned perfectly.

9

RAMBIS

L AST night's hero looked very ordinary stepping through the jetway into the airy sunshine of Los Angeles International Airport. Awaiting Kurt Rambis were his wife, Linda, and two shaggy-haired little boys, Jesse and Jordan, who ran to bear-hug their father's knees. He could have been any Californian returning home, except for the television lights and well-groomed sportscaster with microphone in hand that also were awaiting his arrival.

That night in the city's Fabulous Forum, an adoring crowd would watch Rambis's former teammates award him an NBA championship ring—his fourth—for what amounted to stage hand's work in the Lakers' star-studded "show time" basketball attack. His striking ordinariness and modest talent were so refreshing that he'd become a cult figure in the Land of the Odd and the Abundant. Rambis added to his myth on his first official basketball return to Los Angeles by conducting the interview like any father might, holding three-year-old Jesse in one arm and one-and-a-half-year-old Jordan in the other.

He was glad to be back in Los Angeles, but not because of the ring ceremony, or because he was itching to prove anything to his former team. The hype was in fact distracting him. His father had two of his championship rings, the ones that meant the most to him—the 1982 and 1985 jewels that Rambis's workmanlike play, against Philadelphia and Boston, had helped win. The 1987 ring was in a drawer somewhere in the new home he had purchased in Charlotte. The one he was about to receive meant even less because he felt he had done little the previous season to contribute to the team's success. He'd played very little. As opposed to the rest of his Charlotte teammates, it was Rambis who had walked away from his old team, so the upcoming game wasn't an "I-told-you-so" affair.

The forward was happy to be back in Los Angeles because it had been a long road trip and he missed his family. The Rambises were going to stay the weekend at the house he still owned in Manhattan Beach. He would trade his corduroy sport coat and brown slacks for his favored jeans and T-shirt and roll around on the floor with his boys. He and Linda also planned to catch up with the friends, family, and neighbors they had left behind. Riding the bench with one of the greatest NBA teams of all time had ceased to be fulfilling. The game was more important than a paycheck. His family was more important than the game.

Now, in the airport, with his boys pulling on his shirt collar, he was explaining once more to the media how a native Californian had come to move South. "I had three criteria with my unrestricted free agency. I wanted a location where my family would feel comfortable. The chance to start and play a lot. And I wanted a good contract." Rambis and his agent, Peter Johnson, had asked the Lakers first if they were interested in signing him to a three-year, $1.8-million guaranteed deal. But it was a number he'd correctly figured they wouldn't be interested in, and after a season in which he'd barely broken a sweat, he needed very little reason to walk away. There were no hard feelings between Rambis and the Lakers organization. Dr. Jerry Buss, the owner, and former

NBA great Jerry West, now the general manager, ran a class outfit. He had no disput with the Lakers. He could've stayed on the bench, collected decent money, and provided some necessary insurance in case any of the Lakers' big players went down. But the Lakers and Rambis in a way had grown too good for each other. There was nobody in the NBA better than Los Angeles at putting superstars together on a team. Rambis had too much character to be content with a hefty pay check, one in which he didn't feel he was even earning. He was a throwback to an era where good people with common basketball skills and remarkable effort could play an essential role on a championship team.

If Rambis's career had begun in the early 1970s, he perhaps might have become a West Coast version of John Havlicek. Granted, they were very different players with different assignments. On the floor, Rambis was asked to fill much the same role for the Lakers as Paul Silas had done for those Celtic teams: wax the glass and clear out the middle. Havlicek was much more versatile with an array of basketball skills and statistics far superior to Rambis's. Yet there was something about the way Rambis stood out even alongside Kareem Abdul Jabbar and Magic Johnson that was reminiscent of the former Celtic. Even though he was a limited talent, he excelled at the fundamental components of the game. He could unfailingly block out his man for rebounds, never leave his feet on defense, follow the ball to the basket even if it looked like it was going in. He made the superstars around him look better. Like Havlicek, he was a reminder that amidst the acrobatics and egotism of the supertalented, there were still yeomen who gave everything they had. They gave soul to what was at best a game, at its worst merely show.

Rambis came along in 1981 when athletes were getting better and NBA organizations were poised to become more professional. The Lakers' front office, in particular, brought an uncanny, but systematic approach to creating a team. Their role players were getting so much better than the rest of the league. The tenacious Michael Cooper came off the bench to play both guard positions, as well as small forward, shutting down defensively any of the NBA's top players. He shot from 3-point land, and handled the ball almost as effectively as Magic—though without the flash. NBA All-Star and scoring machine Bob McAdoo was resurrected to provide some pop from the bench. At 6'10", he didn't give anything up in the middle and with his behind-the-head rainbows, he forced the opposition's brawlers to chase him out into the front court.

The niche Rambis had carved out for himself with the Lakers was evolving as dramatically as the show time attack. Rambis had replaced Mitch Kupchak at the 6-point, 6-rebound, twenty-minutes a game position. Both were widebodies, though Kupchak was stouter than Rambis, using sheer strength to shove and bump players across the hardwood. Rambis depended on his coat-rack–like body to bend and hang up the bigger, more agile players. Kupchak was intimidating. Rambis was irritating. But then Riley and West began to find better athletes who could do more at that position— thoroughbreds like A. C. Green, an offensive tackle with sprinter's speed, who could fill the lanes with Magic and Byron Scott without breaking stride, thus adding 10 or 12 points to the equation. Then came Mychal Thompson, a former number-one overall pick in the draft, whose body looked like sculpted marble and who possessed the offensive instincts to score 18 points a game.

The 82-game regular season was a long tune-up for what really mattered, the playoffs. It was a laboratory for the chemistry of the team and the coach, as well as entertainment for fans shelling out $20 a game to watch the greatest players sky and shimmy. The season was so long that there were contrived plateaus. The first 30 games, everyone was fresh, happy to be playing again and eager to show what they were capable of. They set a tone for what might happen the rest of the year. Late December and January were the dog days. The initial burst of enthusiasm had been spent, and players were thinking about saving something for the spring when home-court advantage and playoff spots were up for grabs. A player's financial situation also had something to do with the letdown. Those who didn't have guaranteed money were assured a year's pay after December 27, according to league rules, so the immediate pressure was off after that date. Those whose paychecks were assured were careful not to risk injury or burn out, thus missing NBA crunch-time, when owners, fans, and GMs formed the impressions that dictated the following year's contracts.

Rambis's level of effort never flagged over the course of a season. He gave you everything he had and would win some games for the team on pure persistence. The downside was that come playoff time, Rambis simply didn't have the natural talent to turn his game up. Pure athletes ruled in the postseason. The regular season was forgotten. The games were more physical. Scorers started playing defense. The role players and yeomen who had gotten a team that far were now playing against crazed athletes who may or may not have coasted up to this point. The playoffs were geared toward players such as Orlando Woolridge, the thoroughbred the Lakers had signed in the off-season as a free agent. The 10 points a game he was averaging now at almost midseason were less important than the 14 he perhaps would score off the bench in the Western Conference finals—dunking over Tom Chambers, igniting a Laker rally, sending out the message that "our athletes are better than yours."

Rambis had played in the NBA championship six of his seven seasons in Los Angeles, and was on the winning side four times. His career 5.5-point, 6.2-rebound average didn't reflect his contributions to those teams. Oddly enough, his .592 career playoff field-goal shooting percentage is an NBA record. "When I tried out with the Knicks as a rookie, I tried to do everything in camp. I was running around like Larry Bird, passing, shooting—trying to do too much. I got cut," he said. "I'm not a pretty player, but there are things I do well and when I remember that, I think I'm very good."

He wasn't a franchise player, but Rambis was carrying the Hornets. The game winner the night before in Utah had capped a 15-rebound performance. It was the second time he'd won a game. But once again it was Rambis's intangibles that were elevating the young expansion team.

He was the one guy Harter never worried about. Rambis came to work every day, happy to hear the ball bouncing. He liked to work at practice, usually staying late to shoot that stand-still 15-footer he'd first perfected as a junior high schooler in Ridgecrest, California, near Bakersfield. Even the parlance the forward used to describe the game appealed to the coach. Rambis still called his teammates "ball players" and the team a "ball club." Rambis was raised around sports, but he was anything but a superjock. His father, Mike, was a high school coach and administrator, so a key to the gym was always available to him. He didn't always use it to play basketball, though. Sometimes he and his sister Lerideth and his brother Mike—who was a pitcher in the Cleveland Indians' farm system until he tore up a rotator cuff—roamed the school halls, stopping in their father's classroom to write messages on the blackboard as a surprise. "I always liked playing basketball and it was part of my life, but I could have walked away," Rambis remembered.

The game was simple to Rambis. You played hard because you loved it. Rebounding was the product of desire. Leaders didn't have to say much, but had to show they were leaders at all times. Rambis was demonstrating that with the Hornets. A week earlier at practice, just a couple of days before they'd embarked on this western road swing, Harter had stopped a defensive drill to pull Rex Chapman aside. The most frustrating thing so far for the coach about Chapman's uneven performance was what he perceived as the rookie's lack of defensive fundamentals. Chapman was slight; in fact, Harter was worried about the ten or so pounds Chapman seemed to have lost since the beginning of the season. Too often he was getting straightened up on defense because of poor position, sometimes losing his man after getting caught like this. He also was reluctant to leave his man for double-down defending against the bigger centers. These were correctable, but Harter was losing patience trying to ingrain such habits into the young player's game. Rambis followed the coach and the rookie to the sidelines. He waited for the coach to finish, then stepped in, his back to Harter, making it clear that this was a player-to-player discussion.

"They're coming at you, Rex, because you're a rookie. You got to take it personal or it's gonna keep happening. Stay low, lean into them, don't worry about getting beat. It happens, but make it a pain for anyone to go after you."

It was a caring, simple, and direct approach that left the blank-faced Chapman nodding. Rambis wandered back to the big men without even looking at Harter.

"Kurt understands the game and the things it takes to win that go beyond talent, plus he can relay that in player's terms. You can't pay a guy enough for that," Harter said.

This is what Charlotte was bargaining for when they went after the former Laker in the free-agent market. Rambis was among the first players to benefit from the new collective bargaining agreement. The Players' Association had negotiated what was considered a benchmark agreement for professional athletes: it allowed a player who had five seasons in the league and whose contract was expiring to become an unrestricted free agent. He was his own entity free to cut his own deal with no compensation due his old team. Rambis was pretty sure he would go to an expansion team. Johnson, his agent, had contacted every established team to confirm what Rambis the realist knew already—that there wasn't much of a market for a thirty-one-year-old backup power forward. Unrestricted free agency was more tailored for the Moses Malones of the league. Have superstar, will travel—if the price is right— presumably to bring championships, as the Atlanta Hawks' signing of Malone seemed to indicate.

In Charlotte Rambis found a team looking for a player with star quality for a supporting actor's price. The four-year, $2.4 million-contract he signed was hardly extravagant, considering the NBA average salary is currently $510,000 per year. He'd been a fan favorite in the sprawling, glitz-and-glimmer environs of Los Angeles, so he was certain to excite the already-ecstatic inhabitants of this somewhat provincial Bible-Belt town. Plus, he didn't have to try to be a good citizen. Rambis's commitment to home, family, and worthy causes were genuine. In Los Angeles, Rambis had lent that distinctive mug, as sharp as the tips of his game glasses, to cans of Orange Crush's new lemon-lime soft drink in exchange for a share of the profits being donated to the South Central Boys Club. He agreed, as part of his contract, that he and his family would move to Charlotte and become part of the community. Rambis had traveled to Chapel Hill once for an exhibition game while a Laker and was amazed at how lush the Carolina countryside was, and how friendly the people were. By signing with the Hornets, he had covered all his bases. The $675,000 for the expansion team's inaugural season was an increase of $75,000 over last year. The money was guaranteed and most important, he would start, play as much as thirty minutes a game, and finally, he'd have the opportunity to see how versatile he actually was.

He'd implemented much the same decision-making process as an All-California high school star, when he chose to attend Santa Clara University, a Jesuit university better known for scholarship than basketball. "I wanted to stay close to home and find a school where I could play immediately," he recalled. Before the season Rambis made it clear that he was excited about the possibility of working on his individual game: "When I was first with the Lakers, I was just fighting for a spot on the roster and a paycheck. This is different. I'm looking to excel as an individual as well as helping the team." Thus far, he was doing both, averaging 10 points and 9 rebounds a game, as well as keeping Charlotte in most of the games. His .520 shooting percentage illustrated just how practical Rambis was. Even on an expansion team, where he had the opportunity shoot, call for the ball, and do whatever he thought necessary to elevate himself from journeyman to superstar, he was still a team player. Either all those years as a Lakers role player had warped him, or Rambis had an uncanny sense of his own capabilities. At any rate, Rambis was doing what he wanted now—getting his chance to keep contributing to a team.

*   *   *

Kareem Abdul Jabbar took his master-of-ceremonies role to heart for the Hornets' first visit to the "Great Western's Fabulous Forum"—a name obviously coined by its promoters. Only the six world championship banners and the retired jerseys of Elgin Baylor, Wilt Chamberlain, and Jerry West add any aura to the arena's seedy royal purple, gold, and orange motif. Like a film set, all television viewers see of L.A.'s NBA digs are the courtside celebrities, Jack Nicholson, Walter Matthau, and Dyan Cannon, who pay $250 per ticket to presumably watch the Lakers surgically destroy whoever is in town for the evening. Every day, Los Angelenos ante up anywhere from $8.50 to $23.50 to quietly watch their team from vantage points that range from decent midcourt spots just beyond the camera's eye, to seats so high that they're in complete darkness, which makes you wonder who would sit that high.

This night, 17,505 people were on hand to watch Abdul Jabbar present the 1988 championship ring to his former teammate. The big fella looked at ease with a microphone in his hand. The Jabbar farewell tour was already in full swing and the center, who over the course of his twenty-year career had been cast as a surly, reluctant superstar, had apparently overcome his dislike for the spotlight. As the Lakers visited each NBA arena for the last time this season, Jabbar was always at the center of pregame or halftime festivities, where admiring words and gifts were showered on him for the awesome talents he'd displayed for so long in the league. All that stage time had seemed to pay off.

Chants of "Rambis, Rambis" began as soon as Jabbar stepped to center court. With his trademark goggles around his neck, Kareem looked up in to the darkness of the Forum before beginning his brief remarks. He was surrounded by teammates who stood silently awaiting his praises for Rambis. A phalanx of photographers and camera men lined the nearby free-throw line.

"We have some unfinished business to take care of," Abdul Jabbar finally got out over the din. "Kurt should not be considered a guest. He's been a part of the Laker family. He did a lot to make us a success. He was our teammate and friend and we want to thank him for that and wish him luck in Charlotte."

Rambis, with his long, dishwater-blond hair and thick black athletic glasses that made him look like a welder, had looked out of place when he wore the Laker purple and gold. Jabbar and Worthy, after all, donned their majestic race-car driver goggles and effortlessly ran the floor. Now in his teal uniform, crossing the court to shake Kareem's hand and to accept his fourth championship ring, Rambis looked even more out of place. His former team was a collection of number-one draft picks, elegant athletes and perfect physical specimens who might as well have been in tuxedos. That the gangly Rambis, the corduroy, jean, and T-shirt guy, had once been an integral part of this group seemed astonishing.

There was a full five-minute standing ovation. The A-list, Jack Nicholson, Rob Lowe, John McEnroe and his wife, Tatum O'Neal, stood, politely joining in. The "Rambis Youth"—a pack of teenage imitators who'd adopted the thick black glasses and yellow T-shirts bearing Rambis's jersey number, 31—erupted in their guttural cheers underneath the bucket.

The midday flight from Chicago was so far the most depressing of the season. The Chicago Bulls had blown the team out the previous night. The 118–93 loss was the worst shellacking the Hornets had received since their opening-night, 40-point fiasco against Cleveland. What could have been even worse had been prevented when Bulls coach Doug Collins let Michael Jordan sit out the fourth quarter. The head Bull had already racked up 32 points in three quarters and Chicago was up by 20. Jordan was playing forty-plus minutes a game and even the league's most talented player needed rest. They'd hardly missed him out there.

The season was past the halfway mark and the team was returning to Charlotte for a game with the Atlanta Hawks the next night before taking a five-day break for the NBA All-Star Game. There were no Hornets taking part in the midseason celebration of all that's good and profitable in the game. Tripucka thought he should have been selected to play by the coaches. He was the league's thirteenth-leading scorer with a 22.5 average and already a front runner for the NBA's Most Improved Player award. Mention of the latter honor, though, rekindled bitter memories of his two-year sojourn in Utah. "I always could play. It's just that Utah stole two years from my career," Tripucka asserted. Chapman had been invited to participate in the All-Star Slam Dunk competition on Saturday, but surprisingly, and wisely, had declined. The rookie had missed seven games in December with a lower-back sprain and didn't want to risk aggravating it. When he told beat writers that he didn't want to reinjure it, "doing some silly slam-dunk thing . . . I just want to make it through the season," he'd summed up the mood of the entire team on that anticlimatic return from Chicago.

Most of the Hornets were either asleep, or trying to sleep, in the first-class section of the Piedmont jet—except for Muggsy Bogues, who usually remained wide-eyed and smiling while in the air. The NBA insisted in its rule book that the players travel first-class. Some coaches might bump a rookie to share the spacious quarters, but not Harter. The coach was back in coach with the rest of his coaches, correctly believing that that type of togetherness was counterproductive.

Neither Rambis or Reid, the cocaptains folded into the back row, had ever been All-Stars. But in their combined seventeen NBA seasons, the All-Star break had meant something to them. It marked the halfway point, the rest before the final sprint. Seven times the Lakers had been first in the Pacific Coast division when James, Kareem, Magic, and Pat Riley returned from the All-Star break. At that point, Rambis always noticed the team downshifting for its playoff drive. They were the Lakers and nothing less than a championship was acceptable to the rabid Los Angelenos. They started to play sharper. There were no routine victories. Riley turned up the heat, letting his starters play more, pushing them, looking for routs and the homecourt advantage for postseason.

Only twice had the Rockets and Reid not made the playoffs. They were usually in the hunt at midseason. Reid and Leavell would sit down with the sports page and figure out how many games they needed to win the division, who was playing well, and which games in the second half were playoff tune-ups. The second half was the meat of the season. It was the fun part—they were the games that mattered. Now sitting there on a return flight to a city they were still new in after one more blow-out, the two veterans talked about what the remainder of the season would be like for an 11–33 team. The prospect deflated Reid. At thirty-three, he knew his chances for another run at a championship ring were dwindling. Even though Rambis had chosen his path to Charlotte and was getting the much coveted opportunity to show his wares, the prognosis was sobering.

"We're counting it down, Kurt."

Reid still wasn't ready to count himself out though. The Atlanta Hawks were going to visit Charlotte for the first time. It was the Thursday night before the midseason break officially began and presumably a tune-up for Moses Malone and Dominique Wilkins, who were headed to Houston as All Stars. Reid also was going to Houston, but as a spectator and a returning family man. He'd been haunted by the conversation with Rambis on the plane and in the back of his mind was holding out hope that a trade may be forthcoming that would put him in another hunt for a championship ring. Chicago Bulls coach Doug Collins had contacted Charlotte about Reid in December, looking to add some scoring punch off the bench. But instead, the Bulls acquired Craig Hodges from Phoenix. The interest the playoff-bound Bulls showed whetted his appetite for post season, but he didn't necessarily want out of Charlotte. He was truly enjoying the community and strangely enough felt that he was contributing to its history.

"They're going to remember us no matter how we finish because we're like ambassadors bringing them the game for the first time. For the fans just playing is enough. After everyone wises up that this is a business and the pressure to win starts to build, the Hornets will just be professional athletes and no one is going to care who they are if they're not winning," he said.

There was still more than two weeks left until the trade deadline and Reid interpreted Scheer's lack of interest in his contract discussions and Harter's replacing him with Rex Chapman in the starting line-up four games ago, as a sign he may be on the way out. But first there were the Hawks who were a team stocked with Reid's old friends and teammates.

They had crushed the Hornets by more than 20 points in the teams' two previous meetings. Nevertheless, there was great anticipation on the part of the Coliseum crowd. This was a rivalry Charlotte fans definitely wanted to see develop. Sort of a New South showdown between the region's long recognized "Big Peach" and its upstart neighbor Charlotte, who now in its NBA team had the means to wage a visible battle against the city it so envied. Numerous signs were posted by fans around the arena, including a better than twenty-five-foot masterwork painted in bright flames, "Atlanta Burns."

Harter agreed with the Charlotte fans that Atlanta could be had tonight. The off-season signing of Moses Malone and Reggie Theus that was intended to bring a championship to Atlanta didn't look like it was working out. The Hawks had a better than respectable 28–19 record, but the team was playing poorly. Atlanta coach Mike Fratello was under fire for his seeming inability to harness three explosive scorers, Malone, Wilkins, and Theus into any semblence of team play. Theus was being cast as the chief ball hog. When Atlanta signed him, Hawks GM Stan Kasten (and Theus himself) made much of the smooth shooting guard's willingness to forego his individual game in search of a championship. Theus was a career 18.8 scorer, but like Tripucka, he was cast with a reputation as an effective player only when he was on terrible teams. Over ten years with stops in Chicago, Kansas City, and Sacramento, he'd only been to the playoffs three times. Now there were rumblings from his teammates that Theus would never change and Malone and Wilkins—also irrespressible egos—were fighting him for the ball.

The veterans on the Hornets also wanted to steal a game away from the Hawks. They were happy to be back in Charlotte after their decimation at the hands of Jordan in

Chicago. The week before on the Hornets' home floor, they'd upended Seattle at the buzzer 108–106 in a game that most of the players felt was their most rewarding victory so far. Seattle had come in near the top of the Pacific Division and having won five of their last six games. The Hornets were again without Tripucka and in the midst of another three-game slide. There had been a minor row a few days before the game when the players learned that they'd be expected to pose for pictures from 6:00 to 6:45 P.M.—before the 7:30 tip-off as part of Carl Scheer's Picture Day promotion. No one wanted to deprive the area's children of a photo opportunity with their favorite player, but the veterans, particularily captains Reid and Rambis, thought it was terribly ill-timed. They offered their objections to Scheer and even offered to come in on an off-day for the picture duty. Game preparation was an integral part of a professional player's work day and Rambis especially thought that the two hours before a game were sacred. He told Scheer that he and his teammates had to get taped, loosened up and in a game frame of mind, and that left little time to be congenial. He simply thought it was an unnecessary distraction while preparing for one of the league's better teams. Scheer heard the captains out, but reminded them that the Hornets, besides playing the game, were also trying to build a fan base and such activities as the photo session were vital to the NBA team's success. Reid watched as the mild-mannered Rambis, clearly frustrated, heated up a bit. "But some of us want to win, Carl," he said finally, taking his GM aback.

Eventually, a compromise was worked out so that the players would take 15-minute shifts in front of the fan's cameras. That done they proceeded to run down the superior Sonics in an effort that included every available Hornet. Without Tripucka, the team relied on a balanced, up-tempo attack. Rambis pulled down 13 boards, getting them to Chapman and Bogues who quickly pushed the ball upcourt. Seldom used Ralph Lewis came off the bench for 12 points all on fast-breaks. Reid canned 28 from outside, and on the final play of the game dished a perfect pass off to Kempton for a lay-up that got the victory. "I'd walk miles to see a play like that. It's a professional play," Harter crowed afterward about Reid spotting a double team and dumping off to Kempton.

At the morning shoot around before the Hawks game, Earl Cureton predicted that Charlotte would beat Atlanta. The "Twirl" usually didn't make such statements. But like Reid, he'd been a teammate of Malone's, battling him in practice for a couple years as the 76ers back-up center, and really enjoyed facing, and beating, "Big Mo." Cureton was truly an NBA survivor. For that matter, he was a basketball survivor. Cureton was a product of the Detroit inner-city leagues, and at only 6'1" in 1975 he graduated from Finney High School with little thought of attending college or taking his game to a higher level. One summer day after graduation, Cureton was shooting around by himself at Detroit's St. Cecilia's Gym, getting ready for the night pickup games that drew the city's finest players—players such as Greg Kelsey, Bruce Flowers, and Terry Duerod—when Cleve Edwards came upon him. Edwards, who is now with UNLV, was scouting for Robert Morris College, then a junior college in Coraopolis, Pennsylvania. "He asked me if I wanted to go to college and the next week I was taking my first plane ride and enrolling," he said.

Soon after, Cureton blossomed into a 6'8" center whose knack for finding the glass made him a solid 10-rebound, 18-point-a-game scorer. Robert Morris wasn't very good, especially after they turned into a four-year college in Cureton's second-year. But Earl perhaps has one of the most cherished basketball memories as a result of the little-known college experience. Cureton and Robert Morris faced Indiana State in a Christmas tournament—one of the first Division 1 opponents it was to play in its new four-year status. It was a big game and everyone was talking about the Sycamore's center, Carlton Webster, who was a cousin of former NBA player, Marvin Webster. No one paid much attention to what was the debut of another Indiana State player, a transfer student named Larry Bird. "Nobody had ever heard of him, and when he first stepped on the floor he didn't look that impressive. But as soon as the game started I new that this Bird guy was going to

be a superstar. He was shooting from outside, throwing look-
away passes—I'd never seen a white guy do the things he was
doing. They beat us, but I made the all-tournament team
along with Bird, and I keep a picture they took of us together,"
Cureton recalls.

The next year Cureton transferred to the University of
Detroit, finally acquiescing to a daily courtship by the ubiqui-
tious Dick Vitale. Vitale, who was building a very tough
program at Cureton's hometown university, spoke with Cureton almost daily during his sophomore season. But soon after
Cureton transferred, Vitale took the Detroit Pistons job and
the hopeful center never got a chance to play for him. That
was all right, though. After sitting out a transfer season, he
posted solid enough numbers at Detroit for the Philadelphia
76ers to draft him in the third round. Only Cureton believed
he had a shot at making a talent-laden 76er team that included
Malone, Dr. J, and Doug Collins. Philadelphia was a perennial
title contender with a then unheard of 11 players with guaranteed contracts. Because of sitting out a season due to the
transfer, he still had a year of eligibility left and didn't have to
sign with the 76ers. But he did anyway for three years at the
NBA minimum of $35,000 a year—none of it guaranteed.
And he stuck. Cureton was delighted just to be on the same
court as his childhood heroes. "In those days rookies got beat
on," he recalls. "I carried Mo Cheeks' bags. If I was getting
taped and a veteran walked in I got off the training table. I
wasn't supposed to say much and I didn't. But if you try to
pull that stuff today, you'd start a fight in the locker room.
Rookies don't have as much respect for veterans anymore."

Cureton didn't play much, though he will forever be
remembered in Philadelphia for a baby hook shot over Kareem Abdul Jabbar that he sank to win an NBA final game.
But he got a championship ring in 1983, and was taught some
important lessons to carry with him. The most important came
at the hands of Caldwell Jones. The 6'11" Jones was already
in his fifth year in the league, mostly as a backup center after
spending three seasons in the ABA, when he took Cureton
under his wing to try to teach him the secret of longevity for

NBA big people. For two seasons, Cureton practiced against Jones and watched him hit one 12-foot jumper after another. Cureton thought his teammate had good inside moves, and though Jones had never averaged more than 9 points a game, was certain he could be a dominant scorer. One day he asked Jones, who had twice been named to the NBA all-defensive team and had previously been a leading shot blocker in the ABA, why he didn't take it to the hole more. "He just kept shooting and told me that if he scored 20 points a game one season then they'd expect it from him every year," Cureton recalls. "He said 'Earl, rebounding and defense is what keeps guys like us in the league. Anybody can score, but hell, by doing the things no one else wants to. I'm going to play 18 or 20 years.'"

Good to his word Jones was now playing his 16th season in Portland. By adopting that advice, Cureton was in his ninth season, staring against his old teammate Malone, and hoping that his run might last four or five more years.

There was a moment in the final quarter of the Hawks game that crystallized how the Hornets players felt about their profession, and how the city of Charlotte was enjoying their new major-league status. It began at the Hawks' end of the floor, where Earl Cureton, bent at the waist, leaned into Moses Malone, much like he would a Redwood. Malone went up for a shot with Cureton stuck at his midsection. The ball bounced lightly off the rim, seemingly back into the following Malone's hands, when out of a maze of limbs—Rambis's, John Koncak's, and Malone's—leapt Cureton to snatch it away. He came down quickly and got the ball out to Bogues on the wing, who pushed it up the floor, finding Reid coming off a pick at the top of the key. Reid dribbled once before Spudd Webb fronted him, then did a 380-degree spin and launched a 23-footer falling away. It looked like a laugher. And it was, but it swished giving the Hornets a 98–96 lead. Reid turned to the Hawks' bench and winked at coach Mike Fratello. He was laughing as he got back on defense, where Cureton greeted him with a hand slap and a smile. The play had begun with Cureton's thirteenth rebound and ended with Reid's twenty-second point. Fratello called a timeout, giving a cue to Harter and his players and the packed house, that the Hawks were about ready to cave in.

As his team clustered around him, Harter looked up to find barely contained smiles and arms draped from Rambis to Reid to Bogues to Cureton. The Coliseum crowd was in ecstacy singing, actually yelling, along with a sound system medley of "Shout," "We Will Rock You," "What I Like About You," and finally finishing on "Burning Down The House." The crowd remained on its feet for much of the final minutes, watching their team hold on to win 110–108—Charlotte's thirteenth victory. Afterwards, they refused to clear out, lingering for the post-game radio interview with Reid, who finished with 28 points, and one last rendition of "Shout."

The giddiness extended into the locker room where Harter was explaining a premonition he had on the drive over to the arena. "I had a feeling. No, I knew coming over here we were going to be in it at the end. I thought we might get beat in the last second, but we'd be close," he said excitedly. "I never imagined that we'd win thirteen games at this point of the season. This is fantastic."

Some of the Hawks, however, didn't want Charlotte to get carried away. As Moses Malone made his way to the team bus, a fan tugged at his full length coat and asked for autograph.

"It sure was rough out there," said the middle-aged man.

Malone stopped and glared. "I've seen it a lot rougher in my thirteen years in the league. I don't believe you've seen enough here."

The gentleman winced at Malone's monotone utterance before rushing over to a much friendlier Tim Kempton. If there had been any doubt that this basketball game was any less than a battle of the New South, *The Charlotte Observer* made it official the following morning with a front-page column that once again displayed a community's collective chip on its shoulder. Under the headline, "Golly, Aunt Bee, We Won" referring to television's "The Andy Griffith Show," a columnist took several shots at Charlotte's envied neighbor in a largely unsuccessful tongue-in-cheek piece that pandered to the city's little-brother status in the South. The effort was hardly major league, but did contain an apt description of the impact of the evening on the fans who had been there: "They were so worked up when they left the joint that they were moving at big-city speed."

10

ALL-STAR BREAK

THE Piedmont flight touched down in Houston right on time at 4:15 P.M., a feat hardly noted by the dozen or so Hornets front-office personnel on board. This was a giddy group, buoyed by the previous night's dramatic victory over the Hawks, and anxious to take part in their first NBA All-Star weekend. This was professional basketball's answer to the Super Bowl with all the attending hype, hoopla, and partying. The NBA required the attendance of all owners, general managers, and coaches, perhaps to ensure that the numerous cocktail parties, brunches, and meetings—held under the guise of league business—were well attended.

George and Carolyn Shinn led the Charlotte contingent, which included, among others, Dick and Mari Harter. As mandated by the owner, the men were white-shirted, dark-suited, with touches of teal adorning ties and breast handkerchiefs. Mari Harter and a few other of the women were sporting rhinestone pendants that spelled out "Hornets." The 737 was lurching to the gate when a flight attendant comman-

deered the microphone to welcome all in-bound passengers
to the great state of Texas. "We also would like to thank some
very special passengers for flying Piedmont—George Shinn
and the members of the Charlotte Hornets' organization.
Welcome to Houston," she added cheerfully.

The group seemed pleased with the special recognition,
but toward the back of the cabin, two Texas businessmen (the
loud drawls and eel-skin boots with brown business suits gave
them away), who were struggling mightily to get their brief-
cases out of the overhead bins, seemed momentarily confused.

"Who are they?" asked the taller of the two, finally
freeing a brown leather satchel from the rack.

"I think they're one of those indoor soccer teams,"
answered his traveling mate, shrugging.

Fortunately, the pair were out of earshot of the happy
Hornet crowd. Even if any had happened to over hear the
remark, it surely wouldn't have put a damper on the weekend.
For this was a celebration of the highest order. On Sunday,
basketball fans would be tossed their caviar and champagne
when Akeem, The Mailman, Isaih, Magic, Clyde the Glide,
Moses, and Patrick unleashed the highest-flying, alley-ooping-
est, slam-dunkingest street game before 43,000 fans and
millions of television viewers on the specially constructed
hardwood in Houston's Astrodome, where the sounds of
basketball hadn't been heard in seventeen years. The real
toasts were directed at the league's twenty-five ownership
groups and the equal number of corporate sponsors. They
took place in the suites and ballrooms of the Hyatt Regency
Hotel, the skyboxes of the Summit and Astrodome, and in the
company of fellow millionaires who spent three days congrat-
ulating each other on their success.

The party-giver was a shrewd New York lawyer with the
mind of a Wall Street accountant and the chutzpah of a
Hollywood showman. When commissioner David Stern took
over the league controls in February 1984, the NBA was mired
in sagging attendance, headline-grabbing drug problems, and
a perception that the NBA had become too black. The previ-

ous season, league attendance averages had stalled at 10,220 per game and looked as if they were still dropping. This weekend's host franchise, the Houston Rockets, had changed hands for $12 million, the same amount the Dallas Mavericks had paid three years earlier. Only six of the twenty-three franchises were operating in the black, several were barely functioning and two, Indiana and Cleveland, were hanging by a thread. The NBA's problems, however, went beyond the bottom line. There was an image problem that started at the top with the owners and reached all the way down to the court. Sports franchises in general have always been stigmatized by the sometimes true perception that they were merely hobbies of the idle rich. But former Cleveland Cavaliers owner, Ted Stepien, seemed to take that impression to new heights—that of the *senseless* rich. As soon as Stepien acquired the Cavs in 1980, he'd embarked on a management odyssey that reflected the turmoil gripping the NBA at the time. First, he traded away the Cavs' first-round draft choices through 1986, effectively hamstringing any efforts to bring in young talent. He alienated Cleveland's substantial black community by echoing the sentiments of the league's critics, suggesting that the team would draw better if it had more white players. Then he initiated discussions about moving the team to Toronto, further insulting the locals and ensuring box-office death.

Stern was well equipped for such problems when he became the commissioner. He had been around the league office since 1978, when then-commissioner Larry O'Brien, impressed with the work the youngest partner in the history of the law firm of Proskauer Rose Goetz & Mendelsohn had done on behalf of the league, asked him to become the NBA's first general counsel. The move ended his playing days for the law-firm basketball team, but moved him closer to a world he had admired while growing up in Manhattan, living and dying with tabloid accounts of the New York Knicks. In 1980, O'Brien created the position of executive vice-president for Stern, fully intending him to be a day-to-day troubleshooter. Even then it was clear the aggressive attorney with a penchant for cigars was developing expertise about aspects of sports management beyond his duties as counsel. In fact, he was setting the table for the NBA's future financial success. In 1983, he tackled the two most pressing problems head-on, demonstrating a hard-nosed, yet humane, approach to setting right the troubled league.

First and foremost was the NBA's landmark labor agreement negotiated in the spring of 1983, which had been spurred by a lawsuit filed by the NBA Players' Association regarding the way owners treated free agents. The biggest obstacle Stern faced in working out a labor agreement was the owners he'd been assigned to represent. As a result, the salary cap was conceived—both to protect owners from themselves by essentially making escalating bidding wars impossible, and to placate player demands by promising them a share in the league's revenue pool. The cap is exactly that. Each franchise has a salary pool that they cannot exceed. The figure is arrived at by totaling the NBA's revenues, multiplying it by 53 percent, and divvying that amount up equally among the teams. The cap theoretically brought stability to front offices by putting each franchise on equal ground. The poker game is still on and teams can bet any amount they wish, but now when they reach the $7.23 million (the 1988–89 limit) they have to cash in their chips and go home. Nobody can stay in and clean up.

Stern cut an efficient, no-nonsense figure in Wall Street pinstripes, his aviator glasses, and close-cropped hair. But in his office with his jacket off, leaning back in a chair, he is engaging and quick to smile expansively. Both sides of his nature are reflected in the NBA drug policy, by far the most effective in pro sports. "Tough love" is perhaps the best way to describe the agreement signed by the league and the Players' Association in September 1983. The Players' Association is largely responsible for initiating talks on this comprehensive drug policy. The early 1980s were rife with tragic headlines of gifted athletes such as Michael Ray Richardson, John Lucas, and John Drew who had fallen victim to drugs. The confirmed abuses as well as the rumors and innuendo reported in newspapers that as many as 75 percent of NBA players were using controlled substances were fueling the perception that the league was filled with well-paid, but wreckless and socially irresponsible renegades. That 75 percent of the NBA players were black, as it is also true today, further compounded the league's troubled image.

Bob Lanier, former Detroit Pistons center and president of the Players' Association, was upset with both the public perception of the NBA and its very real drug problems. Lanier sought to have the league kick the troublemakers out. With the support of the majority of NBA players, he pushed for a uniform policy. Stern sat down with Lanier and the Players' Association and after deliberate, mature discussion, they agreed on a system of enforcement that emphasized rehabilitation first, but was backed vigorously by potentially career-ending sanctions. It was the first such arrangement devised, implemented, and monitored jointly by labor and management. The guidelines were unequivocal. The NBA made it easy for players to ask for help. The first time a player voluntarily entered rehabilitation at a Van Nuys, California, clinic, he was suspended for thirty days with pay. The second request for help carried an unpaid thirty-day suspension. The third time, the player is permanently banned from the league. After a two-year period, he can apply to the league for reinstatement, which, along with the players' union, rules on one application. Critics called the voluntary nature of the program soft, but the normally measured Stern vociferously characterized the policy as "humane." The bottom line also came into play. The drug taint removed, corporate sponsors and advertisers were ready to flock back to the game they'd abandoned in the late 1970s and early '80s. Once such emergencies had been settled, Stern and the NBA were able to get on with the show. First, the commissioner turned his sights inward on his own office. He scoured franchise offices for young up-and-comers, like Stern himself, who weren't entangled in the byzantine business practices of the old guard. The NBA office had grown from a 15-man outfit in 1979 to the 115-person machine it is today. The league's licensing subsidiary, NBA Properties, had burgeoned from an overworked and unsophisticated staff of four to forty, ringing up retail sales of league and team paraphernalia of $350 million in 1987–88, compared to the $50 million scratched out in 1981. Stern sensed correctly that the home video market was an untapped resource of vast potential, so the fourteen-person NBA Entertainment, Inc., was created. It created team videos such as the Detroit Piston's *Bad Boys,* which, by the end of the 1988–89 season, had sold more than 20,000 copies at $19.95 a pop.

The NBA would not have been able to join the Smurfs and Transformers as ubiquitous product marketeers if the commissioner hadn't straightened out its diffuse television packaging. When Stern took office, the NBA was playing everywhere to no one. CBS was carrying 8 games in 1983–84, while an additional 170 were tipping off on cable and satellite-fed superstations. The ratings were dismal and the advertising revenues were declining. The television revenues were paltry. Stern decided less was more. He scaled back the cable package so Ted Turner's TBS carried 55 regular-season games, along with 20 playoff contests, and in the process doubled the rights fees. The league, which in 1980 had its championship series televised by tape delay, now has national television deals with CBS for $173 million and TBS for $50 million. Both are set to expire soon and, with an immense increase foreseen, are expected to double.

Stern's administrative prowess had little to do with the basketball legacy of George Mikan, Bob Cousy, Bill Russell, or any other legend of the game. Yet it had everything to do with the celebrity of the Michael Jordans, Charles Barkleys, and Akeem Olajuwons of today's NBA. The commissioner focused fan attention back on the court. He was selling the athleticism of its stars. The NBA was more than on an upswing, as Stern and the owners cautiously proclaimed, it was the *real* thing. The public relations army that the league had marshaled spent much of All-Star weekend spoonfeeding the 750 credentialed media representatives a diet of dizzying statistics that upheld the NBA's "ain't we on a roll" claims.

The league that had earned $118 million in 1981–82 was

expected to gross $400 million during the 1988–89 season. Television ratings had risen by 50 percent since 1980. Franchise values had escalated shockingly: the Portland Trailblazers, which had cost $3.5 million in 1970, had just been sold for $70 million. The Phoenix Suns had sold for $44.5 million in 1987. The NBA was second only to the Olympics as the most widely distributed sports property. The game had been internationalized with television contracts in seventy-six foreign countries. The average yearly player salary of $510,000 was double the 1982–83 figure. Leaguewide attendance was up 9 percent to more than 14,000 a game—a stat that didn't include the two expansion teams, Charlotte and Miami, which had paid $32.5 million each to become part of the show. That, in turn, was nearly three times the $12 million the Dallas Mavericks had paid to join in 1980.

The most dramatic illustration of the Stern touch was a tiny millionaire shuffling through the lobby of the Hilton Hotel named George Shinn. Shinn was less effusive since suffering his stroke, but the Hornets' owner was clearly enjoying his first All-Star gala as a member of the club. He worked the hallways and lobbies slowly, lighting up when approached by fellow owners and their entourage, happily shaking hands. Shinn didn't cause much of a stir in Houston. Here he was just one of the crowd. George Shinn, sports mogul, didn't mean much in the company of Houston's Charlie Thomas, Los Angeles's Dr. Jerry Buss, and Milwaukee's Senator Herb Kohl.

He had plenty to be proud of, though. The Hornets had shattered the all-time expansion season attendance record on January 19 when one Mitzi Roper walked through the turnstile of the Charlotte Coliseum to become the 319,348th person to attend a game. The record, set by Dallas in 41 home games its inaugural season, fell in the 15th game of the season. Charlotte was leading the league in attendance, averaging more than 23,000 a game and selling out its last 12. By virtue of having the NBA's largest arena, the city was on pace to lead the league in attendance, becoming the first expansion team in any major sport to do so. The team's 13–35 record on the floor was more than respectable. The rival expansion team,

Miami, had won only 5 games thus far—they, too, were averaging a near-capacity 14,906 a game. Best of all the Hornets were making money. Lots of it. Enough that Shinn and the lieutenants in his organization, Scheer and organization counsel Spencer Stolpen, were talking about renegotiating the hard-fought $1-a-year lease with the city's Coliseum Authority, so as to regain the bulk of the arena's parking and concessions revenue.

Stern and the NBA had been chided by critics who claimed that the league had just taken the $130 million the four expansion cities had put up and run. They said that for a league that has long tried to shuck its minor-league image, for the right price the NBA had eagerly allowed in the likes of Charlotte and Orlando, Florida. But Stern didn't see it that way. The bigger, more cosmopolitan cities that could get a baseball or football franchise treated basketball as a stepchild. It took Michael Jordan to renew interest in the Bulls in Chicago. But in the Portlands, Salt Lakes, and Sacramentos, smaller one-market cities, the NBA still offered a two-way street. It could lift an area to national prominence, while its smooth-running business operations and marquee brand of entertainment assured ownership groups of making money. Stern thought that the NBA was less daring than it was practical, and that the success the first two expansion teams were enjoying was evidence of that.

The difference between the Miami and Charlotte teams transcended basketball philosophies. That had been apparent as far back as 1985, when the two cities were vying for a franchise. Both had to battle inherent image problems. Charlotte's was that it was too small and minor league. Miami was fighting the rap that it had already failed in sustaining interest in basketball, that its demographics were too diverse, and that its corporate community was disinterested in supporting any more sports enterprises.

But each had strong owners, the kind that Stern had envisioned when he first started thinking of expansion. Ted Arison, the majority owner of the Heat, was probably the wealthiest owner in sports, with an estimated net worth of $1.3 billion. Both organizations also were making money.

"It's better to be lucky than smart," Stern said of his league's successful growth. "All we could do was handpick the type of people we felt would handle all obstacles that come your way when starting a franchise. We just got our guys in place."

Carl Scheer definitely broke ranks for Charlotte's first and only visit to Miami Arena, home of the Miami Heat. Gone were his white shirt, gray slacks, and barely controlled fan fury. The Hornets' vice-president and general managed showed up an a hour before the 7:30 P.M. tip-off as if he'd just stepped off Don Johnson's speed boat. His blue blazer barely concealed Sheer's Florida garb, perhaps a throwback to his law school days. His pastel madras shirt with fly-away collar, tan pants, and gray-blue crew socks made Sheer look right at home in Miami.

Both expansion teams had returned from last weekend's All-Star break to blowouts. The Knicks had posted a misleading 129–117 victory over the Hornets on Valentine's Day, despite a pregame program featuring coaches and players presenting roses to their wives at halfcourt. The Rambises, Kurt and Linda, were clearly the crowd favorites. For the bachelors—Tim Kempton, Brian Rowsom, and Rex Chapman—Scheer's marketing staff had dreamed up a half-time promotion that was part "The Dating Game" and part "Love Connection." The guys were taped earlier on video and a tuxedoed host moderated a question-and-answer session between them and women who had won an essay contest.

The Heat had lost the previous night in Dallas 93–80, returning home dead tired that morning to face their expansion rivals. They were 5–42 and badly in need of a win. Heat coach Ron Rothstein upped the ante of tonight's contest by telling his players that it was no less than "an NBA championship game."

"These guys haven't felt much pressure. I think it's time

to put some on their shoulders. We need to grow up," Rothstein explained at courtside before the game. He also was a rookie coach, who in fact had followed Harter as an assistant at Detroit. Rothstein ran his hand through his naturally curly brown hair, visibly tight about the game. "We got killed in Charlotte. We're at home. We need one."

Harter was his usual dour pregame self, except maybe more irritable because of the incessant newspaper hype about the differences in the two teams' expansion blueprints. But he refused to get drawn into the debate about which strategy was better. "That's your guys' job," he snapped at a variety of persistent beat writers.

Harter just wanted to win. His pre-All-Star break ebullience was gone. He was convinced that opportunities for victory would be few and far between down the season's home stretch. The good teams were prepping for the playoffs. They had seen his team a couple of times, so there was little chance of catching them off-guard. He also was afraid his guys were physically exhausted and emotionally depleted from having scratched out those first 13 wins. The coach's pessimistic streak was apparent after a practice a few days earlier. "We're an older team and we've been playing guys a lot of minutes. Kurt, Boby Joe, Earl," he said shaking his head. "The Heat are a team we should beat, but I don't know."

The Hornets had the better record. They had beaten the Heat once. Charlotte was on pace to win more than 21 games, the average for an NBA expansion team. The Heat looked as if they might win just 9 games, tying the record for the losingest season in NBA history. The Heat players were hearing about it, too. The Miami press was unsympathetic to the expansion excuse. Radio commentator Hank Goldberg had gone as far as calling forward Billy Thompson "a dog" one night on the air. Nobody was throwing softballs here. Earlier in the day, oddsmaker Danny Sheridan had given his nod to the Hornets, making them a 750,000,000-to-1 shot for an NBA title, while the Heat finished as a one-billion-to-1 chance. There were still farsighted concerns about the Hornets' choice of veterans versus the Heat's preference for rookies. Chapman, Charlotte's only rookie, was playing well since being inserted in the starting lineup 11 games ago. He was averaging more minutes per game and had a higher scoring average, 15.2, than any of the Heat's seven rookies. The Charlotte plan also was winning the endorsement of the leadership of the next generation of expansion, Orlando Magic general manager Pat Williams and Minnesota Timberwolves coach Bill Musselman. Both had been monitoring their predecessors closely and at this point were leaning toward following the veteran-rookie formula used by Charlotte.

At game time, the crowd in Miami appeared ready for a pitched battle between the league's two tots. *The Miami Herald* had tried to fuel the rivalry that morning by reprinting a very humorous column by *The Charlotte Observer's* Tom Sorensen that, among other things, claimed that the fact that Julio Iglesias was a limited partner in the Heat's ownership was reason enough to dislike the Miami franchise. Before the game, a Miami radio station gave away orange fly swatters that, when waved by Heat fans, added to the visual feast inside the new Miami Arena, a pink building plopped on the edge of downtown.

The atmosphere inside was decidedly South Florida—loose, casual, and aggressively eccentric. The mostly Biscayne-blue arena seats (some were aqua and forest green) were a soothing backdrop for the tanned, shorts- and sundress-crowd in attendance on this muggy Miami night. The Heat braintrust clearly knew the makeup of their fan base. Waitresses wearing tailed tuxedo tops and shorts took orders for food and drink from courtside fans. The concession stands featured *churros*—long sausage strips—as well as Cuban coffee. A drink called "The Miami Heat," a pink-and-white concoction of pina colada and rum runner, was available for $4. A rock 'n roll orchestra wearing Miama Heat T-shirts was wedged into a floor-level corner to provide rollicking musical interludes during breaks in the action. It didn't appear that The Heat were into too much overprogramming.

A smattering of Hornet fans, most of them occupying a courtside corner, wearing teal sweatshirts and emblazoned ball caps, went virtually unnoticed in the vibrant arena. They definitely knew they were a long way from the Bible Belt when the Miami Heat Dancers appeared in black tights and pink polka-dot wraps that they proceeded to strip off and drop to the floor before their routine had even got going.

Scheer was taking it all in from an aisle seat about ten rows up, parallel to the free throw line at the Hornets' basket. Because he was in enemy territory, there was no courtside ground for him to pace. Scheer grimaced, winced, and squirmed through much of Charlotte's dismal first half. When Dave Hoppen fouled the Heat's Kevin Edwards as he went to the basket at the beginning of the second quarter, he slammed his foot down in the aisle, startling a soft drink vendor. The Hornets seemed wooden much of the first half. Their play execution was sloppy, and they turned the ball over nine times on a variety of bad passes. They were down by 9 at one point, but behind Tripucka's 17 first-half points, they managed to close to within 3 at the end of the second quarter.

The Heat fans were charged up. When Reid picked up a technical foul in the final minutes of the first quarter, they booed and screamed, before bursting into applause when Jon Sundvold hit the free shot. Now they were on their feet, waving their fly swatters at the Hornets as Harter, hands on hips, head shaking slightly as he eyed the floor, led his team off the floor. Scheer got up to wander around.

The Hornets woke up in the second half. Tripucka continued his hot shooting on the way to a 31-point night, bringing the Hornets to within 2 points at 79–77 at the end of the third quarter. The final twelve minutes came very close to Rothstein's prediction of "the battle of the bottom" turning into an NBA championship game. Both teams went at each other in slick, measured attacks. Muggsy Bogues sneaked up behind Rory Sparrow to block his shot early in the fourth, keying a fast break that Chapman finished off with a gliding, shoulder-dipping move between two defenders, switching hands in midair to lay it in off the glass. But Kevin Edwards, a rookie, and Jon Sundvold, the sixth-year shooting specialist of modest quickness, continued to pump in 22-footers at will over Chapman for the Heat. The final three minutes of the game were a duel of desperate wills. The Heat had already been embarrassed once by the Hornets, and hadn't had the chance to notch a victory since beating Sacramento four games ago. Harter was stalking the sidelines, trying to keep pace with Rothstein, who alternated between leaping to his feet from the bench, to scooting quickly toward the scorer's table while waving his arms. At one point, Rothstein picked a phone off the press table and slammed it down three times. As time ticked away, it became clear that this game was to be one won or lost by the veterans. All the talk about whose rookies were coming along better no longer mattered. Chapman, Edwards, and Grant Long were still on the floor, but none of them got anywhere near the ball. Reid stepped into a crease to hit a 12-footer with 2:34 left in the game to put the Hornets up 98–95. After Rory Sparrow, a nine-year vet, answered, Reid then popped a 20-footer, his 13th fourth-quarter point, to make it 100–97. Again Sparrow responded, this time with a 3-pointer with 1:17 left. Billy Thompson hit one of two free throws the next time down the floor to give the Heat a 1-point lead. Then the Hornets had the ball and what looked like a chance to win the game with nine seconds left. The ball went to Reid, who had the hot hand, and he launched it from 18 feet. He missed but Tripucka grabbed the rebound, faded away from a packed middle, and hit a high, arching shot to give Charlotte a 102–101 lead with five seconds left. All of the Floridians at Miami Arena stood through the ensuing time-out; "Let's Go Heat," they chanted as orange fly swatters fanned the air. The two newest and losingest expansion teams were going down to the wire. Scheer was on his feet among the enemy, Harter was pacing up and down the sidelines, watching as the last five seconds ticked away. The ball was inbounded to Sparrow, who'd been instructed to pass to either Jon Sundvold or Kevin Edwards for an outside shot. He bobbed and weaved his way with the ball down center court looking to give it up. Reid had a hold of Sundvold's shirt as the Heat guard tried unsuccessfully to run him through some picks. Sparrow had made his way as far as the free-throw line with no one open and a single second left on the clock. He pulled up for a 15-footer with Holton in his face. The ball had barely ripped through the net before the orange fly swatters began raining down on the court. Rothstein was jumping up and down hugging his players, not unlike Harter had, on the few opportunities his team had pulled out a big win. This time the Heat got to stay on the floor and cheer their fans for sticking with them as Kool and the Gang's "Celebrate" blared from a scratchy PA system.

Afterward in the Hornets' locker room, Harter and his troops looked as if they had just been eliminated from the playoffs. Tripucka was at his customary stool, but this time he had his head in his hands. Harter was off in a corner with Badger and Littles wondering why Holton had let Sparrow back him up so far. Reid was seething at his stall, upset that Holton and Bogues hadn't got him the ball enough when he'd obviously had the hot hand. A red-faced Harter finally met with the press. He snapped his usual responses about how tired his team was, and what little defense they'd played all night. "They're all tough to lose," he growled when someone asked if it was especially painful to lose a close one to an expansion rival. After complimenting the Heat with the usual "they hit the big shots and played well," Harter indicated what some took to be his answer (but which was probably only a knee-jerk response), to which expansion team had the better plan: "They have more talent than we do."

11

GARDEN PARTY

THE Hornets arrived at Madison Square Garden for their fifth meeting with the Knicks fresh from another 28-point blowout at home against Chicago. They had recovered nicely from the previous week's loss in Miami, returning to Charlotte the next night and beating the Indiana Pacers. But a malaise was beginning to envelope the team. Time was running out on any possible trades. The deadline expired that night, February 23, at midnight, shortly after Charlotte played the Knicks. There seem to be no blockbuster trades involving the Hornets in the wings.

Harter's wish for Stuart Gray would have to wait another year. The trade talk was at once infuriating and intriguing to the coach. Two days earlier, the Pacers had obtained Sacramento's LaSalle Thompson, a 6'10" rock, for Wayman Tisdale, making the coveted Gray the Pacers' fifth-string center behind an injured Steve Stipanovich, rookie Rik Smits, and Greg Dreiling, all 7-footers. Still, they refused to deal. "Now they've got all the league's big guys, and won't give one up," bemoaned Harter. The Pacers knew it, and wanted to keep it that way.

But two halfhearted queries by Utah and Atlanta piqued Harter's coaching imagination. The Jazz, in desperate need of a backup to point guard John Stockton, inquired about Holton's availability. The bait was a draft pick, probably a number-two choice, but they did at least suggest a number-one pick. The Atlanta Hawks' query was as fascinating as it was improbable. They were asking about Rambis. Kevin Willis, the Hawks' power forward, had been out for the season and now it was apparent he wasn't coming back at all. The Hawks were looking for a banger of strong character who hopefully could take them down the stretch and into the NBA finals. The Hawks were remarkably talented but the team's chemistry, what little there was, needed a lift as much as they needed a power forward. The addition of the selfless Rambis made sense on paper—especially after the substantial way he had played for 40 games with the Hornets, demonstrating a nice, discretionary shooting touch along with his much-noted boardwork and defense. They talked about giving up a number-one pick in return but Harter didn't put much stock in the Hawks' trade intentions. For starters, a low number-one pick, which Atlanta's good record guaranteed them, wasn't enough for the team's only inside stalwart. Secondly, Harter suspected that the whole front office would be run out of town for making such a deal. Still, he couldn't resist envisioning a trade that would send Rambis to Atlanta for the number-one pick and 7-foot Jon Koncak. The coach had drifted into a sort of reverie earlier in the week in his office just discussing the prospect.

"It would make good business sense. I'd have to have Koncak, along with the draft pick. Face it, we'd get our big guy. He's young and will be around for a while," Harter said, his eyes getting wider as he leaned forward in his desk chair for emphasis. "They'd never give him up. Frankly, we'd never do it. The fans love these guys—especially Kurt. I like 'em all, too. But wouldn't that be a hell of a deal?"

The deal never progressed beyond the fantasy stages,

however, so instead the Charlotte braintrust had spent the last few days trying to peddle either Rickey Green, Ralph Lewis, or Dell Curry for a number-two draft selection. Brian Rowsom, a promising power forward who'd missed 45 games with a foot injury, needed to be reactivated and somebody had to go. When there were no takers, Green was put out of his misery and waived before the team left for New York. After pulling a groin on opening night, the eleven-year veteran had remained on the end of the bench, not doing anyone any good.

Even though the players knew the move was coming, and the veterans, especially Reid, believed it was best for everyone if his contemporary Green was the one released, losing a teammate was still a test of everyone's professionalism. The last few days at practice it was apparent that either Green's or Lewis's days as a Hornet were winding down. Neither showed any trace of concern on the practice court, but on the day prior to the move, Lewis passed a cluster of beat writers surrounding Harter, asking if Lewis would be the one to go. The second-year player had obviously overheard the discussion. He stopped for a moment near halfcourt, about 15 feet from where Harter was holding forth on the sidelines, as if he, too, wanted to hear the answer. But then, thinking better of it, he broke into a "I'm-not-paying-attention" jog, eyes on the floor, until he disappeared through the doorway leading to the dressing room. Harter wasn't answering anyway, but that brief glimpse of a vulnerable Lewis revealed how tough the last few days had been on him. Green, on the other hand, seemed genuinely unfazed by his imminent departure. He was scampering about the court, launching his erratic jumpers, smiling as he knifed between Cureton and Chapman and tugged on their jerseys. Like Reid, he felt that he wouldn't last long on the waiver wire. Veteran point guards were a rare commodity. The better NBA teams were always in the market, especially now in the playoff drive, for some backcourt insurance. Green was worried about his NBA credibility, though. He didn't want to ride the bench on an expansion team any longer. The league might forget about him. The 15-point, 8-assist-a-game seasons he'd posted in Utah were far behind him, but there still was a place for him as a contributing backup. "Somebody'll pick me up. Look at John Lucas. Teams always need guys who can step in and run the game."

The Hornets didn't stand much of a chance against the Knicks in the Garden, especially in the midst of their home winning streak. They had beaten them shortly after Christmas in Charlotte, 122–111, but the loss had been twice avenged by New York, the most recent defeat being the "Valentine's Day massacre" in the Coliseum. Any thunder the expansion team may have had going into the contest was stolen immediately by the news that the Knicks had finally pulled the trigger on a trade for Kiki Vandeweghe. They might as well have called the game off, the way the Big Apple press corps was acting. The Vandeweghe-from-Portland saga had been running almost as long as the Stuart Gray soap opera. When news that the deal was done reached the press room, the New York–Charlotte game and the Knicks quest for a 20th consecutive home win to tie a Madison Square Garden record, became incidental.

The game tipped off before a virtually empty press row and a mostly distracted crowd. The story for the reporters still in the press room and the fans milling about the arena was how the already-formidable Knicks, with players Patrick Ewing, Mark Jackson, and Charles Oakley, had finally added the final piece to what was now a championship-caliber team. The sharp-shooting Vandeweghe brought the Knicks a legitimate halfcourt game—regarded as necessary for the playoffs—to an up-tempo pressing team. The Detroit Pistons or anyone else could no longer double-team Ewing and leave the perimeter open. This little piece of basketball strategy overwhelmed the team from Charlotte all night long. For the first time all season, the Hornets looked like a little-respected expansion franchise. It wasn't so much that they played badly, which they did, getting waxed 139–114 while enduring the humiliation of the Garden crowd calling for—and getting—the seldom-used rookie Greg Butler. Butler, the "people's choice," as the 6'11" center from Stanford University is known in the

Garden, stirred a little bit of suspense in the final moments as the fans yelled for him to shoot his awkward, one-handed jumpers and half-hooks every time he touched the ball. But most striking was how little interest New Yorkers showed in the team from Charlotte. One look at the Knicks' and Hornets' dressing rooms after the game illustrated this point.

In the Knicks dressing room, at least thirty members of the New York media milled around the players, peppering them with questions about the Vandeweghe trade. The journalists weren't unruly, just noisy and forceful, and they didn't want to hear about tonight's game. The *New York Post*'s Steve Pate was pushing Johnny Newman for his reaction to the trade. Newman was the player projected to be the most affected because Vandeweghe was expected to cut into his minutes. Both reporter and player were polite, but there was a real give-and-take going on. Newman was visibly shaken by the trade news and Pate was trying to draw him out. As the Knicks were looking for an edge by acquiring Vandeweghe, members of the Big Apple's competitive press corps were also trying to find an edge *they* could use. In contrast, nobody was pushing anyone around in the near-silent Hornets' dressing room. Harter was barely speaking. Tripucka was giving out quotes to the one or two New York writers who'd rushed in for a comment.

One of the perks for Hornet players was that in press relations they were granted a sort of expansion immunity. It was hard to pick on them. They were immensely popular in the community and the 14 wins they had notched was quite respectable. Several theories about the harmony of press, fan, and team relations were offered by Harter and his players. The coach rarely failed to remind Hornet beat writers that they were new to the NBA and to some degree needed to rely on his perception of how things were progressing. "I'll tell you guys, this team's most amazing feat is that it hasn't lost more than four in a row," Harter had said earlier in the week. "If we keep that up all season, they ought to bronze us and put us in the Hall of Fame. I've been in this league for a long time, and for a team to stay out of a long losing streak shows a lot."

For their part, the players cautiously enjoyed the lack of controversy while waiting for the other shoe to drop. The ex-Laker Rambis didn't believe the utopia would last long. He knew that as soon as the newness rubbed off, just having a team in Charlotte would no longer be enough: "We're getting a chance to make mistakes that I never thought were possible or acceptable after seven years in Los Angeles. There, every loss was treated like a disaster. If we didn't win the championship, the newspapers said we needed to rebuild. That's all part of the game and someday, it'll happen here." Others, like Holton the erstwhile communications major and student of the game, were simply amazed at how little conflict the media was creating. At Christmas, he'd noted how Harter had given the writers each a bottle of Bailey's Irish Creme. He'd thought at the time, "What a media fantasy land." His time at UCLA and his stops in Phoenix, Chicago, and Portland had made him wary of the scrambling press corps eager to dig up any team dirt, or to point fingers at whomever they believed responsible for a loss. That a team that had won just 14 games was still drawing decent notices was beyond him.

It was clear as they dressed after the game mostly undisturbed, in the visitors' Madison Square Garden dressing room, that the Charlotte franchise was the new kid on the NBA block. They had been stomped on the floor, ignored off it, and were ready to return home, where 23,388 fans inside the Coliseum and countless others outside knew who they were. Reid was one of the first players dressed and ready to hit the bus. He slung a leather bag over his shoulder and started down the arena's corridor, weaving unnoticed between the television cameras and reporters still swirling in and out of the Knicks' locker room en route to the press room.

"They're gonna make a run at the ring now. They're a good team. This is a great town," he said, half-smiling. "Sure puts you in your place, doesn't it?"

Charlotte endured one more reminder of how small their inaugural season was in the grand scheme of the NBA. It was early March and the Los Angeles Lakers were in town for their first and only visit of the year to North Carolina. The game had been a sellout prior to the season. The Laker mystique gripped all NBA cities. They were coming off back-to-back championships. Their superstars were affable, telegenic, and together, the most exuberant basketball machine to ever grace NBA floors. They embraced a work ethic grounded in their Hollywood roots. The Lakers not only won, they turned every game into a "show time" production, as if they didn't have enough footage already for their seasonal highlight film. Even in the many blowouts, opposing fans walked away with a distinct Laker memory. It might be Magic Johnson threading a three-quarter court look-away bounce pass with just enough english on it to curl into a streaking Byron Scott's hands at the bucket, or James Worthy taking one step at the free-throw line before lifting into a glide capped by a one-handed finger roll over his paralyzed defenders. The Lakers were simply fun to watch. Where Boston, Detroit, and the Knicks played success-ful, superior basketball, Los Angeles took the game to the level of dazzling entertainment.

This was reason enough to celebrate this basketball game. But there were two more. James Worthy, the former North Carolina All-American from twenty-five miles up the road in Gastonia, was returning home for the first time, and the Kareem Abdul Jabbar farewell tour was making its first and last official stop in Charlotte. The Big Fella was saying hello and good-bye to a pocket of rabid basketball fans who had followed his twenty remarkable years in the NBA either in the newspapers or on television. It hardly seemed fair, but neither did the dilemma basketball fans in North Carolina faced this warm March weekend. The ACC tournament was beginning in Atlanta that same Friday, March 10, prompting the first real loyalty test in basketball country. This was serious business. George Bush's first nationally televised presidential press con-ference in February had had the misfortune of falling on a Wednesday, the night reserved for the ACC conference game of the week. The Charlotte station that carried the ACC contests, WBTV, had relegated the President to tape delay, so as not to preempt the annual classic. The first Friday of the tournament was observed like a holy day in the Carolinas. Businesses either closed down, or their operators winked at employees who asked for the afternoon off or scheduled out-of-office appointments. Tickets to the tourney, which were sold out years in advance, were among the toughest in the nation to get—including the NCAA Final Four—ranging anywhere from $250 to $1,000. Steep, yes, but considering that Tarheel alumni and boosters contributed anywhere from $250,000 to $1 million to UNC for the privilege of purchasing courtside tickets at the Dean Smith Center, or the "Dean Dome," it was hardly prohibitive. The state university at Chapel Hill had taught Shinn and the Hornets a lesson in cashing in on basketball tradition. In 1986, in one of the most brilliant fundraising ploys ever, UNC had made basketball ticket assignments in the new 25,000-seat arena commensurate with booster gifts.

Fortunately for the Hornets, the Tarheels were playing Friday afternoon in Atlanta, allowing their fans to postpone any agonizing soul searching. But Duke and Wake Forest, Clemson and Virginia, were on the night bill and it still was a tough choice. Tom Sorensen, one of the local columnists, thought he might solve the dilemma a couple of days before the Lakers game when he caught Carl Scheer on his usual frantic rounds at the Coliseum. The Denver Nuggets had preceded the Lakers and there was still plenty of time to at least ease the impending fan crisis.

"Carl, is there any way you can televise the ACC games on the scoreboard Friday night?" he asked, adding that some fans had put him up to the query.

The usually fluid Scheer stopped in midstep, crossed his arms, and furrowed his brow in one of the scornful looks he usually reserved for questions he either thought were stupid, or didn't want to answer.

When he saw that Sorensen was serious, Scheer, ever the diplomat, leaned back on a table in the press room and gave what started as a very measured response. There were others listening who believed that transforming the $1-million-plus scoreboard into a big screen and turning the 23,000-seat

Coliseum into a sports bar for one night wasn't that bad an idea.

"No, I don't think we can. I mean, we would like, as a service to our fans, to show ACC tournament highlights, but the timing of it, I don't know. If we could do it before the game, and I assume we can get a transmission . . . but then we've got the ceremony for Kareem. And I'm not going to compromise the show," Scheer said, unsuccessfully searching for a definitive response.

Scheer then cut off the conversation with a response that, though it sounded childish, reflected the protective, ultimately self-interested, vision of a pro basketball executive.

"I don't think it would be fair to Kareem and Magic. I doubt the Lakers would appreciate it."

The Lakers arrived in Charlotte Thursday afternoon, treating their Carolina one-stop as the casual breath-catching opportunity that it turned out to be. The night before they had beaten Miami by 40 points and were still fresh enough to cancel a scheduled practice at the Coliseum. That afternoon at the nearby Registry Hotel, Kareem Abdul Jabbar, still lugging his travel bag, stepped to a microphone in a banquet room for his sixteenth farewell press conference. It was an event once thought unthinkable. Not so much that he'd finally given up a twenty-season career marked by astonishing achievements, but that he'd step in front of reporters and, for sometimes hour-long stretches, candidly reminisce about his years in the NBA. For most of his career, the "Big Fella," as Lakers play-by-play announcer Chick Hearn and teammate Magic Johnson referred to him, was known simply as the man with the sweeping skyhook, impervious goggles, and a never-ending trail of asterisks next to his name in the record books, which highlighted his unprecedented basketball accomplishments. Abdul Jabbar was retiring as the NBA's all-time leader in points scored, shots made, games played, minutes logged, shots blocked, and personal fouls committed. Six times he'd been the mainstay of an NBA championship team.

Standing in front of that room in a blue blazer, gray

slacks, and a maroon sweater over a blue buttoned-down shirt, Abdul Jabbar was far from the distant, guarded soul who'd once appeared to take to heart the villain role in which he'd been cast early in his career by fans and sportswriters simply because he was so expressionless, yet so much better, than anyone else in the game. Instead, he was to the point and expressive. He spoke about his rocky relationship with the press and fans, conceding that at times he'd been overly suspicious and paranoid but he didn't apologize. He'd never wanted to live his life in a goldfish bowl and now he was looking forward to the not-so-distant days ahead when he would not have to. Of his contributions to the game, he said he wanted to be remembered for his consistency, as well as the conditioning and competitiveness that had allowed him to dominate the hardwood for so long. At forty-one, he had no regrets about his career. He'd miss the friendships that had developed over the years, but he was ready to move on. There was no coaching career or front-office position he wished to pursue. His competitive fires were burning out. When asked about the critics who'd said he should retire at midseason when a scoring slump found him spending more and more time on the bench, the Big Fella was frank.

"There was a decision made when the Lakers signed me for the last two seasons [after the 1986–87 championship]. They felt that I didn't have to play up to the standards I'd set. But, if I stayed healthy and stayed with the team, then we could win another world championship," he related. "They made me an offer I couldn't refuse [$3 million for this final year] and told me I could quit whenever I wanted to. The Lakers appreciated what I had brought to the team. I don't think we would have won the title last year if I hadn't played. I was an important part of the team at times. But I know it wasn't the same as in the past."

Kareem Abdul Jabbar was accepting his elevation to "superstar emeritus" of the NBA. He admittedly was being phased out of the "show time" attack as Johnson and Worthy were secured their place as bona-fide heroes. The game's greatest center was coasting through his final year like a corporate chief executive might. He was confident that he'd be remembered for leading his company out of the woods, and didn't mind picking up as many gold watches as he could on his way out.

Yet Kareem sounded a bit wistful about his Charlotte engagement. He had Carolina on his mind. His mother grew up in a tiny rural community in Anson County, outside Charlotte near the South Carolina state line. His father spent part of his military career at Fort Bragg. The two had first met at the base's USO.

"I visited the region once in high school. I've always been curious about this part of the South," said the native New Yorker. "I'm sorry I'm just now getting to play here. I hear nice things about your team and your fans. I started in the NBA with an expansion team [Milwaukee Bucks] so I know things get better."

There was no time on this trip for sightseeing tours, but two vans were waiting outside the hotel. As soon as James Worthy concluded his question-and-answer session, which followed Abdul Jabbar's, the Laker forward was taking his teammates to his parents' home in Gastonia, where Gladys and Ervin Worthy, Sr., were waiting on the NBA's finest entertainers. The fried chicken, stuffing, collard greens, venison, pies and pound cakes, Mrs. Worthy had spent the afternoon preparing were the Lakers' downhome welcome to basketball country.

Before the game, moving through a buffet line in the press room, Gene Littles reminded those within earshot that Kareem had in fact played in Charlotte prior to tonight's game. The year was 1973 and Abdul Jabbar and the Milwaukee Bucks had filled up the old Coliseum for an exhibition game with the Carolina Cougars. Littles knew because he'd been a guard on the old ABA squad: "I took it right down the middle of him because I wanted to say that Kareem had once blocked my shot. But that was before I realized he couldn't block nothing and I blew right by him. We beat 'em, too. Then,

NBA players were physical specimens who'd knock your head off, but they couldn't run with us."

Littles was the Hornets' director of player personnel. His eleven years in the collegiate and professional coaching ranks hadn't eroded his greatest asset to the franchise—a player's mentality. It had been forged in six seasons in the ABA and a solid NAIA Hall of Fame career at nearby High Point College. Littles was the one guy in the Charlotte organization who joyfully embraced his job. Where Harter wrestled with the pressure to win and Scheer juggled a myriad of responsibilities that came with stocking a team as well as the stands, Littles relished his role as chief talent scout and player liaison. Most of the time he was on the road looking for players at the more-than-fifty college and CBA games that he attended throughout the season. Littles didn't seem to mind the travel, nor did he object to the assistant-coaching duties assigned to him prior to the season, jamming his already-frantic schedule. He liked being around players, liked watching them, liked assessing their talents, and, after ferreting out any weaknesses or hidden potential, he liked shaping their individual game. This was especially true of Chapman, to whom he'd devoted most of his instruction. Littles still was fit enough at forty-five to take the basketball to the rookie, get him in the air, and lift up for a compact 18-foot jumper. Whenever he was with the team, at home or on the road, Littles spent time with Chapman either showing him the little things to do on the floor, like hooking an arm around a defender to get an extra push on the way to the bucket, or just talking to the soft-spoken rookie, telling him old ABA stories. He left the offensive schemes and double-down talk to Harter and Ed Badger.

Littles's time might have been better spent tonight in Atlanta scouting the ACC tournament, but the lure of the Lakers had proved too strong. He paused now to put his Kareem story in its proper perspective.

"It's amazing that Kareem's been around twenty years. He's only four years younger than I am. Chapman was around two years old when Kareem was a rookie," he mused. "We don't have a chance tonight against the Lakers, but it will be something for these guys to remember. I'll always remember that exhibition game—now they're getting their shot at a memory."

Scheer need not have worried. The farewell pregame show for Kareem went off without a hitch. Kurt Rambis handled the emcee chores, as the Laker center had done for him in Los Angeles at the ring ceremony. Besides his Laker heritage, Rambis was a natural for such duty. He joked about his qualifications. He had obtained an American Federation of Television and Radio Artists card for a featured role in Fox's "It's Garry Shandling's Show," and had starred in two local television commercials. Those performances ranged from throwing a Charlotte radio personality into a hoop accompanied by the line, "What a basket case!" and promoting a contest entitled "Californian Dreaming," whose prize was a West Coast swing with the team.

Rambis took his role in the Kareem show seriously. They had been teammates for seven years. Abdul Jabbar was already the league's greatest player the first time they'd met at training camp in 1981. Rambis, who had been cut by the New York Knicks the previous year and was coming off a season in Greece, was an unknown, last-minute addition to the Lakers. That summer, then-Laker coach Paul Westhead had been looking for an inside banger when he spotted Rambis in a San Francisco summer league. He invited him to try out, but Rambis at first declined. He had decided to play another season or two in Greece, see more of Europe, and then maybe decide on graduate school. He didn't believe he was good enough for the NBA, and the prospect of being a training-camp punching bag for veterans didn't much appeal to him. But Westhead persisted, at one point becoming so exasperated that he told Rambis he was the first anonymous free agent he'd ever had to talk into playing basketball. When Rambis reported, the veteran Lakers pushed on him as he'd expected, but the free agent pushed back. He made the team and after Mitch Kupchak went down early in the season with a knee injury, Rambis moved into the starting linup and stayed there all the way through the Lakers' championship campaign. Abdul Jabbar watched Rambis that first year and encouraged him through his rookie battles. At that point in his career, Kareem was the offense's focal point, posting his 23-plus points a game and calling for the ball at crunch time. His work habits and collegiality is what impressed Rambis the most. They were aspects of professionalism he'd worked hard to emulate: "Kareem set the tone for the Lakers, he recounted on his last trip out west. If he wasn't an asshole and Magic wasn't an asshole, how could you be an asshole?"

Charlotte presented Abdul Jabbar with an oversized rocking chair made of cherry wood and mahogany that showed off the state's furniture craftsmanship. The Big Fella was cleaning up on his farewell tour. His love for jazz music was much publicized, so he had already received a saxophone, a flute, and numerous rare jazz records, as well as art work, a computer, basketball memorabilia from his career, and keys to various cities. Kareem admitted at his press conference that the Milwaukee Bucks, for whom he began his career, so far had given him the best goingaway present—a 1988 Harley Davidson motorcycle. The chair was a precocious gift from the upstart organization, but Kareem took it in stride, even moving the ubiquitous Hugo the Hornet, who was wearing goggles and a Laker T-shirt, out of the way so he could try it out.

He spoke briefly to the crowd, telling them about his mother's roots in North Carolina and how he regretted saying hello and good-bye to them at the same time. He was given a warm and respectful standing ovation by the Coliseum crowd, but not quite as enthusiastic as the one given James Worthy as the other Lakers were introduced. It somehow was appropriate because Worthy was a homeboy who'd first worn Carolina blue and white. In Carolina basketball history, even Kareem's legend didn't quite match the return of a Tarheel.

The Lakers quickly launched a 13–0 first-quarter salvo that featured Kareem's skyhooks and Worthy's drop-step moves around the smaller Tripucka, which he finished up with his patented finger rolls. Charlotte was never in the game, but as expected, the sellout crowd of 23,388 were. The Lakers put on a show, rolling up a 129–90 victory. Afterward Magic Johnson pulled on a Hornets T-shirt to conduct a televised postgame interview. It was the type of unaffected gesture that had made the Laker guard one of the most popular players in the league.

But it did little to console Harter or his players, who despite Littles's wish, didn't play well enough to walk away with cherished memories. Harter was absolutely morose after the game. This was his team's sixth straight loss, which was bad enough, but what hurt him the most was looking out on the floor and realizing that even if his team had played their best game of the year, the outcome hardly would have been affected. He felt bad for his players and he felt bad for himself.

"In my thirty-seven years in the game, I've seen a lot of different teams, but this was the most mismatched game I've seen since the late fifties when I coached freshmen and would have to go down to Navy to play guys three and four years older than us," he said. "You swear after nights like that that you won't ever get outrecruited again. The problem with tonight is that I can't go out and recruit a new team. Until we get better players we're going to have a lot more nights like this."

12

HOMECOMING

THERE wasn't much Harter could do but coach. His team was now in Denver four days after losing to the Lakers, two days after blowing a game they should have won at home against the Sacramento Kings. After seven losses in a row, he no longer talked of Charlotte being immortalized in the Hall of Fame. The Hornets were 5:31 away from their eighth loss in a row, but in the time-out huddle, down 115–88, Harter was remarkably patient.

"Give me five hard minutes, guys. Let's score twenty and hold them to under one hundred thirty. Nothing good is going to happen unless we play defense. We got to get it back to get out of this," he said in an even, yet urgent tone. "Let's make the extra pass and get back on defense. Cut off the lanes, Rex. We've got to work within the framework. Come on, now, five hard minutes."

As his team broke for the court, Harter stood up from his one-knee crouch, tucked his purple handkerchief deeper into his breast pocket, and turned toward Ed Badger. Both men shrugged before taking their seats, as if looking for some divine intervention. It didn't look like they'd get it tonight. Despite wholesale substitutions and the insertion of Bogues into the starting lineup for a sputtering Holton, Harter's team had never been in the game. At one point in the third quarter, down by 37 points, the Hornets had appeared to be unraveling. The normally patient Reid and Rambis had taken Harter's twenty-second time-out as a cue to face down their young teammates, Rex Chapman and Dave Hoppen. Not five feet from each other near midcourt, Reid took on Chapman and Rambis confronted Hoppen.

One cocaptain was upset that Chapman, after not getting a call for what he thought was a back court foul, had stayed downcourt to plead his case to referee Joe Crawford, instead of trying to stop another Nuggets break. The other was irked that Hoppen had let Blair Rasmussen, considered a soft inside player, move him out of the lane for an easy score.

"If you don't get the foul, you still have to get back on 'D,' Rex," Reid squealed, before regaining his composure and leaning in for some quieter counsel.

"He walked right in on you, Dave. You can't let that keep happening," Rambis was heard to say in his dry monotone.

Harter had looked on, letting the players finish before offering his own resigned, quiet words of encouragement. There was no need for histrionics or scoldings. His team was beat up, tired, and frustrated. They had reached their lowest point of the season. Tripucka was again in street clothes with back spasms. They had given up a dreadful 34-plus first-quarter points over the last 10 games, which had taken them out of the contests before the players had hardly had a chance to peel off their warm-ups.

Even though Harter knew from the season's outset that a prolonged losing streak was inevitable, it didn't make it any easier. It wasn't so much the losses that bothered him, but the way the streak was shaking *his* confidence and his *players'*. They were sinking into the abysmal feeling that the thrashings might never end. He's seen it happen in Detroit during his second year as an assistant when a vastly more talented team led by Isaih Thomas and Bill Lambeer dropped 11 in a row. "You never understand why it happens. But when it does, it goes beyond the court and gets into your mind," he recalled. "You're playing hard, trying not to lose. But that's all you're doing. You start expecting to lose and unless you get lucky, or catch someone on a down night, there's not a lot you can do. At least in baseball, you can change pitchers or bring in your stopper."

This time his fourth-quarter pleadings were mildly successful. The Hornets had outscored Denver 14–10 through the final minutes with a scoring burst led by Ralph Lewis and Dell Curry. The two reserves had come off the bench to score a season-high 17 and 21 points respectively in the 125–102 loss. Lewis was pleased. His eighteen minutes of game time and 7–11 shooting was a much-needed tonic for the team's twelfth man. He'd survived the February cut, but he knew that his place on the team was precarious at best. One more trip back to the minors was all it would take to dash his NBA dreams. He'd spent two years in the CBA after being cut by Boston as a rookie out of LaSalle University. Lewis was a well-spoken, gentle guy who was primarily kept around—as most of the league's twelfth men are—to work hard in practice. At a slight 6'6", Lewis was ill suited for the front court, but also lacked a consistent shooting touch and the ball-handling skills to play guard. So basically he hustled, running the floor baseline to baseline, sacrificing his body in the middle to grab sneaky rebounds. "I know I've got better players in front of me, but this goes a long way. All I can do is sit down there on the bench and be ready when I get a shot." He had made the best of his shot tonight.

Carl Scheer was waiting outside the locker room as the team made its way off the floor. Just in front of him was the runway leading to the court, where for ten years he had stalked as he mined the joys and heartaches of the Denver Nugget franchise he'd essentially given birth to and nurtured. Harter stopped and draped his arm over his boss's shoulders. "I'm sorry, Carl, we just can't get it going," he apologized.

This was Scheer's homecoming and the coach felt badly

that the team hadn't given him a grander return. Soon a cluster of reporters pinned down the two men. From Harter they wanted game analysis, from Scheer they wanted comparisons.

"This is a very special place for me and just to sit here in the stands and look at the banners brings back a lot of memories. I could barely come around when I was last here," Scheer explained, referring to his notable absence when he was in town as the CBA commissioner.

Denver, the city at the foot of the Rockies, had been much like Charlotte during Scheer's ten-year stay with the Nuggets. The sleek, mirrored buildings of downtown reflected the city's cosmopolitan aspirations. The all-important fan base was comprised of button-down go-getters who wanted to be entertained. Scheer had accomplished some noteworthy milestones with his teams in Denver. He'd introduced the Slam Dunk contest to the NBA, which was now a part of the league's All-Star weekend, after first showcasing it here as part of the ABA midseason break.

Scheer was good copy in Denver in those days. He'd brought in crowds to see the hybrid ABA, then had helped bring the basketball stepchild into the NBA. He'd been the guy out front for the Nuggets and basketball in the city. The local investment group, of which he was one of more than thirty, had relied on him to put a basketball team together as well as to market it and oversee its business operations. He'd been compulsive about managing the team, partly because that was his nature had partly because he'd had to be. The hometown ownership group had been undercapitalized. Even when McNichols Arena was consistently filled, high interest on outstanding loans had undermined the franchise's financial stability.

Scheer's intense personal relationship with his coach, Larry Brown, had also been in the public domain. The two were inseparable, spending long hours in the office, speaking by phone at night, drawing crowds as they played racquetball or jogged together. Both were boy wonders putting together championship-caliber teams that regularly self-destructed in the playoffs. So in 1979, when Brown quit after four seasons in Denver, walking out on a long-term, lucrative contract, the soap-opera breakup only added to Denver's Carl Scheer lore. Business was at the crux of the dissolution of Scheer's and Brown's basketball relationship. Several of the trades thought to have been initiated by Brown were not working out. In 1978, Brown asked for, and got, George McGinnis from Philadelphia for Bobby Jones. It turned out to be a loser as Scheer had sensed, and when Brown next suggested trading popular veteran Dan Issel, Scheer had heard enough. Their parting was bitter. After Brown left, he blasted Scheer in the newspapers, saying his boss's "ultimate goal was to be president of the basketball world. He is the most ambitious man I've ever seen." The fallout hurt Scheer deeply. He vowed never again to mix friendship with business.

His halcyon days may have been behind him, but now he was back in Denver, head held high, the chief basketball executive of one of the NBA's most-talked-about franchises. Scheer's boss, owner Shinn, was "Mr. Basketball" in Charlotte, but after eighteen years in the executive trenches that suited Scheer fine. His team had lost tonight, but he knew better days were ahead for his expansion Hornets. He would diligently chart those days and hopefully would lead Charlotte to a championship. That he was back was all that really mattered.

Next the team was in Seattle with a day off before having to play the Supersonics. They had a full day to relax, lick their wounds, and try to recapture the winning attitude that somehow had been eluding them. Reid, however, was in no mood for contemplation. The veteran forward was livid. Prior to embarking on the road trip, his attorney had forwarded him an item from one of the Houston papers that quoted Scheer as saying that Charlotte was not going to guarantee the remaining two years on Reid's contract. This wasn't the way Reid had understood it. He believed he had a commitment from as far back as training camp from Scheer to at least discuss, if not actually guarantee, one of his final two years.

The two had danced around the issue all season, especially when Scheer and the organization intermittently asked why Reid hadn't moved his family to Charlotte. He'd repeatedly explained that they weren't coming until he was offered some security. Now near a luggage carousel at the Seattle–Tacoma International Airport, a very upset Reid began outlining what he thought was a gross injustice.

"I've done everything Carl and Dick have asked of me here. I came off the bench when I was asked to, I'm the third leading scorer, and I haven't missed a game. I've been involved in the community. Now Carl goes to my town and says he isn't going to guarantee me without even talking to me. He lied to me. I don't want to come out blazing, but I'm going to have to go through all this bullshit again. Hell, I'll go on TV and say it. It's just not right."

Reid was among the most popular players in the community. Even Scheer had been very complimentary about the veteran's contributions to Charlotte. He made anywhere from three to five appearances a week at various civic and church functions when the team was in town. He and Tim Kempton had been a godsend for the team's administrative assistant, Fletcher Gregory, who handled the players' personal-appearance scheduling. What had started for Gregory as a two-hour-a-week task had ballooned to an almost-three-hour-a-day job. The majority of the player visits were gratis, and in Reid and Kempton he'd found two guys willing to go to schools and church groups at a moment's notice. His versatility on the floor also had been vital to the team. So far Reid had played small forward, shooting guard, and at the point. Harter had asked a lot of him and Reid had responded as the inveterate professional that he was. Now he felt that the organization had used him and was trying to discard him, and that Scheer was going back on his word.

This perceived betrayal opened an old wound in the veteran. For ten years, he'd watched some of his peers cuss out general managers, cry in the newspapers, and abuse alcohol and drugs off the court, only to be welcomed back by teams waiting with fat contracts to reward their talents. "It makes you wonder where nice guys finish," he said, "when guys come out of drug and alcohol clinics and teams are lining up to sign them. We're professionals and I know it's a business, but look who's getting all the money and attention."

Deep down he knew it would really be a business decision. Charlotte was interested in developing younger talent who presumably would lead the playoff charge four or five years down the road. As valuable as he was now as an experienced hand, Reid was worth even more as trade bait. His unguaranteed contract was rare in the NBA. The right team—especially one in the playoff hunt—might be willing to give up a number-one draft choice or decent big man for a player of Reid's immediate talents, knowing that they would not be encumbered with a long-term contract. Like the Hornets, they could keep him as long as they needed him and only have to pay him for his time served. Reid longed for another opportunity at a championship ring, but not at the expense of job security. At thirty-three, he needed to be durable on the court as well as resilient off.

While the players were getting a much-needed day of rest, the man who was working the hardest probably was the happiest. Trainer Terry Kofler spent most of his afternoon in his room at the Westin Hotel, patching up the battered and demoralized basketball team. Road trips were in a lot of ways tougher on Kofler than on any of the players and coaches. Besides taping players and monitoring their injuries, Kofler functioned as travel agent, den mother, and whipping boy between road games. He was the Hornets' lifeline—dispensing the $50-a-day meal money, lining up hotels, chartering buses, and ensuring that baggage got on and off the plane intact. Kofler was brusque, efficient, resourceful, and in many ways embodied the team's expansion spirit. Like his players, Kofler had been somewhere else the previous year with nary a thought of moving to Charlotte. Until August, he was the assistant athletic director at Xavier University in his native Cincinnati. But then a call came from Ed Badger, the Hornets' assistant who had been hired from the rival University of

Cincinnati, suggesting that he apply for the post of team trainer. Kofler had also dreamed of working in the NBA. His wife, whom he had married the previous month, pushed him to interview for the job, and then encouraged him to take it. He was now living in the Embassy Suites in Charlotte, while his wife was in Cincinnati fulfilling the last of her business commitments. They had just bought a house and over the summer planned on making Charlotte their new home.

Kofler was having a ball with his first professional team and when he wasn't presiding over 6:00 A.M. baggage calls, he was an animated conversationalist. He got along well with the players, and on this overcast off-day—in the midst of a losing streak—Kofler had his hands full. Tripucka was out with back spasms that made it painful for him to sit on airplanes, as well as to endure the team's many bus rides. Rambis, a voracious reader ("anything but basketball books"), was holed up in his dark, disheveled hotel room with ice packs on both feet—a postpractice ritual he'd started in Los Angeles— reading *Presumed Innocent*. Holton had pulled a groin at practice, and along with Bogues, Cureton, and a few others, made Kofler's room look like a hospital waiting room.

Surveying the scene, the trainer shook his head.

"You guys look bad," he said.

"We're losing and we're on a West Coast trip," Holton replied. "That's what it'll do to you."

These were soul-searching times and Harter was more dour than usual before the next day's game with Seattle. The Supersonics had lost five games in a row themselves and were returning home from an East Coast trip without their coach, Bernie Bickerstaff, on the bench. Bickerstaff had just returned to Seattle after spending five days in a Milwaukee hospital for a bleeding ulcer, fatigue, and dehydration. He was the NBA's second coaching casualty this year. Sacramento's Jerry Reynolds had collapsed on the sidelines previously and had had to be taken by ambulance to the hospital for a stress-related illness. The Hornets' coach felt for his two peers, but wasn't kidding when he said, "The only way to prevent it from happening is to win. This game will kill you. Ask any coach."

The way the Hornets played against Seattle, Harter might have expected to fall at any moment. His team did break its string of horrendous first quarters, closing at the buzzer with a respectable 7-point deficit. But Seattle's 32-to-16-point run in the second quarter effectively blew Charlotte out of the game. With Holton and Tripucka out, Harter was down to ten men. Without Bogues, who dished out 14 assists in his second game as a starter, the outcome would have been far worse than the 108–88 final.

The 5'3" Bogues was a crowd pleaser, who thus far had posted a respectable 8.7 assists a game as Holton's backup. In Charlotte, he was a hero as soon as he was selected in the expansion draft, and owner Shinn, hardly a Goliath at 5'6", had taken credit for bringing the Wake Forest University grad back to North Carolina. "Muggsy was my pick. I wanted somebody I could see eye to eye with," Shinn joked.

The jury was still out on whether Bogues truly belonged in the NBA. He was a poor-to-fair outside shooter, connecting on just 42 percent of his shots, which begged opposing point guards to slough him off on defense, knowing that he was too small to penetrate as effectively as he had in college, and which also freed them to help out inside. Although he was an excellent backcourt defender, leading the team in steals with his sneaky low-to-the-ground harassment, he pretty much got abused on the defensive end of the floor. It was simply a matter of size. With no zone defenses allowed in the NBA, Bogues was regularly posted up by opposing guards ranging from 6'3" Mark Jackson to 6'8" Magic Johnson. The result was either an automatic bucket or an awkward double-team by one of the Hornets' inside players, which inevitably left someone open for an easier basket. This frustrated Harter who, though he appreciated how Bogues's quickness and passing skills could pick up the tempo of a game, thought Bogues disrupted his team's already spotty defense. "Sometimes on defense it's not like three on two. It's like three on one-and-a-half because of his size," Harter complained.

But Bogues was determined to prove that he was more than an NBA sideshow as many in the league suggested he was. Many basketball people snickered when the Washington Bullets made him their number-one selection, the twelfth overall pick, in the 1987 draft. The Bullets were floundering at the gate, as well as on the floor, when they selected the Baltimore-bred Bogues. The tiny guard was a local legend at perennial basketball powerhouse Dunbar High School, where in 1983 he had led his team to the mythical national championship with an undefeated record. Bogues was voted Dunbar's most valuable player on a roster that included two other 1987 first-round picks, Reggie Williams of the Los Angeles Clippers and Reggie Lewis of the Boston Celtics. He was an exciting player with decent numbers on mediocre Wake Forest teams, but most NBA people were aghast when the Bullets took him in the first round. When he ended up deep on the Bullets bench after several poor outings and coach Wes Unseld's decision to install a halfcourt offense, which made Bogues's helter-skelter skills superfluous, the Bullets were lashed by critics who accused them of using their draft pick as a gate attraction. Washington already had another questionable talent in 7'6" Manute Bol, and with the addition of Bogues, they boasted the NBA's tallest and smallest players.

Bogues recognized that his appeal went far beyond the basketball court. He was especially popular with kids. Teenage girls wrote him letters enclosing their pictures, and he perhaps was the only NBA player who was patted on the shoulder by young fans and basketball contemporaries alike. His buddy, Earl Cureton, was not the only veteran compelled to throw an arm over his shoulder. In every game he played, it was inevitable that at some juncture an opposing player would reach down and affectionately buff the muscular little Bogues's head. The Lakers' Michael Cooper, after spending a night chasing Bogues around like a careening pinball, likened the experience to playing with one of his sons: "I thought I was playing one-on-one with my six-year-old on a Dr. J bucket." Bogues seemed to enjoy all of the attention. Off the court, his electric smile never failed the youngsters who were always clamming after him. On the floor, though, it was all business. Only once did he ever lose his composure during a game, and that was against the Knicks the last time Charlotte was at Madison Square Garden. He and Mark Jackson spent much of the first quarter poking and pulling on each other. The two had been teammates on some international squads during their college days and were notorious for horsing around. On an inbounds play, Jackson was caught pulling on Bogues's shorts by one of the referees, who barked, "All right you two quit screwing around and play ball." At that Jackson snapped to attention and shot back in mock seriousness, "Yes, sir," cracking up Bogues and most of press row.

But Bogues believed wholeheartedly that he belonged on the floor with other pro ball players. He was hurt deeply when the Bullets didn't protect him in the expansion draft, though the jilting was softened somewhat when he found he was returning to North Carolina. Financially, he was solid. The Bullets had signed him to a four-year $1.1-million deal, with all but the final year guaranteed. He really wanted to start in the NBA. He wanted to prove what he had claimed all along: "Everyone's been telling me I was too short ever since I started playing ball. But when we put our sneakers on and get out on the floor, my heart makes me as good as anyone else."

And on this night, so was his play.

13

FINALE

SHORTLY after April Fool's Day, as the Hornets' honeymoon season was winding down, the business of professional basketball was writing the final chapter of Charlotte's Cinderella story.

The Hornets were a success. Just two years after Shinn and Charlotte were selected by the NBA, the franchise was well on its way to leading the NBA in attendance, averaging more than 23,000 fans a game—a record for an expansion team in any sport. Teal and purple were the city's most popular colors, and the lively Hornet, its most recognizable logo. The elusive "Ch" factor, touted by civic leaders as the key to Charlotte's identity problem, was officially proclaimed dead. No longer did the rest of the country mix up the "Queen City" with Charleston, South Carolina or West Virginia, Charlottesville, Virginia, Chapel Hill, or any other place whose name started with the letters "ch."

George Shinn, who'd started out nearly four years before as the "little millionaire who could," was about to realize his dream of becoming Charlotte's first bona-fide sports mogul. In the first week of April, Shinn's plan to buy out his initial partners, Felix Sabates, Rick Hendrick, and Cy Bahakel, was made public after months of financial positioning and discussions. Shinn had agreed to sell his twenty-six-school Rutledge College Educational System earlier in the spring for a reported $33 million in cash. His financial situation had blossomed substantially since that May 1985 afternoon when he first met NBA commissioner David Stern, and now Shinn's sports holdings included two minor-league baseball teams, the Double A Charlotte Knights and Single A Gastonia (North Carolina) Rangers. He was building a new 10,000-seat stadium for the Double A Knights across the state line in York County, South Carolina, that could be converted, if necessary, into a larger venue for a professional baseball or National Football League franchise, both of which Shinn was continuing to pursue. The Hornets were projected to make a profit of anywhere from $4 to $8 million, according to Shinn and team officials. The revenue would be applied to retiring the partner's $16-million-plus bank debt.

Hendrick and Sabates, both limited partners who each owned 7 percent of the team, did not resist the buy-out. Shinn agreed to pay them 40 percent of their $1.25-million investments immediately and the rest, plus an undisclosed additional amount, over five years. Hendrick had never intended to become an active basketball owner. He had his racing interests and had got involved only to help Shinn out; "We're close enough and good enough friends, he's like a brother to me. If he wanted a team, then I wanted him to have his team."

Sabates also agreed to relinquish his portion of the Hornets. But he was ambivalent about giving it up. Sabates was proud of his early involvement in securing the team, and like the rest of the city, had got caught up in Hornet mania. He was a very visible fan, rising often from his midcourt seat to cheer the team on. "I'm sorry that I'm not going to be part of it after five years. I am not so sure I would have gone in to begin with if I had thought that George was going to pull his option," Sabates said. "He told me that he didn't think he would exercise the option, but he always wanted to own one hundred percent of the team. I would have liked to stay with it. I am a little disappointed."

Shinn's relationship with broadcast executive Bahakel was not as easy to dissolve. Bahakel had started as a small investor, but had ended up with a critical 35 percent when the NBA was scrutinizing Shinn's financial package. The two had wrangled almost from the beginning about the television rights and Bahakel's role as general partner. Bahakel believed he had increased his investment at a time when Shinn needed it to allay the NBA's financial concerns, and charged that commitments made to him were forgotten when partnership agreements were drawn up after the franchise was awarded. The two butted heads almost immediately after the June 1987 partnership agreement was signed, when Bahakel threatened to withhold his $4,812,500 portion of a payment to the NBA unless his television station, WCCB-TV, was given television rights for more than the year provided in Shinn's original agreement. The ploy brought Shinn to the negotiating table, where he agreed in November 1987 to give Bahakel the television rights for ten years in exchange for a buy-out option.

Now both men were accusing each other of not living up to their agreements, and of wanting to take the lion's share of the riches that Charlotteans had showered on their team. Shinn's argument hinged on the fact that Bahakel was reneging on a contract by not accepting the buy-out. "It looks like Cy has seen how well we're doing and doesn't like the deal he made," Shinn said. Bahakel claimed that Shinn had falsely induced him to increase his investment after being tipped off by Dallas's Sonju that the expansion committee was worried about Charlotte's financial clout: "I was told by George that I'd be a general partner in every sense of the word. If I'd have known that I was giving him six million dollars to be kept in the dark about operations, and that then he ws going to buy me out in a year, I wouldn't have invested." Both Bahakel and Shinn resolved to take their grievances to North Carolina Superior Court.

In tightening his grip on the sports market in Charlotte,

Shinn also had lost the services of Max Muhleman. The sports consultant who had become synonymous with the NBA effort was no longer serving Shinn in any capacity. Immediately after the franchise was awarded, Shinn heaped praise on his friend and employee. He went public with what he had been telling Muhleman privately throughout the long, uncertain process. "No individual has meant more to me over the past three years," Shinn told *The Charlotte Observer* on April 6, 1987. "He and I made all the key decisions on management and business. We've been a one-two team. . . . The two of us will be the main players in managing the team."

The two spent the better part of the summer trying to find the right role in team operations for Muhleman. Both had sacrificed a lot of time and money trying to get a team for Charlotte, and Muhleman believed he had an understanding with Shinn that he'd be taken care of once they were up and running. Shinn first suggested that he take a key front-office job with the team, but he wanted Muhleman to give up his business: "I did consider that," Muhleman related. "But the salary he offered would not have enabled me to do it." They then discussed an executive consultant role, where Muhleman would sit on the team's executive committee, sharing some responsibilities for running the Hornets with Shinn and Carl Scheer, who by then had been named the team vice-president and general manager. Muhleman tried to arrange such an agreement on a guaranteed basis for two or three years, but Shinn agreed only to a month-to-month retainer. According to Muhleman: "That was kind of shocking to me because the job we had done was substantial." Still, he agreed.

In August 1987, Muhleman was contacted by NCNB's Hugh McColl, Jr., who asked him to meet with a group interested in trying to bring an NFL team to Charlotte. Jerry Richardson—a former Baltimore Colt and fast-food magnate from Spartanburg, South Carolina—and his two sons who had played college football in the Carolinas, wanted Muhleman to find out when and if the NFL was expanding. The Richardsons asked him to keep the query confidential. Muhleman complied, but told them that if they ever reached a formal working relationship, he wanted to tell Shinn. He knew of Shinn's previous interest in football, but didn't believe that there was a conflict now that Shinn was busy readying his basketball franchise. In fact, he thought Shinn might be interested in discussing a minority role in the Richardsons' bid. But after agreeing to a deal with the Richardsons in November and telling Shinn a few weeks later, Muhleman found he had badly misjudged Shinn's aspirations. The basketball owner fired Muhleman and announced that he too was going to pursue an NFL team. He also was incensed to learn that Hugh McColl had put the Richardsons in touch with Muhleman and had appeared at a press conference to pledge NCNB's support to their NFL effort. Shortly afterward, Shinn arranged for the Hornets' financing, as well as that of his own business, to be shifted to NCNB's crosstown rival, First Union. The Shinn group had not been entirely satisfied with NCNB's terms, even though it had been the bank of record from the outset and McColl had come through with the key phone call to Thomas at Shinn's hour of need. Bahakel had asked Shinn to shop the banks as part of his coming into the deal; "I presented the same proposal to First Union that I did to NCNB and they gave me a much better deal. When you're looking at something in the millions, one [percentage] point [of a fee] is an enormous amount of money." But the Hornets' managing partner conceded that bruised feelings played a part in the move. "There was some sense of betrayal. I had made my interest in the NFL known and they were part of my team."

As the Hornets' inaugural season was approaching its end, the team that had brought the NBA to Charlotte, that had ridden in Corvette convertibles down Tryon Street in a late-April 1987 tickertape parade before 30,000 appreciative Charlotteans, had been winnowed down to one. George Shinn was the reigning sports mogul of the Carolinas.

The scene was strangely familiar. Robert Reid had finished his pregame warm-up and was on the sidelines signing autographs when Rickey Green appeared under the basket, chasing down an erratic jumper. The two looked almost the same as they did six months ago on opening night. But tonight there was no symphony warming up at courtside, or fans in tuxedos and evening gowns entering the arena. Instead, the action was outside, in the Charlotte Coliseum's parking lot and on its promenade, where thousands of fans had arrived early to celebrate the Hornets' last home game as an expansion team. Green was now wearing a Milwaukee Bucks uniform. As the two veterans had expected, he was picked up within a week of being cut by the Hornets by a veteran team on its way to the playoffs.

Little had changed for Reid, except tonight's uniform. Carl Scheer had asked the league, and been granted, permission for the team to wear its away, or teal, uniforms—a further treat for the hometown crowd as part of tonight's "FANtastic FANale." The rock music and block party going on outside also were part of the festivities. Reid was ninety-six minutes away from concluding his eleventh season in the NBA. There was tonight's game and a season-ending contest in two days with the Celtics at Boston Garden. Three nights earlier, he'd ripped an 18-footer in the second quarter of a 121–105 victory over New Jersey at the Meadowlands. It was his 10,000th NBA point. The ball that he'd shot pass the milestone was at his Charlotte apartment on the couch waiting to be returned to his home in Houston. One more souvenir of an accomplished career. The Hornets had announced shortly before tip-off that he was being given an island vacation. He still hadn't wrested a guaranteed contract away from the Charlotte management, and wasn't sure where he would be playing basketball next year. Three weeks earlier, Reid, through his agent, had faxed a letter to Scheer, asking that he be waived. The Hornets' general manager had once again promised to talk about it after the season was over. "Maybe I'll be back. Maybe I'll be in Europe," he told Green. "I've had a good year. I can still get up and down the floor. Somebody's gonna need me."

The month of April had started for the Hornets' coach with a public admission of something he had long known.

Sitting in a metal folding chair after practice one morning, his hands clasped behind his head, Harter had blurted to that day's gathering of beat writers, "I've come to terms with the fact that we're a relatively terrible team." No one argued with him, but he continued anyway. "I mean, there are terrible teams in this league—the Clippers, San Antonio—Sacramento sometimes is all right—and us. None of us is very good."

There was some reason for Harter to be so concerned about his team. They had lost the previous night to Golden State and were in the midst of another four-game slide. Denver's Doug Moe had proclaimed Miami as the better expansion team after the Nuggets had thrashed Charlotte out West. Moe's comments would have been ignored, if Harter and the rest of the organization hadn't tacitly agreed with him. Gene Littles was second-guessing himself and the rest of the staff's strategy after the Hornets had picked up former Celtic, and most recently Los Angeles Clippers center, Greg Kite, from the waiver wire the previous weekend. "Miami can go down their roster and point at their young guys and say, 'Seikaly is better than he was at the beginning of the season, Edwards is better now, so is Long,'" Littles said. "We can only say that about Rex. Reid, Kelly, and Kurt are as good as they're ever going to get."

Ralph Lewis was cut to make room for Kite. The Hornets' twelfth man had made it through 69 games before falling off the end of the bench. Kite was Charlotte's second new addition in the past ten days. Former North Carolina State point guard Sidney Lowe was plucked from the CBA after Holton went down with a stress fracture of his foot. Kite's acquisition was an act of desperation, Lowe's one of necessity. There were still 12 games left in the season, but already the coach was thinking about next year. The month that had started so fraught with anxiety for Harter and his staff was winding down nicely. So was the season. Almost as soon as Harter uttered his summation of his team's talents, something remarkable had happened—the Hornets started playing like at least a mediocre NBA team. They lost 5 more games after acquiring Greg Kite, matching the longest losing streak of the season at

9, but then just as quickly turned it around and won 3 of 5—including two in a row on the road—against New York and Philadelphia. The Big Apple, which had roughed them up so badly on previous visits, seemed kinder after they upset the Knicks 104–99. The previous night Ewing and Company had clinched their first division title in eighteen years. After the game, when Rambis and Kite visited Mickey Mantle's sports bar on Central Park South for dinner, they were given a standing ovation. "I think they were cheering everyone who walked through the door," Rambis cracked, "hoping it was Mickey Mantle."

They weren't mistaken for legends at home against the Bucks. The Hornets dropped their last home game, finishing the season by losing 13 straight at home. The game was practically a sidelight to the Carl Scheer–orchestrated Fan Appreciation activities. Besides the street party, there were special performances by a Blues Brothers lip-synching duo, backed by four leggy lovelies and postgame concert by Otis Day and the Knights, the group that had popularized the Charlotte crowd's theme song, "Shout." The all-day, all-night extravaganza made for an odd evening. The Coliseum rocked with appreciation when a banner that read, "Charlotte Hornets, 1988–89 NBA Attendance Champions, 950,064," was unfurled before tip-off. But at time-outs, the usually raucous crowd was quiet as they waited for Hugo the Hornet to do his best Vanna White impersonation, posing before the new Chevrolet, Kawasaki jet ski, or Kentucky Fried Chicken go-cart that the Hornets were giving away. The crowd also proved that the organization had underestimated them, when, in the fourth quarter, a chant went up for Dell Curry. Curry, who had found his way out of Harter's doghouse, had been on fire in the last 12 games. The guy, who'd been on his way to Indiana at midseason for a fifth-string center, had scored 31 the previous game in New Jersey, and was on his way to a 23-point night against the Bucks. Never before had the Charlotte crowd second-guessed their beloved team. They had rumbled slightly at particularly bad plays, but they had never

booed and certainly never chanted for a player. Harter continued coaching as if hadn't heard, but after the ball changed
possession eight times, he finally acquiesced, sending Curry in
for Chapman to a thunderous standing ovation.

The significance of the moment wasn't lost on the coach.
When asked about the crowd response after the game, he
lashed out, in effect welcoming the crowd to the NBA, while
acknowledging the expansion honeymoon was over.

"My job is to coach, and the players' responsibility is to
play. That's it," Harter said. "It's unfair for a rookie [Chap-
man] to play his heart out and hear that. But when you come
here early and the firewater has a chance to flow, that's what
happens. That's a good way for us to leave this building
because that's how it's going to be for the next couple of
years. We're not going to win enough to keep everyone
happy."

The irony of the evening wasn't lost on Curry. For the
first time all season, he had a crowd around his dressing stall
after the game. Everyone wanted to know how he felt about
finding his game so late in the season. Cureton, who was
getting dressed in the next stall, waited for the pack to move
on to Tripucka before tapping Curry on the shoulder.

"I didn't know you'd lost your game, Dell," he chided.
"Where did you lose it?"

"They know best. Whatever they say I just agree with
them," Curry smiled back.

There was still one game left. The end of the Hornets'
initial year took place, appropriately enough, in Boston Garden—the rickety old warehouse of an arena where modern
basketball was born. The Garden was celebrating its sixtieth
birthday anniversary by opening a Boston Garden Hall of
Fame. The eclectic group being inducted included the Celtics'
Red Auerbach, the Bruins' Bobby Orr, the late John F. Kennedy, and the Rolling Stones—all Garden stalwarts.

Somehow the basketball team in teal, pinstripes, and
pleats looked like they didn't belong on the uneven parquet
floor with the esteemed green-and-white of the Celtics. But

this final game actually meant something. The Hornets could keep the Celtics from the playoffs for the first time in nine years if they won. These were not the Celtics of old. Larry Bird had sat out the season with bone spurs, leaving rookie coach Jimmy Rodgers a mixture of seasoned warriors, such as Kevin McHale and Robert Parish, and young players not yet part of that winning Celtic tradition. Brian Shaw and Reggie Lewis hardly inspired awe. The Celtics were battling the Washington Bullets for the final Eastern Conference playoff spot. They had lost two of three going into this game and now needed to beat Charlotte, and hope Philadelphia defeated Washington to clinch a playoff birth.

Harter was treating the final contest like it was a playoff game. His team hadn't beat Boston all year, though they'd come very close the previous week at the Coliseum before falling 113–108 in overtime. Harter had insisted all year long that the Bullets were better than the Celtics and deserved to be in the playoffs. Now he had a chance to do something about it. His 20–61 newcomers could prevent the Celtics from getting an opportunity to hang a sixteenth World Championship banner alongside the others already hanging from the Boston Garden rafters.

The Hornets stayed close for much of the first half. Tripucka, who had been awarded the team's Most Valuable Player award by the fans, kept them in it with his outside shooting. The Garden crowd, which at first seemed indifferent to the Sunday afternoon showdown, came alive in the fourth quarter as the Celtics stretched out a 20-point lead. But the Hornets had one last run left for the season. Chapman stole a pass at midcourt that he took in for a twisting lay-up that ignited a 13–0 run, cutting the Celtic lead to 7, 110–103. That was as close as they got, however, as Boston held on to win, 120–110.

Afterward, in the team's small dressing area, the usual postgame routine was underway. The coach was at the doorway, once more crestfallen, telling the microphones, "We did a lot of good things. You try to play as hard as you can. But we didn't play defense, and just couldn't keep it together inside." Tripucka was drawing his usual media crowd, today telling them, among other things, about how he'd blown his shoe out in the first half and had to borrow one from team beat writers, Tucker Mitchell: "I played like a writer today—from the left side." Chapman dressed quickly. Reid dawdled. And Rambis, who hadn't suited up because of an ankle injury, leaned back on a bench and took the whole scene in. As a Laker, his last games on the Boston parquet usually were in June, during the championship series. "I've seen the Lakers and Celtics do many amazing things on this floor," he said. "But I have no regrets. This year in Charlotte has been a hell of a season."

EPILOGUE

A
S the NBA draft approached, the season had been over for weeks. Superstar Michael Jordan was roaming the Carolinas from golf course to golf course. This was his chosen reward for an unprecedented performance in the playoffs, where as a point guard he was posting 40-plus games, dishing off dozens of assists and single-handedly defeating the young powerhouses, Cleveland Cavaliers and New York Knicks.

The Knicks, who had hoped for so much after obtaining Kiki Vandeweghe, were further set back after the playoffs when coach Rick Pittino decided to rejoin the more familiar college ranks at Kentucky. The Detroit Pistons "Bad Boys" first stopped Jordan and the Bulls, then easily dispatched Los Angeles—who were without Byron Scott and Magic Johnson—in four straight games in the final series. Kareem Abdul Jabbar had played well throughout the NBA playoffs, but without the full services of the Lakers' backcourt he simply hadn't been enough, as he once was, to fend off the explosive Piston team.

The day after Detroit won their championship rings, the dispersal draft was conducted for the newly franchised Orlando Magic and Minnesota Timberwolves teams. As a result of that draft, Robert Reid and Kelly Tripucka both sympathized with Detroit's Rick Mahorn, who became the latest casualty of the league's callous attitude over loyalty to team member practices. When the Pistons had left Mahorn unprotected for the draft, the Timberwolves called their bluff and snatched him away. The burly forward with a nasty reputation was the heart of the bruising Pistons. In twenty-four hours he went from being a world champion to being a member of the NBA's newest franchise. Like Reid, Mahorn had been caught in a numbers crunch. Although he had been a starter and had earned veteran status in his four years at Detroit, he was considered old and battered at thirty. Mahorn was making $600,000 a year and was certainly affordable for a new team lacking strength and leadership.

Like he did with Tripucka, Detroit GM Jack McCloskey bumbled the notification of his outgoing employee. The Pistons were in the midst of a city-wide parade when McCloskey found out Mahorn was a Timberwolf. Mahorn had just finished leading thousands of appreciative fans in cheers, kissing his teammates, and shaking hands with his coach and general manager when he was told he was Minnesota bound. The crowd was certainly unaware of it. As Mahorn drove away from the adulation outside The Palace in Auburn Hills, Michigan, he fought back tears, saying to a reporter, "It's . . . a business deal, it's a business deal."

It was a phrase Charlotteans had been hearing a lot that final week in June. The George Shinn–Cy Bahakel range war over ownership of the Hornets was escalating into a full blown shoot out. On June 26, Bahakel sued Shinn for $110 million and accused him of deceit and fraud. Bahakel was countering a Shinn suit filed for $6.9 million in May for refusing to sell his 35 percent of the team. Bahakel also requested the court that the the Hornets be placed under the control of a court appointed official until all suits were resolved.

The two men's public legal fight piqued even more interest in Charlotte. Business disagreements are common in Charlotte's thriving financial arena, but they were rarely played out in the newspapers and television airways. Bahakel was characterizing Shinn as a "dictator," contending that Shinn made a verbal agreement to not only share management of the team, but to split profits and exclusive TV rights as long as their partnership agreement lasted. Bahakel claims the verbal committment was made by phone on March 13, 1987. The Dallas Mavericks' Norm Sonju called Shinn to warn him of Charlie Thomas's—the Houston Rockets' owner and an expansion committee member at the time—concerns about Charlotte franchise's financing. Bahakel said Shinn pleaded with him that evening to up his original $1 million investment to $6 million, in order to save Charlotte's chances at landing an NBA team. Bahakel cites an April 26, 1987 article in *The Charlotte Observer* that outlined such a scenario. No one disputed that article at the time, which appeared three days after the NBA announced Charlotte would receive a franchise. But Bahakel says both in his suit and publicly that when the ensuing partnership agreements were negotiated, Shinn coerced him into signing the buyout cause by threatening to announce that Charlotte's franchise hopes had been jeopardized by Bahakel's reneging on his financial commitment.

"I felt that I've been used like a credit card," said Bahakel. "I'd never in my life filed a personal statement of wealth, but I did it for the NBA because I was told by George that we needed the clout."

Shinn denies that the conversation between he and Bahakel on March 13, 1987, ever took place, and that there never was an oral agreement made. He says that the newspaper report was not accurate and that it was NCNB's Hugh McColl, Jr., who put the expansion committee's fears to rest by phoning Charlie Thomas. "I never needed Cy [Bahakel]. He wanted in for more, so I cut back Felix [Sabates] and Rick's [Hendricks] shares," Shinn said. "This is about honor and Cy is showing he doesn't have enough to keep an agreement."

Initially the North Carolina Superior Court Judge Frank Snepp agreed. He ordered Bahakel on July 31 to release his interests in the NBA team to Shinn. It was a brief proceeding, but Bahakel avowed to appeal the decision terming it "a gross miscarriage of justice."

Whatever the outcome of the lawsuits, the dispute has lifted the lid on the ill-feelings among the four men who brought NBA basketball to Charlotte. Like Bahakel, Sabates, and Hendrick said that Shinn never mentioned a buyout agreement when they were stalking a team. They go on to say that when partnership contracts were drawn up there were several other surprises that they had no choice but to agree to besides the buyout clause—including a provision that Shinn be referred to as managing partner in all public and media outlets. Sabates is especially verbal about Shinn's posturing as the one-man band who orchestrated Charlotte's leap into the big time. "George would like everyone to believe that he did it all, but the truth was he had a dream, we all helped out and Max Muhleman did all the work. We didn't know what we were doing. What did we know about the NBA, or landing a sports franchise?" Sabates said.

Charlotte's year of national attention and glorious basket-ball was now disintegrating into charges of greed and status. The one thing that was not hurt at all by the squabble, however, was the financial health of the Charlotte Hornets organization. After leading the league in attendance in 1988–89, the organization received more than 24,000 requests for the 1989–90 season tickets—4,000 more seats than were allotted for season packages and more than 1,000 seats more than the coliseum could even hold. Licensing revenues, which the organization clung to fiercely, powered what began as a $32.5 million investment into a franchise. It was now estimated to be worth $90 million.

The bad form coming out of Charlotte was duly noted by NBA officials. Commissioner Stern, early in the dispute, heard both sides out and confidently projected that it could be cleared up without legal action. "I believe a large part of our success is that we don't do our negotiating or arm twisting in the newspapers," was Stern's only comment. Norm Sonju, the spiritual father of Charlotte's expansion efforts, had been called in to mediate at the behest of Shinn and Bahakel. When he too was unable to broker an agreement he also became exasperated with both men.

However, there still was some basketball business that needed attending to, and that's what had brought 16,000 people to the Coliseum in late June. The Hornets were drafting fifth in their second draft. It was yet another evening of promotional gimmicks, a chance for the Hornets to sell their yearbook and video to their eager audience. All the members of the 20–62 expansion team were invited but only Sidney Lowe and Tim Kempton were on hand that evening. The team had gone their separate ways for the summer.

Coach Harter had said at mid-season that perhaps all of the charter Hornets would be back for a second season, but as the year unwound and the focus shifted to the business of winning basketball games that appeared doubtful. Several players were free agents and not yet signed, Michael Holton being the most prominent. He was an unrestricted free agent, able to shop himself without limits to all NBA teams. Holton was about to enter that tier of NBA players he so longed for: well paid, guaranteed, and valued. He was leaning toward the Hornets, but had not yet struck a deal. Greg Kite, who finished the year in Charlotte, also was an unrestricted free agent, but it was doubtful that he'd be resigned. Dave Hoppen and Sidney Lowe were restricted free agents who could entertain other offers, but Charlotte could match any offer another team made and keep them. They both were still negotiating with Carl Scheer.

Of those on the team who were secure, Kelly Tripucka was guaranteed a roster spot for two more years. His wife, Janice, had given birth to Travis Bond Tripucka on May 3, and he was enjoying fatherhood. Kurt Rambis wasn't going anywhere. He had made it back to California for part of the summer and participated in his eighth NBA championship series, however, this time he was a member of the media, covering the Detroit–Los Angeles games for a California television station. Rex Chapman was splitting his time between Kentucky, Charlotte, and his weight room where he was busily preparing for his second season. Earl Cureton was home in Detroit, playing basketball everyday on his familiar playgrounds and gyms. Brian Rowsom had been re-signed and was working out with Dell Curry and Muggsy Bogues in Charlotte. Curry and Bogues are virtual gym rats and mainstays of the area pro-am and summer leagues. Robert Reid was in Houston taking care of his businesses and spending time with his family. He was exploring various basketball options, waiting he thought in vain for Scheer to offer some contract security.

After spending a lot of time discussing the potential of the several college stars available on the draft Harter, Scheer, and Gene Littles were now in the end of June at the Charlotte Coliseum waiting to show off their expertise at spotting future stars. Harter looked tan and rested. He had drawn excellent notices for his handling of the Hornets. He had even been mentioned as a possible new coach for the Portland Trailblazers, which he found flattering but he never acted on it. There was a groundswell of support among the public and sportswriters for extending Harter's two-year contract or possibly enlarging his salary. Scheer had indicated at a year end review that wasn't yet up for discussion. The talk of a local coaching hero assuming the Hornets' coaching position still was floating around, but if it bothered Harter, he didn't show it. He was too busy getting ready for next season.

There was little suspense for the Charlotte braintrust, or the Coliseum crowd, this draft night. That the Hornets would select North Carolina's J. R. Reid as the fifth pick was a foregone conclusion. Shinn had made sure of that. He had gone public the week before with a proclamation that if Reid was available when it came time for Charlotte to select, that the homeboy would be trading in his Carolina blue for Hornets' teal. Shinn prefaced his statement by saying that if there was only a marginal difference between Reid and whoever else might be available, that the team would naturally go with the North Carolina product because that's who the fans wanted to see. Marketing was obviously at the heart of Charlotte's basketball interests. Shinn was scorched by the national press for his statement, and was compared to such meddling owners such as the Yankees' George Steinbrenner and former Cleveland Cavaliers' owner, Ted Stepien. "I don't care what anyone says. They don't have a right to stick their nose in my business," Shinn explained on draft night. "I've invested $32.5 million in this team and I said I was going to be an active owner. If I just signed the checks and cheered like one fellow in Miami suggested, I wouldn't be much of a business man."

When Reid decided to make himself available after his junior year, the team's draft scheme, overseen by Littles and Scheer, was thrown into a tizzy. They liked Reid's bulk and strength at 6'9" and 245 pounds, but they both questioned his offensive skills. Like all the other teams, they coveted Duke's Danny Ferry, Arizona's Sean Elliott, and Louisville's Pervis Ellison, but figured they'd all be gone by the fifth spot. Littles and Harter had been high throughout the year on Oklahoma's Stacey King—a willowy 6'11" scorer—and figured that he might still be around. They also liked Louisiana Tech's Randy White and Michigan's Glen Rice. When White was measured at 6'6" shortly before the draft, they lost interest. They already had too many shooters as well at the 2 and 3 positions to consider Rice seriously.

Shinn's statements, however, were an affront to Scheer, Littles, and Harter's basketball expertise. The trio had 50-plus years of basketball experience between them and their scouting staff, had seen over 100 college games and compiled countless hours of video tape in evaluating their potential selections. Shinn, a former vocational school operator and car dealership investor, had just finished his very first season in organized, let alone professional, basketball. They had not only been shown up by their owner, but Shinn had said if Charlotte passed on J. R. and he went on to become a star it "would never be forgotten."

The draft went as expected. Ellison went to Sacramento first, Ferry to the Los Angeles Clippers second, Elliott to San Antonio third, and Rice to Miami fourth. The resonance in the Coliseum escalated as the Charlotteans anticipated the selection of J. R. Reid. It was down to King and Reid, but any thoughts that Harter, Littles, and Scheer might pull a surprise move were dashed when it was learned by the press that Reid was already in town at The Registry Hotel and awaiting the impending selection. Scheer made the announcement to the crowd at a podium set up at one end of the arena before it was announced on WTBS. The GM conveyed to the crowd that that the Hornets had selected "the best player available." The crowd mostly roared, although some hardy boos underscored the celebration. When Reid was brought into the Coliseum about twenty minutes later he was greeted with a predominantly welcoming chorus. He wore a white Hornets cap with his dark suit and said all the right things in the brief interview. Upstairs in the Coliseum's crown club, Shinn crowed about Reid's selection. "J. R. was down here on Sunday and me and Dick both spent a great deal of time with him. He told us he wanted to play here because it was close to his family home in Virginia. He answered everything right. I looked him in the eye and told him about my commitment to the community and how I expected the same from my players. I asked him point blank about drugs and he told me he was stronger than that. He even had a white shirt on," Shinn said with a smile.

The crowd's interest in the draft waned after the Reid selection and the Coliseum began to empty. Harter and Littles remain locked away in a locker room that served as a draft command center. They still had a number two pick to go. A deal was in the works and the two basketball men were tidying it up. They had decided the Hornets needed help at the point guard, as well as more big men. The Seattle Supersonics had offered 7-footer, Alton Lister, but wanted Dell Curry in return. This time Curry was deemed too valuable. His performance down the season's home stretch had revived interest in him within the organization. When a run on point guards late in the first round left the Hornets without any coveted options, a deal was completed for Stuart Gray. Harter finally had his fifth-string center, grabbing him from Indiana for Tennessee's Dyron Nix, who the Hornets selected in the second round on behalf of the Pacers. "He's tough. We've gone from being one of the weaker teams to at least now having a chance," Harter said with a gleam in his eye. "We're going to be more physical and able to bounce people back."

The curtain had now been officially pulled on the Charlotte Hornets' inaugural season. The honeymoon was over. New players were now in place to shape a new Charlotte team at training camp in October. Orlando and Minnesota were now the expansion patsies.

When NBA commissioner Stern was discussing how professional basketball had managed to prosper in the 1980s, he offered a very simple explanation. "The popularity of the sport comes from the intensity of the game and its athletes. When they go out on the court it doesn't matter how much Larry Bird or Magic earn from endorsements. It matters who can put the ball in the hole and who can stop 'em. Our players live by that and for that. That is at the core."

Similar sentiments were expressed to me over the season by Rambis, Reid, Harter—virtually every one connected with the NBA. At the time though Stern was also conceding that most of the time that basic truth was being overshadowed by the business and entertainment nature of the NBA.

On draft night I was again reminded of Stern's comment when I saw Hornet Tim Kempton answering a barrage of pointed questions from the press. He was a backup center who'd been all the way from Italy to the Los Angeles Clippers plying his trade. No one thought he'd ever even play in the NBA when he came out of Notre Dame. But through dogged work he kept landing on a team upon team until he found a home in Charlotte. Now he was hitting the weights hard, as well as maintaining a busy appearance schedule in the community. He did these things because it was important to him and not for the Hornets organization. Now with the acquisition of Reid and Gray his future looked bleak. They were there ready to knock him out of a job. The press wanted to know what he thought of his chances. Kempton began by complimenting the organization's selections, saying Reid was a great college player and Gray would certainly help in the middle. He then looked at the pack of reporters and said earnestly of J. R., "He'll have to give one hundred percent on the floor because I want to play the game just as much as he does. Maybe even more."

Charlotte Hornets'

1988–89 Season

GAME-BY-GAME

(Courtesy of *The Charlotte Observer*)

Cleveland 133, Hornets 93

GAME 1

Date: Nov. 4.
Site: Charlotte.
Attendance: 23,388.
Highlights: After playing Cleveland to a 26–26 tie in the first quarter, Charlotte was held scoreless for spans of 2:46 and 2:57. Cleveland turned a 34–32 deficit with 8:41 left into a 66–42 halftime lead. The most significant damage was done by Cavaliers shooting guard Ron Harper, who finished with 22 points, and center Brad Daugherty, who scored 20. The Hornets lost starting point guard Rickey Green in the first quarter when he pulled his right hamstring.
Quote: "Every time I looked up, I saw one of their guys push our guy out of the way and dunk it through. We can only get better than that. That's for sure."

—**Harter**

Detroit 94, Hornets 85

GAME 2

Date: Nov. 5.
Site: The Palace, Auburn Hills, Mich.
Attendance: 21,454.
Highlights: The Hornets stayed in their first road game far longer than they lasted in their home debut. The Pistons pulled away to a 20-point, fourth-quarter lead en route to the victory. Charlotte's best moments of the night may have been the first 2 minutes of the third quarter, when the Hornets cut the lead to 50–46 on Michael Holton's 2 jump shots and Robert Reid's 15-footer. But the Pistons went on a run that opened a 56–46 edge. The Pistons shot 11 of 18 in that quarter as Detroit built an 18-point margin.
Quote: "We played a little bit better tonight but we still don't have players clicking on all cylinders."

—**Rambis**

Hornets 117, L.A. Clippers 105

GAME 3

Date: Nov. 8.
Site: Charlotte.
Attendance: 18,865.
Highlights: Earlier in the day, Hornets principal owner George Shinn suffered a mild stroke when a small blood vessel burst in the right frontal lobe of his brain, just above his right eye. With Tripucka scoring 24 points and Bogues and Reid hitting key shots down the stretch, the Hornets held off the Clippers for their first win.
Quote: "This one is for you, George. We'll bring you the ball tomorrow. Get well fast."

—Tripucka

Washington 95, Hornets 87

GAME 4

Date: Nov. 11.
Site: Capital Centre, Landover, Md.
Attendance: 12,731.
Highlights: Turnovers plagued the Hornets late in the game, allowing the Bullets to run off 8 straight points to turn a 2-point deficit into an 80–74 lead with 7:54 remaining. Turnovers weren't the only problem, however. After shooting 56% from the field in the first quarter, the Hornets were 30% (7 of 23) in the final period. Rex Chapman continued to shoot with abandon, making 3 of 15.
Quote: "Each one of us is upset. Twenty-three turnovers! We're a much better passing team than that."

—Reid

Atlanta 132, Hornets 111

GAME 5

Date: Nov. 12.
Site: The Omni, Atlanta.
Attendance: 16,155.
Highlights: After closing a 15-point, fourth-quarter deficit to 3, the Hornets missed 7 of their next 9 shots. In less than 3 minutes, the Hawks' lead was back to 11, after Moses Malone hit two straight inside baskets. Malone scored his sixth straight double-double with 21 points and 10 rebounds.
Quote: "I just can't see us allowing that many points down the stretch. We can't give up the way we did."

—Tripucka

New Jersey 106, Hornets 99

GAME 6

Date: Nov. 15.
Site: Charlotte.
Attendance: 21,748.
Highlights: Charlotte not only lost its third game in a row in the fourth quarter, but also lost its best young inside prospect, power forward Brian Rowsom, to a foot fracture. The Hornets allowed Joe Barry Carroll 10 points in the final period on a slew of jump hooks.
Quote: "We let him [Carroll] get all he wanted."

—Hoppen

Dallas 104,
Hornets 93

GAME 7

Date: Nov. 17.
Site: Reunion Arena, Dallas.
Attendance: 15,512.
Highlights: After leading by one at the half, the Hornets shot 14% in the third quarter, scoring only 12 points and the Mavericks held a 14-point edge going into the final quarter. Not surprisingly, 12 points was the Hornets' low in a quarter, and the second fewest in a quarter for a Mavericks opponent.
Quote: "They came out in the third quarter on a mission. We seem to have a spot where we let up in all of our games and can't come back."

—**Holton**

Hornets 107,
San Antonio 105

GAME 8

Date: Nov. 19
Site: HemisFair Arena, San Antonio.
Attendance: 10,863.
Highlights: The Hornets made their big move early in the third quarter, scoring 10 of the period's first 14 points for a 60–45 lead with 9:14 remaining. The Spurs made up the deficit and former Duke star Johnny Dawkins hit a 20-footer with 45 seconds left, making it 105–105. Kelly Tripucka (31 points) made 2 free throws with 3 seconds left, giving the Hornets the win.
Quote: "What I told George [Shinn] and Carl [Scheer, the Hornets' vice president] last spring is that there would be so many games when we'd get the ball to him [Tripucka] in the last minute. This is example no. 1"

—**Harter**

Detroit 99, Hornets 93

GAME 9

Date: Nov. 22.
Site: Charlotte.
Attendance: 23,388.
Highlights: The Hornets made a run at the lead late in the third quarter when Kurt Rambis tipped in a Holton miss, cutting the margin to 67–65. But Detroit hit the boards hard, getting two uncontested lay-ups in a 12–2 run to finish the period and essentially the game. Joe Dumars capped the run with a breakaway lay-up for 2 of his 26 points. Tripucka made 5 of 17 shots.
Quote: "Obviously they weren't going to let me get anything going. I was on the floor more than I was standing up."

—**Tripucka**

Boston 114, Hornets 109

GAME 10

Date: Nov. 23.
Site: Boston Garden.
Attendance: 14,890.
Highlights: After playing a superb first half to build a 9-point lead and trailing by only 2 with a minute left in the game, the Hornets finally succumbed to the Celtics. Guard Danny Ainge hit 4 free throws in the last 15 seconds and Reggie Lewis hit an off-balance 12-footer with 37 seconds left to hold off the Hornets.
Quote: "It came down to one or two plays. We're not satisfied with just coming close any more. Close doesn't help."

—**Tripucka**

Philadelphia 123, Hornets 116

GAME 11

Date: No. 25.
Site: The Spectrum, Philadelphia.
Attendance: 10,588.
Highlights: The Hornets recovered from an 11-point second-quarter deficit to lead by 8 on Reid's 15-foot jump shot with 4:50 remaining. But Charlotte's offense shut down in a hail storm of missed shots and turnovers. Reid's jumper proved to be the Hornets' last points for nearly 4 minutes. Tripucka's 2 free throws with 55 seconds left ended the Hornets' scoring for the night.
Quote: "It was a classic game against a team like that. They were very loose with nothing to lose, hitting jumpers and threes. When that happens, it's too late."
—Philadelphia 76er Mike Gminski

Washington 120, Hornets 113

GAME 12

Date: Nov. 26.
Site: Charlotte.
Attendance: 23,388.
Highlights: For the third game in four nights, Charlotte played hard without finding a victory. The Hornets trimmed a 24-point deficit to 4 in an electric fourth quarter but could come no closer. Tim Kempton scored 11 straight points in the final period to bring Charlotte back from a 96–72 deficit. But Washington rallied with 6 straight points in the last 5 minutes.
Quote: "We have to start playing hard for 48 minutes. We can't expect to get down 20 very often and come back to win."
—Kempton

Hornets 99, Miami 84

GAME 13

Date: Nov. 29.
Site: Charlotte.
Attendance: 23,388.
Highlights: The sellout crowd turned NBA ugly and booed Rony Seikaly relentlessly, while Rex Chapman, whom the Hornets had picked instead of Seikaly in the draft, was winning the game with two sensational streaks of play and earning player-of-the-game honors. Seikaly shot 1 for 10 from the field, 2 for 8 from the line. Chapman scored 22.
Quote: "The booing didn't bother me. Charlotte's crowd is more like a college crowd. It's a great help for the Hornets, like a sixth man for them."

—Miami Heat Rony Seikaly

Hornets 109, Philadelphia 107

GAME 14

Date: Dec. 1.
Site: Charlotte.
Attendance: 21,716.
Highlights: The Hornets built a 23-point third-quarter lead—their largest this season—only to see the Sixers dash it with Ron Anderson's jump shots and Charles Barkley's drives. But Barkley crashed into Chapman and drew a charge to cancel a tying basket, and the Hornets held on. Tripucka had put the Hornets ahead for good with a lay-up with 4 seconds left.
Quote: "[Drawing the charge from Barkley] was a reaction play. If I had it to do over, I might not step in. The call could have gone either way. It could have been on me, he could have hit the free throw, and . . ."

—Chapman

Houston 108, Hornets 104

GAME 15

Date: Dec. 3.
Site: The Summit, Houston
Attendance: 16,611.
Highlights: After a 17-point second-half lead, the Hornets twice fell behind by 6 and trailed by 4 entering the final minute. With 26 seconds remaining, Tripucka slipped free on the wing, took a pass and cashed in a 3-pointer, bringing Charlotte within one at 105–104. The Rockets ran down the clock and made free throws down the stretch to hold on. Reid scored 24 points against his former teammates.
Quote: "When the game slowed down to a walk, it went to more of a power game."

—Harter

Hornets 96, New Jersey 95

GAME 16

Date: Dec. 9.
Site: Charlotte.
Attendance: 23,388.
Highlights: Rex Chapman scored 24 points, plus 3 steals, 6 assists, and 4 rebounds in a victory over the Nets before a sellout crowd. After taking a 10-point edge with 2:26 left, it took 2 free throws by Muggsy Bogues with 10 seconds remaining to ice the game. John Bagley hit a 3-pointer with a second left, but Tripucka successfully inbounded the ball to Kempton to kill the clock.
Quote: "We wanted to contain Joe Barry Carroll and also hit our shots. I think we did a good job on both counts."

—Chapman

New Jersey 121, Hornets 112 (OT)

GAME 17

Date: Dec. 10.
Site: Brendan Byrne Arena, East Rutherford, N.J.
Attendance: 9,460.
Highlights: Charlotte couldn't pull down a rebound with a 2-point lead following a missed hook by Carroll with 18 seconds left in regulation and, given another chance, Carroll hit a second hook to tie the game. The Nets went on to win in overtime. Carroll scored 22, including 7 in overtime.
Quote: "All we have to do is grab a rebound with a 2-point lead in regulation and the game is ours. We did a lot of good things, but we've got to make a big defensive play in a close game on the road, and we didn't."

—Harter

Indiana 115, Hornets 104

GAME 18

Date: Dec. 13.
Site: Market Square Arena, Indianapolis.
Attendance: 8,670.
Highlights: The Hornets were outrebounded 61–37 by the Pacers in the game and outscored by 18 points in the fourth quarter. Charlotte shot 40% from the field and 64% from the free-throw line. Pacers point guard Vern Fleming had a triple double with 13 rebounds, 12 assists, and 10 points.
Quote: "We just had a lot of guys who didn't play well. Our bench people really didn't do it at all. They've been picking us up. Tonight, they were shooting us down."

—Harter

Hornets 115, Indiana 106

GAME 19

Date: Dec. 14.
Site: Charlotte.
Attendance: 22,601.
Highlights: The Pacers had taken a 1-point lead, their first of the second half, in the final 4:37. Tripucka responded with a 20-foot jumper, and led the Hornets to victory with his game-high 40 points. Rickey Green contributed 10 points, 4 assists, 2 rebounds, and 1 steal. Tripucka took a full-court pass from Rambis for a breakaway dunk with 44 seconds left, the closest thing basketball has to a victory lap. Chapman strained his back in the second quarter and missed the rest of the game. The injury would put him on the disabled list.
Quote: "Rickey Green did a neat job, no, a super job, of getting me the ball in the right spots."
—Tripucka

Dallas 107, Hornets 98

GAME 20

Date: Dec. 16.
Site: Charlotte.
Attendance: 23,388.
Highlights: The Hornets were charged with 28 personal fouls to 16 for the Mavericks. Although Charlotte scored more field goals (44 to 38), Dallas had 21 more points from the free-throw line. Rambis grabbed a career-best 21 rebounds. Chapman went to the injured list and Curry joined the active roster.
Quote: "It's nice to achieve [the career record of 21 rebounds], but it's meaningless. We played hard but didn't play well."
—Rambis

Detroit 100, Hornets 91

GAME 21

Date: Dec. 17.
Site: The Palace, Auburn Hills, Mich.
Attendance: 21,454.
Highlights: The Pistons scored 5 straight points over 30 seconds to take a 17-point lead with 1:17 left in the third quarter of a game that the Hornets never led. A desperation full-court press by the Hornets in the last minute scored 8 points and kept the final score from looking as one-sided as the game.
Quote: "We did some good things, but we didn't play smart enough at times. We gave them opportunities and easy baskets."

—**Tripucka**

Milwaukee 125, Hornets 115

GAME 22

Date: Dec. 20.
Site: Bradley Center, Milwaukee.
Attendance: 15,075.
Highlights: Terry Cummings led all scorers with a 37-point performance but it was Ricky Pierce who buried the Hornets, scoring 17 fourth-quarter points. The Hornets made up a 10-point deficit in the second period and led throughout the third quarter but the defense faltered and Pierce put them away in the fourth quarter.
Quote: "The way Ricky [Pierce] played in the fourth quarter put a lot of pressure on their defense."

—**Milwaukee Buck Terry Cummings**

Milwaukee 112, Hornets 100

GAME 23

Date: Dec. 21.
Site: Charlotte.
Attendance: 23,010.
Highlights: The Bucks scored 11 straight fourth-quarter points, highlighted Jack Sikma's 3-pointer with 7:17 remaining, ending a Charlotte rally. Charlotte overcame a 12-point Milwaukee edge in the last 6 minutes of the third period, leading 82–81 entering the fourth.
Quote: "I've hit a couple of those before. It really helps our guards' post-up game. Our guards spread [the defense] and then I can one of those, and it helps our whole game."

—**Milwaukee Buck Jack Sikma**

Hornets 103, Chicago 101

GAME 24

Date: Dec. 23.
Site: Charlotte.
Attendance: 23,388.
Highlights: The return of Michael Jordan to North Carolina was spoiled by Rambis, who tipped in the game-winning basket at the buzzer. Reid and Holton took turns guarding Jordan (33 points) and got plenty of help for double-team defense.
Quote: "It's very difficult to play against Michael Jordan. But it's a Merry Christmas game for the people of Charlotte, and they deserve it."

—**Harter**

Houston 97, Hornets 95

GAME 25

Date: Dec. 26.
Site: Charlotte.
Attendance: 23,388.
Highlights: Charlotte had the ball for the final 34 seconds and had three times put the ball in play, going for a tying basket. The Hornets failed each time to get off a shot. The result was a loss after a bizarre finish that produced only one basket—the decisive one—in the last 3:29. With 1:10 left, Akeem Olajuwon dunked an alley-oop pass from Buck Johnson for a 97–95 Houston lead.
Quote: "Our defense was good the last 2 minutes, and so was theirs. Theirs was just one basket better."

—**Harter**

Cleveland 122, Hornets 98

GAME 26

Date: Dec. 28.
Site: The Coliseum, Richfield, Ohio.
Attendance: 17,353.
Highlights: Charlotte scored only 2 points in the last 4 minutes of the first quarter and blew its sole lead of the game (20–16) on a plague of turnovers. Three Cleveland substitutes scored in double figures and Charlotte's bench was outscored by Cleveland's 53–32. Charlotte was led by Reid's 19.
Quote: "Both nights [against Cleveland] I thought we stunk the joint out. I give [our players] credit for all the games in-between, but we can't play like we did opening night and tonight."

—**Harter**

Hornets 122, New York 111

GAME 27

Date: Dec. 30.
Site: Charlotte.
Attendance: 23,388.
Highlights: Power forward Rambis grabbed 16 rebounds and tied a career-high 21 points while Earl Cureton added 10 rebounds and 15 points as the Hornets' inside game powered them to victory. The Knicks never led but cut an 11-point, second-quarter deficit to one with 8:26 left in the third before Cureton scored back-to-back buckets to push the margin back to 5.
Quote: "We tried to push [Ewing] back farther from the basket. And we doubled-teamed him, even triple-teamed him. We sat people in his lap."

—Rambis

New Jersey 109, Hornets 106

GAME 28

Date: Jan. 3, 1989.
Site: Charlotte.
Attendance: 23,388.
Highlights: Lester Conner made a 3-point shot from well behind the line as the 24-second clock expired to smother a Hornets rally with 47 seconds left. With its 10th sellout in 15 home games, Charlotte surpassed the Dallas Mavericks' previous expansion record of 319,347 over 41 home dates in 1980–81. The Nets outscored Charlotte 12–7 in the last 3:43 for the win.
Quote: "All I wanted to do was get one up. I didn't want the clock to run down without us getting a shot. That shot took a lot of wind out of their sails. It was so loud my ears were ringing. They feed off their crowd."

—New Jersey Net Lester Conner

Washington 109, Hornets 86

GAME 29

Date: January 4.
Site: Capital Centre, Landover, Md.
Attendance: 4,832.
Highlights: The Hornets missed 9 of their first 10 shots and allowed the Bullets to make 12 of their first 15 en route to a 29-point halftime lead. The Hornets set marks for fewest points in a quarter (10) in the second period and a half (30) in the first.
Quote: "I think this is the worst we've played except at the start of the season. We were lackadaisical and didn't concentrate."

—**Bogues**

Boston 115, Hornets 92

GAME 30

Date: Jan. 6.
Site: Boston Garden.
Attendance: 14,890.
Highlights: Charlotte had cut a 17-point third-quarter deficit to 4 before Robert Parish took Hoppen inside with 1:33 left in the quarter, drawing Hoppen's third foul. From there the Celtics scored 6 straight points to build a 12-point lead and rolled away.
Quote: "With Larry Bird out, you can see [Parish is] the guy who has to carry them. He's not a dominating guy, but he had what they needed when they needed it."

—**Reid**

Hornets 107, Washington 104

GAME 31

Date: Jan. 7.
Site: Charlotte.
Attendance: 23,388.
Highlights: Holton, who promised a win before the game, delivered, hitting two free throws in the last second to clinch the emotional victory. Charlotte had squandered all but 1 point of a 16-point fourth-quarter lead before Chapman hit a desperation 3-pointer with 2 seconds left on the 24-second shot clock and 10 seconds left in the game. Then Holton's free throws sealed the victory.
Quote: "This was special. We really needed this one."
—Chapman

Utah 114, Hornets 92

GAME 32

Date: Jan. 9.
Site: Charlotte.
Attendance: 23,388.
Highlights: Utah forward Karl Malone hit 12 of his first 17 shots, pushing the Jazz to a 33-point lead at one point and an easy victory over Charlotte. Malone scored 38 points and had 19 rebounds. The Hornets were outshot 60% to 38%, outrebounded 26–13, and committed 10 turnovers to Utah's 8 in the first half.
Quote: "They just knocked us out of our socks. We've got to find some players who can knock them out of theirs."
—Harter

Chicago 106, Hornets 101

GAME 33

Date: Jan. 11.
Site: Charlotte.
Attendance: 23,388.
Highlights: Charlotte went scoreless for 2:05 down the stretch before Tripucka (24 points) finally stopped the drought with 2 free throws with 42 seconds left. Former Clemson star Horace Grant responded with a 15-foot jumper to settle things for good. Chicago had to take a bus from Atlanta due to fog at Atlanta's airport. It started on a runway at 8:20 A.M. and ended in Charlotte at 4 P.M.
Quote: "I think Michael [Jordan] took himself out of the game tonight in the first half. He saw Michael [Holton] moving over to help out, and saw [Scottie] Pippen shooting the ball well, so he said, 'I had 48 points last night, you guys shoot.'"

—Reid

New York 106, Hornets 89

GAME 34

Date: Jan. 12.
Site: Madison Square Garden, New York.
Attendance: 16,943.
Highlights: After a 48–48 score at the half, the Knicks exploded in the third quarter, outscoring the Hornets 32–13 to take a 80–61 lead entering the fourth quarter. The Hornets shot 17% and scored just 3 points more than their all-time low in a quarter.
Quote: "It's really simple. We turned it over a couple of times and their press got more intense, more comfortable. Then turnover, turnover, turnover, the ball goes all over the arena and it's show time in the Garden."

—Holton

Philadelphia 116, Hornets 109

GAME 35

Date: Jan. 15.
Site: Charlotte.
Attendance: 23,388.
Highlights: Charlotte missed 8 straight shots between 9:54 left and Kurt Rambis's lay-up with 6:28 to go. That gave the Sixers a chance to score 8 straight and reverse the game's momentum. Philadelphia score 20 points in the last 6:02—only one by Charles Barkley, who finished with 24.
Quote: "Most teams aren't going to let Barkley have the ball down the stretch. It's the price you have to pay to guard players in this league who are literally unguardable."

—Philadelphia 76er coach Jim Lynam

Hornets 127, Philadelphia 122 (OT)

GAME 36

Date: Jan. 16.
Site: The Spectrum, Philadelphia.
Attendance: 10,116.
Highlights: Chapman hit a 3-pointer to send the game into overtime in the final 15 seconds of regulation. Tripucka hit the put-away basket with 26 seconds left in overtime, giving Charlotte an 8-point lead. Tripucka finished with 40 points. It was the Hornets' first win in overtime, their first game won after trailing to begin the fourth quarter, their first road victory in the last twelve tries, and their first two victories over the same team.
Quote: "Just when we needed it, we got a confidence-builder on the road. That put us in double figures [for victories], and you can't beat that."

—Tripucka

Milwaukee 118, Hornets 106

GAME 37

Date: Jan. 18.
Site: Bradley Center, Milwaukee.
Attendance: 16,145.
Highlights: After scoring the first 8 points of the fourth quarter, the Bucks hovered at about a lead of about 20 until both coaches emptied their benches with 4 minutes left. The Hornets couldn't keep the Bucks off the offensive boards in the third quarter, giving up 8 rebounds and 12 follow-up points in that period alone.
Quote: "We gave them too many easy baskets. We didn't play any kind of defense in the second half."
—Chapman

Phoenix 126, Hornets 112

GAME 38

Date: Jan. 19.
Site: Charlotte.
Attendance: 23,388.
Highlights: Mark West blocked 3 Hornets shots down the stretch to stop a Charlotte rally that had cut the deficit from 15 to 7. Charlotte collapsed offensively late in the third quarter, making only 1 of their final 12 field-goal attempts to trail 96–87 entering the final period. The deficit grew to 15 with 5:21 left.
Quote: "Every time we'd make a run, they'd hit a big basket. Our crowd never got a chance to get into it."
—Chapman

Atlanta 137, Hornets 113

GAME 39

Date: Jan. 21.
Site: The Omni, Atlanta.
Attendance: 16,371.
Highlights: Charlotte shot 56.5% from the floor, despite the absence of Tripucka (flu), but Atlanta completely dominated the boards, 46–25, allowing the Hornets their lowest rebounding yet. The Hornets were whistled for 31 fouls and the Hawks cashed in with 36 free throws (in 46 attempts). Chapman made his first start of the year for Tripucka.
Quote: "We had no answers to stop their offensive games. We can do some things on defense. We cannot play some people who cannot play defense."

—**Harter**

Phoenix 106, Charlotte 103

GAME 40

Date: Jan. 24.
Site: Arizona Veterans' Memorial Coliseum, Phoenix.
Attendance: 11,089.
Highlights: Hampered by illness and fouls, the Hornets couldn't counter one final run by the Suns. Charlotte fought back from a 10-point deficit only to see Suns guard Kevin Johnson hit a 15-foot jumper with 7 seconds left for a 5-point lead. Chapman, in his second start in place of leading scorer Tripucka, who was out because of illness, led the Hornets with 23 points. The Hornets also played without Hoppen, who was also ill.
Quote: "I think that was as well as we could play tonight. Kevin Johnson just rose up and shot the ball so well. We played well overall defensively."

—**Harter**

Hornets 89, Utah 88

GAME 41

Date: Jan. 26.
Site: Salt Palace, Salt Lake City.
Attendance: 12,444.
Highlights: Rambis, left all alone under the basket, hit a follow-up shot at the buzzer for the win. Charlotte overcame a 13-point halftime deficit with 8 straight points at the end of the third period for a 68–68 tie entering the fourth quarter. The Hornets took the lead for the first time in the second half on 3 straight points by Cureton.
Quote: "The ball just bounced down on the ground. I said, 'Whoa here!' when the ball came to me. Everybody was a little surprised. It was an easy lay-up."

—**Rambis**

L.A. Lakers 114, Hornets 97

GAME 42

Date: Jan. 27.
Site: The Forum, Inglewood, Calif.
Attendance: 17,505.
Highlights: Rambis was honored before the game by his former teammates when Kareem Abdul Jabbar presented Rambis with his NBA championship ring from 1987–88. Abdul Jabbar topped his previous personal best of 16 points this season with 6:51 left in the third quarter, and ended with 19 as the Lakers breezed past the Hornets.
Quote: "La-La Land. Jerry West. Wilt Chamberlain. Elgin Baylor. I look up at the banners and see all the players I grew up idolizing. And if you're not careful, you look up at all those stars at courtside. You wonder who's here, where they're sitting, how they got the seats, and how much they paid for them."

—**Tripucka**

Portland 130, Hornets 118

GAME 43

Date: Jan. 30.
Site: Memorial Coliseum, Portland.
Attendance: 12,848.
Highlights: The Trail Blazers pulled away with 10 straight points in the third period, highlighted by Clyde Drexler's floating transition dunk and a Jerome Kersey scoop shot. The Hornets went scoreless for 2:40 in the period, to trail 85–75, and Portland glided to victory. Drexler scored 30 of his 32 points in the first three quarters. Charlotte got 26 points from Tripucka and a season-high 22 from former Trail Blazer Holton. Charlotte's last lead of the game came at 64–63 with 55 seconds left in the half, but another Drexler drive and free throw, plus Kersey's drive with 8 seconds left, gave Portland the 68–66 halftime edge.

Boston 107, Hornets 94

GAME 44

Date: Feb. 1.
Site: Charlotte.
Attendance: 23,388.
Highlights: The Hornets hustled and ran to cut the deficit to 3 early in the second quarter. But they never led and never really threatened to throughout the second half. Much has been asked of Parish in the absence of Celtics superstar forward Larry Bird and Parish responded, collecting his 30th double-double of the season with 24 points and 24 rebounds. Holton led the Hornets with 21 points. Cureton had 15 rebounds.
Quote: "Outrageous!"
—Harter

Hornets 108, Seattle 106

GAME 45

Date: Feb. 3.
Site: Charlotte.
Attendance: 23,388.
Highlights: Kempton converged on the basket, preparing for a possible offensive rebound as Seattle's defense converged on Reid. Kempton was left totally alone along the right baseline for the winning basket with 2 seconds left. The Sonics' last hope was dashed when Kempton swatted away the Sonics' inbounds pass and Reid grabbed the ball as the final horn sounded.
Quote: "This team is better than anybody else we've beaten. We played so well together."

—**Reid**

Cleveland 110, Hornets 91

GAME 46

Date: Feb. 5.
Site: Charlotte.
Attendance: 23,388.
Highlights: The Hornets led twice—at 2–0 on a Rambis lay-up and 6–4 on one by Reid. In less than 5 minutes after Reid's lay-up, Charlotte trailed by 11. The closest they got the rest of the game was 7. Cleveland had five players score in double figures (three scoring over 20) while Charlotte was led by Rambis's 16.
Quote: "This [Cleveland] team just has so much talent! Mark Price—jump shot, jump shot, jump shot . . . Ron Harper—fast break after fast break . . . Brad Daughtery—you think about double-teaming him and he always finds the open man . . . and Larry Nance—he didn't even play. If he'd been in there on defense, he would have blocked everything."

—**Reid**

Chicago 118, Hornets 93

GAME 47

Date: Feb. 7.
Site: Chicago Stadium, Chicago.
Attendance: 17,385.
Highlights: Jordan scored 16 of his game-high 32 points in the third quarter and gave the Bulls an 89–69 lead entering the fourth quarter, then he went to the bench to watch. Tripucka kept the Hornets in the game in the first half with 22 points, but the Bulls held him to 5 in the second half as they pulled away.
Quote: "Michael could do no wrong tonight. He always plays great. Tonight, there was that much more."

—Harter

Hornets 110, Atlanta 108

GAME 48

Date: Feb. 9.
Site: Charlotte.
Attendance: 23,388.
Highlights: Tripucka took a charge from Hawks guard John Battle in the last 4 seconds, missed the first of 2 free throws, then watched Hawks center Moses Malone miss a shot that could have tied the game. Reid matched season highs with 28 points and 9 rebounds.
Quote: "All day coming over here I was thinking, 'We can stay with them, we can stay with them . . . we can lose at the end.' If we'd lost this game in the last 3 seconds, I would have shot myself."

—Harter

New York 129, Hornets 117

GAME 49

Date: Feb. 14.
Site: Charlotte.
Attendance: 23,388.
Highlights: Charlotte trailed 58–55 at halftime, after leading by as many as 8 in the second quarter, but the Knicks extended their 3-point halftime lead to 11 with 5:42 left in the third quarter on a series of dunks and drives.
Quote: "Patrick Ewing [the Knicks center, or 5-spot], was passing when we came back to double-team him, and he opened up the 4-spot. And [Johnny] Newman terrorized us at the 3-spot. . . . We didn't control [Trent] Tucker at all at the 2-spot. . . . Mark Johnson and Rod Strickland did what they wanted at the 1-spot. When you get beat at all five spots, you're probably not going to win."

—Harter

Miami 103, Hornets 102

GAME 50

Date: Feb. 17.
Site: The Miami Arena.
Attendance: 15,008.
Highlights: Tripucka grabbed a rebound off Reid's 20-foot miss for a 10-foot basket and a 1-point lead with 5 seconds left. But in the midst of a broken play, guard Rory Sparrow swished a 15-foot jump shot at the buzzer. Charlotte allowed the Heat to shoot 51% in the first half and lead by as many as 9. Miami was last in the NBA in field-goal percentage (44%) coming in.
Quote: "It was a 17-foot jump shot with a hand in his face. It hurts a little more when you get beaten at the buzzer."

—Holton

Hornets 119, Indiana 114

GAME 51

Date: Feb. 18.
Site: Charlotte.
Attendance: 23,388.
Highlights: With just over a minute left and the Hornets clinging to a 4-point lead, Rambis pulled in an offensive rebound, feeding Tripucka for a reverse lay-up to seal the victory. The Hornets outrebounded the Pacers 41–38, and were 10–4 when outrebounding their opponents.
Quote: "There was no secret to my rebounding. I was just in the right place at the right time. When we outrebound a team, it's always good notice that we're playing well."

—Rambis

Chicago 130, Hornets 102

GAME 52

Date: Feb. 22.
Site: Charlotte.
Attendance: 23,388.
Highlights: Dave Corzine's 3 baskets in the game's first 5 minutes helped the Bulls to a 20–7 lead they never relinquished. Five Bulls scored in double figures in the first half. By the end of the third quarter, Chicago led 108–82. Rowsom saw his first action since the season's sixth game, when he went out with a stress fracture in his foot. Jordan led all scorers with 24 points, Chapman led the Hornets with 22.
Quote: "My conditioning is still not quite there, and my timing is off a little bit. The only way I can get those things back is to play. I wanted to be able to contribute, not just be out there floundering around."

—Rowsom

New York 139, Hornets 114

GAME 53

Date: Feb. 23.
Site: Madison Square Garden, New York.
Attendance: 16,130.
Highlights: The Knicks turned 14 first-quarter Charlotte turnovers into 10 points and scored the most points the Hornets were allowed in a half to lead 77–58 at halftime. Mark Jackson had a career-high 7 steals, as many as all the Hornets combined.
Quote: "We may have to make some changes in our rotation. I'll think about that after I see the tape of the game."

—Harter

Hornets 124, San Antonio 113

GAME 54

Date: Feb. 25.
Site: Charlotte.
Attendance: 23,388.
Highlights: Charlotte put together a well-rounded effort paced by Tripucka's 40 points. Rambis pulled down 22 rebounds and scored 16 points, Chapman scored 21 points, Cureton had 17 points and 12 rebounds, Holton had 18 points and 9 assists.
Quote: "I had a talk with myself on the way over here, told myself I had to play well. I know if I play well, we all tend to play well."

—Tripucka

Boston 112, Hornets 87

GAME 55

Date: Feb. 28.
Site: Charlotte.
Attendance: 23,388.
Highlights: Charlotte scored 4 points in the last 6:30 of the game as Boston ran away with the lead. Boston starters McHale, Reggie Lewis, and Parish combined for 42 first-half points to 13 from Tripucka–Rambis–Cureton. Tripucka had all 13 of those points. By halftime the Hornets trailed 59–33. Lewis finished game-high honors of 28 points. Tripucka led Charlotte with 21.
Quote: "They were blocking everything in sight. Kurt has to carry us on nights when we don't shoot well."
—Harter

New Jersey 114, Hornets 103

GAME 56

Date: March 2.
Site: Brendan Byrne Arena, East Rutherford, N.J.
Attendance: 8,011.
Highlights: Nets forward Chris Morris scored a career-high 31 points, including a dunk with 58 seconds left that served as an exclamation point on the victory. Charlotte had built a 74–59 lead with 10 minutes left in the third quarter. Five minutes later, New Jersey had outscored Charlotte 19–4 to tie the score at 78–78. Morris had 11 of those 19 points.
Quote: "We were nonaggressive—just not competing enough in the fourth quarter. We had played so hard, so aggressive in the first half. This is a game we should have won."
—Tripucka

Atlanta 133, Hornets 109

GAME 57

Date: March 3.
Site: The Omni, Atlanta.
Attendance: 16,371.
Highlights: Dominique Wilkins had 35 points before going to the bench late in the third quarter with Atlanta ahead by 24. The margin grew to 34. Wilkins gave the Hawks a 19-point lead in 18 minutes on 1 of his 6 dunks.
Quote: "Dominique was on fire tonight, jumping over everybody. I don't think [Rambis's injury] is a legitimate excuse for this. We need Kurt's rebounding to be the team we want to be. But we could have had Wilt Chamberlain at center and still gotten beat like that."
—Harter

Washington 114, Hornets 101

GAME 58

Date: March 5.
Site: Capital Centre, Landover, Md.
Attendance: 6,661.
Highlights: With the game tied at 86–86 and 7:49 remaining, the Hornets crumbled and the Bullets took off on a 14–1 run. Washington beat Charlotte on the boards 26–16 in the second half. Malone led all scorers with 34.
Quote: "We played harder than we've been playing. We did a lot of the things we hadn't been doing—playing unselfishly and putting the ball in the right people's hands for open shots. But they were making all the momentum plays in the second half."
—Holton

Denver 112, Hornets 99

GAME 59

Date: March 8.
Site: Charlotte.
Attendance: 23,388.
Highlights: Tripucka scored his 10,000th NBA point just 12 seconds into the game. Unfortunately, the Hornets' offense went straight down hill from there. The Hornets shot 38% from the field in the first half to spot the Nuggets an 8-point halftime lead. Charlotte trailed by as many as 21 in the third quarter, after Denver reeled off 10 straight points to start the third quarter.
Quote: "It's the same old story—we don't have the athletes to compete with these teams and they're fighting for their lives in the playoff race. When you don't connect on your shots, they'll run the ball down your throats. We didn't have enough plugs for the dike."
—Tripucka

L.A. Lakers 123, Hornets 90

GAME 60

Date: March 10.
Site: Charlotte.
Attendance: 23,388.
Highlights: Charlotte gave up 13 points before scoring 4 and looked like toy soldiers in the path of the two-time NBA champions. Charlotte missed 6 of its first 7 attempts and for the second straight game shot 38% in the first half to the Lakers' 63%.
Quote: "You feel naked as a jaybird in games like this. You think you're improving, and you see so many flaws."
—Reid

Sacramento 114, Hornets 105

Game 61

Date: March 12.
Site: Charlotte.
Attendance: 23,388.
Highlights: The Hornets trailed by 9 points after the first quarter, wasting a career-high 37-point effort from Rex Chapman. The Sacramento lead spread to 15 at halftime and 20 with 6:12 left in the third quarter before Chapman and Tripucka shot the Hornets back into the game. After the Hornets cut the lead to 2, Wayman Tisdale pushed Sacramento back to an 11-point lead in 2½ minutes.
Quote: "They're a small team that needs to get into transition. When you're scoring on them, they have to play five-on-five and that's tough on them. We can score."

—Sacramento Kings coach Jerry Reynolds

Denver 125, Hornets 102

GAME 62

Date: March 14.
Site: McNichols Sports Arena, Denver.
Attendance: 10,522.
Highlights: Once again Charlotte fell behind early, this time by 17 points after the first quarter and 33 points at the half. Tripucka remained on the bench with back spasms.
Quote: "The key to whether we win or lose is defense. We can score 100. But they're scoring 130."

—Lewis

Seattle 108, Hornets 88

GAME 63

Date: March 16.
Site: Coliseum, Seattle.
Attendance: 9,665.
Highlights: Charlotte finally broke out of its string of dreadful first quarters. But the second quarter was a very different story. Charlotte had trailed by only 7 points entering the second quarter, primarily on 10 first-quarter points from Chapman. The Hornets failed to score the last 4:06 of the first half against Seattle. The Supersonics outscored Charlotte 14–2 on a variety of drives by Dale Ellis and Xavier McDaniel. Chapman's drive with 4:06 remaining accounted for Charlotte's last points of the half. The result was a 23-point halftime deficit and a loss.
Quote: "Ellis is a very hard player to contain."

—Harter

Hornets 108, L.A. Clippers 105

GAME 64

Date: March 17.
Site: Los Angeles Memorial Sports Arena.
Attendance: 10,758.
Highlights: The Hornets led 56–53, their first halftime lead in 8 games, on a buzzer-beating 3-pointer by Curry. In the last 3 minutes of the half, Charlotte went on a 12–2 run on 3 baskets each from Reid and Rambis to take a 49–43 edge with 2:40 left. The third quarter swayed back and forth, with the Clippers opening a 6-point lead by outscoring the Hornets 9–2. Two minutes later the Hornets responded with 5 straight points from Curry to close the gap to 2 and went on to win, breaking a 9-game losing streak.

Golden State 124, Hornets 117

GAME 65

Date: March 19.
Site: Oakland Coliseum Arena.
Attendance: 15,025.
Highlights: The Warriors took control early in ther fourth quarter with a 10–2 run built around breakaway lay-ups. When the Warriors couldn't find the fast break, they beat the Hornets with long jump shots by Chris Mullin, who had 27 points, Terry Teagle (20), and Rod Higgins (14). The Hornets were without leading scorer Tripucka, who was hospitalized with back spasms.
Quote: "We do that against everybody. As soon as we're in position [when the opponent's shot is released], we take off."
—Golden State Warrior Mitch Richmond

Hornets 117, Sacramento 110

GAME 66

Date: March 20.
Site: Arco Arena, Sacramento.
Attendance: 16,517.
Highlights: After building a 20-point edge early in the third quarter on the shooting of Chapman and Reid, the Hornets outlasted a Sacramento run in the last 2 minutes of the game for the win. Bogues hit 2 free throws with 49 seconds left, pushing the lead back to 8. Three Hornets scored 20-plus points—Chapman (25), Reid (24), and Curry (21).
Quote: "I thought we wouldn't have to sweat in the fourth quarter. But they didn't give up. It would have been nice if we didn't have to go the whole way, but these guys don't give up, just like we don't."

—Reid

Washington 102, Hornets 97

GAME 67

Date: March 23.
Site: Charlotte.
Attendance: 23,388.
Highlights: Three offensive rebounds by the Bullets on the same possession drained the clock and with it the Hornets' chances. Trailing by 8 with 4:32 left in the third quarter, Chapman hit a lay-up to start a rally. Curry made a 20-footer and a 3-pointer, then Rambis hit a free throw and a 19-footer to cut the deficit to 3 with 1:24 remaining in the quarter. That was as close as Charlotte got the rest of the night.
Quote: "[Bernard] King plays very, very hard, and he's a smart player. Once he's on with that shot, he's taking it again and again. And [John] Williams—he's a point guard, a center and a forward. Those two are great players."

—Reid

Detroit 113, Hornets 101

GAME 68

Date: March 25.
Site: Charlotte.
Attendance: 23,388.
Highlights: Pistons guard Joe Dumars (18 points) and forwards Mark Aguirre (17) and Dennis Rodman (16) ran the Hornets defenders into the ground while center Bill Laimbeer was setting up outside for 18 points in standing jump shots. Holton likely will be placed on the 5-game injured list to treat a stress fracture just above his right ankle. Tripucka missed his 6th game in the last 7 with back spasms. Curry came off the bench for the Hornets to score 18 points.
Quote: "It's far more important to get Mark [Aguirre] more involved in the offense. We have a lot of room for improvement in that sense."

—Detroit Piston Bill Laimbeer

New York 121, Hornets 105

GAME 69

Date: March 27.
Site: Charlotte.
Attendance: 23,388.
Highlights: Knicks center Patrick Ewing tied a career-high with 45 points as he led his team to victory. The Hornets trailed 94–86 entering the final quarter, making up 4 points with their last two possessions of the period. But New York pushed its lead to 17 with about 4 minutes left on a follow shot by Knicks swingman Johnny Newman.
Quote: "This one is sweet. I'm so happy. We were at the bottom when I first came here [three years ago]. Now we're close to the top."
—**New York Knick Patrick Ewing**

Golden State 113, Hornets 104

GAME 70

Date: March 30.
Site: Charlotte.
Attendance: 23,388.
Highlights: Mitch Richmond's 2 offensive rebounds in the last 5 minutes shut down a Hornets rally and extended Charlotte's home losing streak to 8. Chris Mullin's 36 points kept the Warriors ahead for most of the last three quarters. But when the Hornets closed an 18-point, fourth-quarter deficit to 8, Richmond was the difference.
Quote: "[Richmond's] a great player—a very tough, strong player. They got 2 or 3 big offensive rebounds by just rooting us out of there. Sure, people will be talking about their shooting, but I really think this game was won on strength."
—**Harter**

Portland 124, Hornets 121 (OT)

GAME 71

Date: April 1, 1989.
Site: Charlotte.
Attendance: 23,388.
Highlights: Portland's 16-point third-quarter lead slipped away in regulation when Reid hit a 3-pointer with 19 seconds left to force an overtime. After Drexler drove the lane for a basket and collected the foul Charlotte never led again. Drexler had 9 points in the overtime.
Quote: "Kite made more big plays tonight than the other big guys [Tim Kempton and Dave Hoppen] had the last month. He's definitely our starting center next game."
—Harter

Chicago 121, Hornets 101

GAME 72

Date: April 4.
Site: Chicago Stadium.
Attendance: 17,578.
Highlights: With 6:34 left in the first quarter, Jordan and the Hornets each had 10 points. By halftime the Bulls had pulled in 30 rebounds to Charlotte's 13 and led 69–48. Jordan scored his sixth consecutive triple-double with 33 points, 12 rebounds, 10 assists.
Quote: "Michael Jordan at point really improves them as a team. He seems to distribute the play to all the others, where before it was more a game of isolation or one-one-one for him."
—Rambis

Philadelphia 118, Hornets 108

GAME 73

Date: April 7.
Site: Charlotte.
Attendance: 23,388.
Highlights: The Hornets had recovered from an 11-point third-quarter deficit to trail 107–102 with 1:32 left when Barkley stole an inbounds pass and drove for an uncontested lay-up to end the game. Barkley had game highs of 31 points and 20 rebounds. Charlotte outshot the Sixers 50% to 38% in the first half, but trailed 55–50 at the half. The Sixers outrebounded Charlotte 55–32.
Quote: "They were really working in there—making great plays. But they were never ahead, and that's important. It's hard always running from behind, because there's a lot of pressure—you have to score off every possession."
—Philadelphia 76er Charles Barkley

Cleveland 122, Hornets 116

GAME 74

Date: April 9.
Site: Richfield Coliseum, Richfield, Ohio.
Attendance: 19,276.
Highlights: Charlotte couldn't retain a 9-point lead built in a brilliant first half, then watched Cleveland's inside game take over down the stretch. Former North Carolina center Brad Daugherty put the Hornets away with 6 of the Cavaliers' last 8 points. Daugherty finished with 22 points, and former Georgia Tech point guard Mark Price led the Cavaliers with 35.
Quote: "Price is such a smart player. He uses screens very well. And he's getting the calls, the way he's playing."
—Bogues

Atlanta 112, Hornets 105

GAME 75

Date: April 10.
Site: Charlotte.
Attendance: 23,388.
Highlights: Moses Malone scored 24 points and the Hawks held Charlotte scoreless for nearly 4 minutes late in the game to cruise to the 112–105 win. Malone also had 14 rebounds. The Hornets outshot Atlanta 56% to 51% in the first half, yet still trailed by 9 at halftime.
Quote: "We are playing well and we played good ball tonight, but we just can't get over the hump."

—**Curry**

Hornets 104, New York 99

GAME 76

Date: April 12.
Site: Madison Square Garden, New York.
Attendance: 18,385.
Highlights: One night after the New York Knicks clinched their first divisional crown in 18 years, the Hornets shocked the Knicks 104–99. Hoppen, who first hit Kelly Tripucka with a long baseball pass for a lay-up, made two clinching free throws with 6 seconds left.
Quote: "We're going to savor this for a long time—on the road, against a top-notch team."

—**Tripucka**

Hornets 119, Philadelphia 115

GAME 77

Date: April 14.
Site: The Spectrum, Philadelphia.
Attendance: 14,321.
Highlights: The Hornets shot a team-record 58% and led in the second half for all but about 4 minutes. Charlotte put the Sixers away with consecutive jumpers by Rambis and a 20-footer by Tripucka with 2:03 to play.
Quote: "I want a recount. . . . We want the Sixers in the playoffs."
—Ed Badger

Indiana 115, Hornets 105

GAME 78

Date: April 16.
Site: Market Square Arena, Indianapolis.
Attendance: 11,860.
Highlights: Forward Chuck Person started the assault on Charlotte, hitting 8 of his first 9 shots for 19 first-quarter points. He finished with 37 points and Rik Smits had 27, leading the Pacers.
Quote: "The way Person was leaking out [of the lane], hitting those jumpers, it was hard for [Rambis] to get to the boards."
—Reid

Boston 113, Charlotte 108 (OT)

GAME 79

Date: April 17.
Site: Charlotte.
Attendance: 23,388.
Highlights: Robert Parish made consecutive follow-up baskets in the extra period to give the Celtics a 5-point lead and secure the victory. Parish finished with 21 points and 22 rebounds (10 of Boston's 21 offensive rebounds). Charlotte was outrebounded 73–44. Chapman hit a transition dunk with 53 seconds left in regulation to force the overtime.
Quote: "I'll be very honest. It's a game we should have had. It's a game we shouldn't have lost."

—**Reid**

Hornets 121, New Jersey 105

GAME 80

Date: April 18.
Site: Brendan Byrne Arena, East Rutherford, N.J.
Attendance: 8,991.
Highlights: Win number 20! Robert Reid reached a milestone by scoring his 10,000th career NBA point. The Hornets built a 10-point lead, with 10:33 left, and stretched it to their widest margin of victory this season (16 points). Dell Curry led all scorers with 31 points.
Quote: "I remember looking up at the clock and thinking we're up 13, and the next 4 minutes are enormous to our season. It means we're over that plateau of expansion. There are established teams that haven't won 20 games in a season."

—**Curry**

Milwaukee 117, Hornets 110

GAME 81

Date: April 21.
Site: Charlotte.
Attendance: 23,388.
Highlights: The Hornets closed out their home season in front of their 30th straight sellout crowd, but Milwaukee spoiled the party and handed Charlotte its 13th straight loss at home. Charlotte's bright spots were guards Rex Chapman and Dell Curry, who combined for 45 points. Larry Krystkowiak (23) and Ricky Pierce (21) did much of the Bucks' damage.
Quote: "We did not have a good night, but we played hard down the stretch. I couldn't say our team did a good job defensively. Our [small forwards] got ripped apart, our [power forwards] got ripped apart. Krystkowiak was the best player on the floor."

—Harter

Boston 120, Hornets 110

GAME 82

Date: April 23.
Site: Boston Garden.
Attendance: 14,890.
Highlights: Charlotte played the Celtics close in a game Boston had to have in order to make the playoffs. Boston moved out to a 20-point lead in the fourth quarter, then watched as the Hornets made a stirring run—scoring 13 straight points to cut the lead to 110–103.
Quote: "What better way to end the season than beating Boston on its home floor and keeping them out of the playoffs? Most teams in our position would have had trouble finding incentive to play the last 15 games of the year, but we took those 15 games and made them our playoff season."

—Tripucka